DATE DUE

50
/ 3

*A Publication of
the California State Colleges*

Napoleon III
and the Working Class

A STUDY OF
GOVERNMENT PROPAGANDA
UNDER THE
SECOND EMPIRE

DAVID I. KULSTEIN

Department of History, San Jose State College

A Publication of
THE CALIFORNIA STATE COLLEGES

TO MY MOTHER

Contents

Preface   ix

I   *Introduction: Bonapartist Propaganda Before the Reign of Louis Napoleon*   3

II   *Propaganda Media: The Press*   38

III   *Other Propaganda Media*   69

IV   *The Imperial Message to the Working Class*   94

V   *Government Propaganda New Style—Workers Organizations—Bonapartist Agents*   120

VI   *The Government Press and the New Propaganda: The Crises of the 1860's*   151

VII   *Economics Instruction for Workers*   170

Conclusion: An Evaluation of Government Propaganda   197

Bibliography   206

Index   243

Preface

Propaganda was not invented in the nineteenth century. Since its purpose is to move people to accept or to reject things, usually in the area of politics, it is probably as old as mankind's earliest communities. In the ancient world, the oratory of Homer's heroes, the poetry of Virgil, the campaign slogans still to be found on the walls of Pompeii, were kinds of propaganda. At all times, and even in the most despotic of regimes, the value of public support has been recognized, and attempts have been made to elicit that support.

In the nineteenth century, however, propaganda took on a new and very important position. The propaganda that first appeared during the French Revolution differs from earlier efforts in two ways. In the first place, earlier propaganda was usually an attempt to influence the opinion of a privileged minority; Homeric speeches were directed to Homeric heroes, not to the ordinary Greek infantryman or camp-follower. Propaganda since the French Revolution, on the other hand, has been directed primarily at the masses. In the second place, earlier propaganda was specific and intermittent. Even when propaganda did seek to enlist mass support, as it did during the Crusades, the English civil war of the mid-seventeenth century, and the Fronde, it was a great, but temporary effort that was abandoned when the crisis calling it forth came to an end. From the time of the French Revolution, however, popular support has been solicited continually by all interest groups as a matter of course. Propaganda, as a consequence, has been omnipresent in modern political life.

This was especially true in France, the home of the Revolution, after the Second Republic proclaimed universal manhood suffrage in 1848, and the Second Empire maintained it. Henceforth, public opinion in the widest sense could no longer be ignored. And, although peasants were far more numerous in nineteenth century France, this meant particularly the opinion of workers. The working class had revealed its power by the important part that it had played in the overthrow of the Restoration and July Monarchies. Moreover, uprisings such as took place at Paris and Lyons in 1831 and 1834 and later the "June Days" aroused anxiety among the upper classes that worker discontent threatened property rights. Workers, therefore, must be persuaded of the justice of the economic and social order.

The potential political strength of the working class and fear of its wrath led to two different propaganda messages for workers. On the one hand, each of the dynasties, parties, and ideologies contending for power in France disseminated its own propaganda message. And, on the other hand, those groups satisfied with the social order often cooperated in the preparation and the distribution of propaganda defending it.

This monograph examines the organization, the media, and the contents of pro-government propaganda among workers during the Second Empire. I became interested in the problem while preparing a doctoral dissertation, *Louis Napoleon and the Social and Economic Policy of the Second Empire.* My research indicated that a wide gap existed between what the Second Empire actually did for the working class and what many contemporaries (as well as some recent historians) believed that it had accomplished. This tendency to exaggerate the improvements of the condition of the working class during the Second Empire is due, in part, to Bonapartist propaganda.

A few definitions and comments on method and problems are needed. The terms propaganda and propagandist suggest, of course, dishonesty and venality. However, many pro-government

[x]

propagandists during the Second Empire acted from altruistic motives. Such sincere and dedicated Bonapartist missionaries believed that workers had more to gain from cooperation with the government than from opposition to it. I have, therefore, used the term propaganda to describe any effort to influence opinion regardless of the motives of the propagandists.

The mere use of the term "class" immediately warns the twentieth century writer that he must define it—a warning which I shall not, however, heed. Government propagandists during the Second Empire did not worry about a definition. They appealed indiscriminately to all kinds of workers, those who produced in their homes, in small workshops, and in the factories. Moreover, propaganda to workers was often indistinguishable from propaganda to that even more inclusive category, *le peuple*, defined by the *Nouveau petit Larousse* as "the most numerous and poorest, the least cultivated inhabitants of a town, country, etc."

I have also limited my study primarily to propaganda to workers *qua* workers. This may, at first, seem to be an arbitrary and unrealistic distinction. After all, French workers were also Frenchmen who shared the attitudes of members of other classes on many matters; for example, pride in their country. There are two reasons for stressing government propaganda that appealed to the class interests of workers. First, this was the most common kind of propaganda. Second, propaganda based upon other concerns of the working class cannot usually be distinguished from propaganda for the liberal bourgeoisie, who often shared the attitude of the more thoughtful workers on many matters; for example, the cause of the suppressed nationalities and the question of personal liberty.

The two main problems I faced in preparing this monograph are related: a disappointing lack of material on some questions, and an overwhelming abundance on other questions. The government of Napoleon III revealed, of course, only a part of its propaganda organization and activities. Thus, although secret agents and secret funds frequently were involved in the dissemination of propaganda, the tie between the government and its agents is not a very well documented relationship. On the other hand, I have been able to examine only a fraction of the propaganda material that appeared during the Second Empire. There were, for example, hundreds of newspapers that printed pro-government propaganda.

I wish to acknowledge the advice and aid of the late George Bourgin whose command of the *Archives nationales* spared me many hours of work, the librarians and archivists at Widener Library, the *Archives nationales*, the *Bibliothèque nationale*, the Archives of the Ministry of Foreign Affairs, the *Bibliothèque de l'Institut*, and Madame Willemetz, archivist of the *Imprimerie nationale*. I wish to thank Dr. William J. Brandt of the University of California whose suggestions on style and organization were especially valuable.

I am also grateful to the San Jose State College Foundation for aid in the preparation of the manuscript.

It is the burden of scholars' wives to listen to and type their husbands' manuscripts. My wife, Edith Kulstein, has been superhumanly patient. Finally, without the advice and encouragement—even when separated by 3,000 miles—of the late Professor Donald C. McKay of Harvard University and Amherst College, my master, colleague, and generous friend, this book would not have been written.

Napoleon III
and the Working Class

Introduction: Bonapartist Propaganda Before the Reign of Louis Napoleon

From the very beginning of their dynasty the Bonapartes grasped the importance of propaganda in the new France that had emerged since 1789. "To attach no importance to public opinion," said Napoleon I, "is a proof that you do not merit its suffrage."[1] Unlike the previous rulers of France, Napoleon who claimed to be the popular choice, could not afford to neglect public opinion. The Emperor, concludes a recent student of his propaganda, "was the first sovereign to talk to his subjects directly and frequently."[2] He sometimes also spoke to his subjects (and enemies) indirectly through the articles he had printed in the official newspaper, *Le Moniteur*, some issues of which were distributed not only in the armies and schools but throughout the countries occupied by France.[3]

The Queen Hortense, Louis Napoleon's mother, had an equally perceptive awareness of the need for propaganda in the post-Revolutionary world, and her advice to her sons anticipated the propaganda message and techniques of Napoleon III. She re-

[1]Robert Holtman, *Napoleonic Propaganda* (Baton Rouge, 1950), V.

[2]Holtman, *Napoleonic Propaganda*, 246.

[3]Jacques Driencourt, *La Propagande, nouvelle force politique* (Paris, 1950), 46.

minded them that their title of prince was of recent origin and told them what they must do to earn respect for it:[4]

When those who own property fear for their interests, promise them to be a guaranty of it. If the people suffer show them that you also are oppressed. Let them understand that there is no salvation without you. In a word, the role of the Bonapartes is to present themselves as the friends of all; they are the mediators, the conciliators. And I mean this not only in the human sense of the word but in every sense. You must believe that it is not impossible for you to become literally an idol, something like the Redeemer, the intermediary between the rigorous destiny of heaven and human interests; men like to seek protection from a visible providence. It is so easy, moreover, to gain the affection of the people. They have a childlike simplicity. If the people see that one is interested in them, they are silent. Only when they believe that there is injustice or treason do they revolt. Without giving yourself to anyone do not rebuff anyone.

Hortense also advised her sons on propaganda technique: repeat your message over and over again, adapt it to suit the interests and intelligence of your hearers.[5]

Louis Napoleon, the Emperor's nephew and from 1832 the recognized Bonapartist pretender, inherited, therefore, a tradition of appealing to public opinion, as well as a claim to the throne of France. From the beginning to the end of his political life Louis Napoleon believed that in France a government could endure only if it were based upon popular support. In August 1833, he insisted to his friend Heeckeren, "A popular government alone has a chance to last in France. What is built up with-

[4]*Mémoires de la reine Hortense* (Paris, 1927), III, 192; Georges Duval, *Napoléon III, enfance, jeunesse* (Paris, 1894), 73-74.

[5]Frédéric Loliée, *Rêve d'empereur*, 6th ed. (Paris, 1913), 130-131: "On finit par faire croire ce que l'on dit à satiété; on obtient toujours ce que l'on demande sans se lasser et sur tous les modes, depuis le ton de la litanie jusqu'au rythme fier de l'ode héroique." And: "Chaque paire d'oreilles est prédisposée à des sensations particulières, chaque esprit est touché d'un genre particulier d'arguments. Employons donc toutes les cordes de la voix, toutes les sortes de raisons."

out the People is overthrown by the People."[6] The following year he repeated this view to a former tutor, Vieillard: Although a party might gain power in a state, it could not consolidate this power without the confidence of the people.[7] And from the prison of Ham, Louis Napoleon proclaimed that the "reign of castes is over; one can govern only with the masses. It is necessary, therefore, to organize them so that they can formulate their wishes and to discipline them so that they can be guided and enlightened concerning their own interests."[8] To govern, he continued, no longer meant to dominate the people by force and violence but to appeal to their hearts and reason. In 1855, soon after the taking of Sebastopol, Napoleon III reaffirmed his belief in the force of public opinion, "At the stage of civilization in which we are, the success of armies, however brilliant they may be, is only transitory. In reality it is public opinion which wins the last victory."[9]

However, despite his recognition of the need for popular support, Louis Napoleon at first addressed his propaganda to political leaders, usually members of the opposition, to men of letters, and to army officers rather than to the masses. (He was particularly eager and hopeful of gaining followers in the army). In the early 1830's, Louis Napoleon distributed his works to leading Frenchmen and responded eagerly to their comments. His correspondents included Lafayette and Chateaubriand; the latter assured the Pretender of his respect for Napoleon I, even though his first loyalty was to the Bourbons.[10] During these years Louis

[6]Baron d'Ambès, *Intimate Memoirs of Napoleon III* (London, n.d.), tr. I, 68. Baron d'Ambès is a pseudonym for Heeckeren, the man who killed the poet Pushkin in a duel.

[7]Georges Duval, *Napoléon III, enfance, jeunesse* (Paris, 1899), 129-130.

[8]*Extinction du Paupérisme; Oeuvres de Napoléon III* (Paris, 1856-1869), II, 122.

[9]Lynn M. Case, *French Opinion on War and Diplomacy* (Philadelphia, 1954), 1.

[10]André Lebey, *Les trois coups d'état de Louis-Napoléon Bonaparte, Strasbourg et Boulogne* (Paris, 1906), 80.

Napoleon also wrote a number of pamphlets and books which he stated in a frank letter to Vieillard were all intended to make himself known to different elements of the population.[11] His *Manuel d'artillerie* (1834), for example, he hoped would "gain some hearts in the army and prove that if I do not command troops I at least have the necessary knowledge to do so."[12]

The message of Louis Napoleon's early propaganda was primarily political. He exploited political dissatisfaction with the July Monarchy and contrasted what he described as the lowly state of France with the glories of the Empire. He tried particularly to convince republicans that their views and those of the Bonapartists were not irreconcilable. In the *Rêveries politiques,* for example, he expressed the hope that Bonapartism and republicanism, "the two popular causes," would unite; "with the name Napoleon one no longer fears a return of the Terror, with the name Republic one no longer fears a return of absolute power."[13] Louis Napoleon also proclaimed his respect and the respect of the Bonapartes for the rights of the individual, one of the great gains of the Revolution. War had made the dictatorship of Napoleon I necessary, but had the Emperor conquered England and Russia, he would have surrendered his wartime powers and established a liberal regime.[14] The early propaganda rarely sought to exploit the discontent of the workers, although an article in a proposed constitution drafted by Louis Napoleon declared that, "Public aid is a sacred debt. Society owes subsistence

---

[11]Taxile Delord, *Histoire illustrée du Second Empire*, nouvelle ed. (Paris, 1880-1883), I, 57-59. The most significant of Louis Napoleon's early works are: *Rêveries politiques* (1832) and *Considérations politiques et militaires sur la Suisse* (1833). Both are in the official *Oeuvres de Napoléon III*. However, the *Oeuvres* does not give the entire text of the *Rêveries politiques*. For the unabridged work, see Charles Edouard Tremblaire, *Oeuvres de Louis-Napoléon Bonaparte* (Paris, 1848), I.

[12]Duval, *Napoléon III*, 277.

[13]Tremblaire, *Oeuvres*, I, 71-72.

[14]*Oeuvres de Napoléon III*, II, 336.

to unfortunate citizens, either by obtaining work for them or by assuring the means of existence to those who are unable to work."[15]

During the 1830's, Louis Napoleon, like many other Bonapartists, relied excessively upon the power of the name he bore. Thus, after a brief stay in Paris in 1831, Louis Napoleon said, "The people are Bonapartist. If I had not been ill on May 5, 1831, and had gone down to the Place Vendôme and cried 'Vive Napoleon' everybody would have followed me. Louis Philippe knew it, and that is why he made me leave [France]."[16] Five years later, on the eve of the Strasbourg attempt, Louis Napoleon still believed that the prestige of his name was the sole arm he needed to overthrow the July Monarchy.[17]

The planning and the execution of Louis Napoleon's attempted *coup d'état* at Strasbourg in 1836 provide an example of the limitations of Bonapartist propaganda at this time.[18] Although many republicans and workers who might have given support 'to the *coup d'état* lived in and about Strasbourg, the conspirators made only slight attempts to gain their cooperation.[19] Instead, Louis Napoleon relied entirely upon the military. The plan was to win over the garrison at Strasbourg to the Imperial cause, seize the city, and then march on Paris with the expectation that the

[15]Tremblaire, *Oeuvres*, 75.

[16]Ivor Guest, *Napoleon III in England* (London, 1952), 13-14.

[17]Fialin de Persigny, *Relation de l'entreprise du prince Napoléon Louis et motifs qui l'y ont déterminés* (Geneva, 1836), 9.

[18]For the Strasbourg attempt, see Lebey, *Les trois coups d'état*; Félix Ponteil, *L'Opposition politique à Strasbourg sous la Monarchie de Juillet (1830-1848)* (Paris, 1932); A. Mathiez, "Le prince Louis-Napoléon à Strasbourg," *La Revue de Paris*, XXII (November 15, 1899), 294-322.

[19]Armand Laity, a participant in the Strasbourg attempt and the author of what might be termed the official Bonapartist version, wrote that although Louis Napoleon had spoken to several civilians in Alsace and Lorraine, he apparently did not tell them of his plans, *Relation historique des évènements du 30 Octobre 1836. Le Prince Napoléon à Strasbourg* (Paris, 1836), 26.

people, still loyal to the memory of Napoleon I, would join the conspirators, just as they were supposed to have rallied to the Emperor in 1815. Even the very modest efforts made to gain civilian support in Strasbourg was in order to influence the garrison. Heeckeren, one of the conspirators, relates that he "undertook to foment a popular rising," but with the hope that "the echoes would stir the soldiery."[20] Louis Napoleon, in fact, feared popular participation. Shortly after the Strasbourg failure, in a detailed account of the attempt to his mother, he wrote that he had relied upon the army "particularly to avoid the disturbances which often accompany popular movements."[21]

The political emphasis of the manifestos that Louis Napoleon issued at Strasbourg was also typical of Bonapartist propaganda at the time.[22] A proclamation to the French people denounced the July Monarchy, a government which lacked a popular mandate, for its political failures and cowardly foreign policy, and closed with a rousing appeal to revolutionary and Napoleonic sentiments: "Men of 1789, men of March 20, 1815, men of 1830 rise! Look at those who rule you; look at the [Imperial] eagle, emblem of glory, symbol of liberty, and choose!" The proclamation did not, however, entirely ignore the economic and social grievances of the population. It attacked the government for betraying the commercial interests of the nation and for suppressing workers' movements. It charged the July Monarchy with forgetting its origins on the barricades and with filling "our towns with blood."

What Louis Napoleon and the Bonapartists did not yet understand was that France was becoming more industrialized and the number and importance of workers was increasing. Although

[20]D'Ambès, *Intimate Memoirs*, I, 102.
[21]*Oeuvres de Napoléon III*, II, 68-69.
[22]For the text of these proclamations, see Lebey, *Les trois coups d'état*, 142-144.

France did not experience an industrial revolution until the last decade of the nineteenth century, production and the number of workers employed in industry increased significantly after the close of the Napoleonic wars.[23] For the working class this period of early industrialization was, indeed, a "bleak age." Surveys by public officials, economists, and reformers have left a grim portrait of conditions in the industrial towns of France—conditions that aroused cries of horror from upper class observers.[24] Despite these reactions it is possible that the condition of the French worker, objectively measured, improved slightly during this period; historians are not agreed.[25] But the important fact was that the workers themselves did not think so. Compared with the progress of other social classes, their own state seemed to be worse than ever before. For a number of reasons workers believed that they were not receiving their share of the increasing wealth of society. The growing concentration of workers around factories and mills made their poverty, which under the system of domestic production had been almost private and hidden, public and clear for all to see. A new attitude towards the old problem of poverty also contributed to the belief that the condition of the working class was worsening. As Ernest Renan wrote, a guid-

[23]From 1812 to 1827 cotton production tripled; the number of looms in use at Lyons increased from 7,000 in 1814 to 42,000 in 1842. G. de Berthier de Sauvigny, *La Restauration* (Paris, 1955), 301-302. According to a contemporary census, by 1851 French industry already employed 4,110,000 persons. Henri Sée, *La vie économique de la France sous la monarchie censitaire (1815-1848)* (Paris, 1928), 66-67.

[24]The best known of the many surveys of working class life is M. Villermé, *Tableau de l'état physique et morale des ouvriers employés dans les manufactures de coton, de laine et de soie* (Paris, 1840), 2 vol. For other surveys, see Hilde Rigaudias-Weiss, *Les enquêtes ouvrières en France entre 1830 et 1848* (Paris, 1936).

[25]Villermé, for example, believed that despite the deplorable conditions of many workers, the working class as a whole was better off than in earlier centuries, *Tableau de l'état physique*, II, 1-6. An early historian of the working class wrote that the severe crisis of 1847 caused less hardship than the crisis of 1817, which, in turn, was accompanied by less suffering than seventeenth century crises when thousands starved to death. F. du Cellier, *Histoire des classes laborieuses en France* (Paris, 1860), 401-402.

ing principle of nineteenth century social thought was "the tendency to regard individual suffering as a social evil and to render society responsible for the misery and the degradation of its members."[26]

Although the working class in the first half of the nineteenth century lacked, "an original conception of economic and social organization,"[27] many workers sought to defend their interests by means of both traditional institutions and techniques, as well as new ones. Thus, the *compagnonnage*, condemned by Church and state during the Old Regime, survived into the post-Revolutionary period in certain crafts. Workers also organized illegal trade unions or resistance societies, often behind the façade of authorized mutual aid societies.

In 1830, the discontent of the Parisian workers erupted into political action. Towards the end of July, *"les trois glorieuses,"* many Parisian workers descended into the streets to help overthrow the unpopular Charles X. The Revolution of 1830 marked the beginning of the working class as a political force in France. Workers, after the arrival in power of Louis Philippe, did not return peacefully to their workshops and factories. The Revolution had deepened an economic depression which had lingered on since 1825, and workers expected help from the new regime which owed so much to them. However, when workers' representatives called upon the government for assistance (usually a minimum wage), the authorities, faithful to the doctrines of liberal economics, replied that they could not interfere with the terms of the contracts between workers and their employers. At the same time, the government, which in the period after the July Revolution had tolerated illegal strikes, began to enforce the

[26]Cited in Maxime Leroy, *Histoire des idées sociales en France*, vol. II, *De Babeuf à Tocqueville*, 2nd ed. (Paris, 1950), 11-12.

[27]François Dutacq, *Histoire politique de Lyon pendant la Révolution de 1848* (Paris, 1910), 30-31.

law, as well as to suppress demonstrations and to ban many workers' organizations.

The July Revolution and its aftermath had a double impact
on French workers. Hitherto, most workers had believed that the
interests of the working class and the liberal bourgeoisie were
the same, and they had, therefore, been willing to accept the
guidance of the latter. Now, the more class-conscious workers
began to doubt that this community of interests existed. The
events of 1830 also gave workers a new sense of self-confidence.
"We are now the most important part of society," boasted a workers' newspaper in September, 1830.[28]

In the 1830's and the 1840's, workers demonstrated their discontent through both economic and political action. Although
they were illegal, there were frequent strikes and several strike
waves: 1833-1834, 1839-1843, 1847. Some workers also played an
active part in republican political movements and in the various
socialist schools that flourished during these years.[29] In 1831 and
1834, violent worker uprisings at Lyons and Paris had to be suppressed by troops.

The usual response of the upper classes and the government
to strikes, riots, and other evidence of worker dissatisfaction was
repression. The bourgeoisie, wrote Heinrich Heine, "has an in-
stinctive terror of communism, or of those dark and dreadful
forms which would come swarming like rats out of the ruins of
the present regime."[30] Villeneuve-Bargemont, a Catholic social
reformer, exclaimed: "Today it is no longer only the political
order which is involved, but perhaps the very existence of soci-

[28]Edouard Dolléans, *Histoire du mouvement ouvrier*, 4th ed. (Paris, 1948), I, 57.

[29]In 1847, the Prefect of Police at Paris reported that the influence of the writings
of Cabet, Leroux, and Proudhon among workers was growing. E. Levasseur, *Histoire des classes ouvrières et de l'industrie en France de 1789 à 1870*, 2nd ed. (Paris,
1904), II, 64-65.

[30]Heinrich Heine, *French Affairs. The Works of Heinrich Heine*, tr. (London,
1893), VIII, 233.

[11]

ety. The warning signs of a social revolution are everywhere."[31] And a month before the outbreak of the Revolution of 1848, de Tocqueville warned of a social revolution that was brewing in the minds of French workers—a revolution that threatened the institution of private property.[32]

The government of Louis Philippe, being interested primarily in the opinion of the small minority of Frenchmen who had the franchise, the *pays legal*, could only respond to worker agitation with fear and repression. Some perceptive followers of the other dynasties and movements contending for power in France saw, however, in the dissatisfied working class a potential ally.

The Legitimists, heirs to the feudal and Christian tradition of responsibility for the lower orders, were particularly apt to respond sympathetically to the complaints of workers and to see in these complaints a way to strengthen their cause. Many Legitimists founded charitable institutions and some devoted their lives to the aid of the needy. They also inspired and dominated the new school of social Catholicism which sought a Christian solution for the problems of the working class.[33] Such Legitimists believed that although the working class was being misled by the liberal bourgeoisie, "the revolutionary party in every state,"[34] it was not yet irretrievably lost to the Bourbon cause.

The Restoration Monarchy was also interested in public opinion and how to influence it. Thus, a circular to the prefects from the chief minister Decazes stated that popular songs provided a "sufficiently accurate picture of the various changes in public

[31]Alban de Villeneuve-Bargemont, *Economie politique chrétienne* (Paris, 1834), I, 24-26.

[32]*The Recollections of Alexis de Tocqueville*, tr. ed. by J. P. Mayer (London, 1948), 12-15.

[33]For the origins of Social Catholicism, see J.-B. Duroselle, *Les débuts du Catholicisme sociale en France 1822-1870* (Paris, 1951), Part I, Ch. 4.

[34]Statement by the Ultra minister Villèle, cited in René Rémond, *La droite en France de 1815 à nos jours* (Paris, 1954), 36-37.

opinion."[35] It also urged the prefects to use the many peddlars who traversed France "to disseminate useful truths."

After the Royalists' exclusion from the government following the fall of Charles X in 1830, Legitimist propaganda to workers became more daring. In fact, at times, it resembled the propaganda of republicans and socialists with whom royalists occasionally cooperated against the common foe. Although a Legitimist plan for a newspaper for workers came to nothing,[36] other channels of propaganda frequently were used to express concern with the misery of the poor. The followers of the Bourbons denounced the alliance between the bourgeoisie and the government of Louis Philippe and the "fraud" perpetrated on the workers of Paris in July, 1830, by bankers and industrialists. "Liberal ministers," warned a Legitimist newspaper, *La Quotidienne*, "we shall defend the people against you."[37] "The men of the right," announced another Legitimist newspaper, "are the true defenders of the popular interests."[37a] A royalist, P. Charnier, helped found the *Devoir mutuel*, an organization of silk workers at Lyons.[38] When the Orleanist monarchy repressed workers harshly after the Lyons and Paris insurrections of 1831 and 1834, some Legitimists sought to gain sympathy for their cause among workers by attacking the government's policy. A government is always wrong, wrote *La Quotidienne*, when it refuses to heed the pleas of the people for bread.[39] In 1834, the government charged the Abbé Peyraud, a Legitimist, with manufacturing weapons for

[35]Paul Leuilliot, *L'Alsace au début du XIXe siècle. Essais d'histoire politique, économique et religieuse (1815-1830)*, v. III, *Religions et culture* (Paris, 1960), 340.

[36]André Armengaud, *Les populations de l'Est-Aquitain au début de l'époque contemporaine. Recherches sur une région moins developpée (vers 1848-vers 1871)* (Paris, 1961), 343.

[37]Duroselle, *Les débuts du Catholicisme social*, 201.

[37a]Duroselle, *Les débuts du Catholicisme social*, 201.

[38]Dolléans, *Histoire du mouvement ouvrier*, I, 59 ff.

[39]Duroselle, *Les débuts du Catholicisme social*, 201.

revolutionary workers at Lyons; a Bourbon newspaper defended the Abbé and protested against the insensitivity of the government to the needs of the working class.[40]

It must be kept in mind, however, that Legitimist propaganda of this kind was the work of a handful of men; the great majority of royalists remained aloof from, if not hostile to it. Republicans, on the other hand, believed that the support of workers was vital to their success. As a result, even before 1830, they had directed much of their propaganda at the working class. Before the July Revolution, however, the republican message to workers was usually political. It attacked the alliance between throne and altar, the political power of the Church, the privileges of the nobles; it reaffirmed the principles of the French Revolution and demanded more political and personal freedom.

After the July Revolution, however, republican propaganda sought also to exploit the economic and social grievances of the working class. In 1830, a manifesto of the *Amis du peuple*, a republican club, demanded social and economic reforms as well as the familiar political reforms that republicans had been demanding since 1815.[41] And in the 1840's *La Réforme*, a leading republican newspaper, declared that the ultimate objective of the republicans was a profound reform of the economic and social order. As a consequence of this emphasis on the social problem, the term "republic" came to mean for many workers not merely a form of government, but also to suggest a new social order in which their lot would be greatly improved.

Republicans disseminated their message among workers through many media. They organized republican societies for workers; they often supported strikers verbally and financially. They distributed newspapers among them. In 1848, *La Réforme*

[40]Duroselle, *Les débuts du Catholicisme social,* 202.

[41]Georges Weill, *Histoire du parti républicain en France (1814-1870),* 2nd ed. (Paris, 1928), 31.

did much to arouse the workers of Paris against the July Monarchy. The pamphlet was another widely used medium for republican propaganda; in one three-month period republicans distributed more than six million pamphlets.[42] Republicans also used the theatre, a form of entertainment very popular with the working class. And in evening courses for workers, founded by republicans after 1830, teachers frequently mixed propaganda with their lessons.[43]

Bonapartist propagandists among workers in the first part of the nineteenth century were more active than their Legitimist and Orleanist rivals, but not until the Revolution of 1848 did they effectively challenge the republicans.[44] The retired Imperial officers and the romantic youths and adventurers who led the Bonapartist cause usually failed to exploit economic discontent. Typical of their attitude was the exclamation of an indignant Bonapartist when he learned of a pamphlet written by Louis Napoleon in the prison of Ham defending the domestic sugar beet industry against the importers of colonial cane sugar: "To be an imprisoned Bonaparte and to discuss the sugar beet!"[45]

The most widely used formal medium of Bonapartist propaganda was the press.[46] In December 1814, there appeared the pro-Bonapartist *Nain Jaune*, a newspaper read by Louis XVIII

[42]Dolléans, *Histoire du mouvement ouvrier*, I, 80.

[43]One institution for adult education, *L'Association libre pour l'éducation du peuple*, enrolled 2,500 workers in the forty-six courses it offered, Dolléans, *Histoire du mouvement ouvrier*, I, 80.

[44]This introduction to Bonapartist propaganda before 1848 is not intended to fill the need for a detailed study of the subject.

[45]Frédéric Loliée, *Rêve d'Empereur*, 6th ed. (Paris, 1913), 162.

[46]Two interesting studies of the press during this period have recently appeared: Charles Ledré, *La presse à l'assaut de la monarchie 1815-1848* (Paris, 1960); Irene Collins, *The Government and the Newspaper Press in France 1814-1881* (London, 1959). However, in view of the important role played by the press in the nineteenth and twentieth centuries, there is a great need for more research on newspapers.

himself. (He may even have contributed anonymous articles to it.)[47] In March 1817, two Bonapartists founded the *Bibliothèque historique,* and although the newspaper's circulation never reached 2,500, the government feared its influence. The following year the *Minerve* appeared and by January, 1819, had reached a circulation of 10,000, a figure exceeding that of most contemporary newspapers. In the provinces, the *Bibliothèque historique* and the *Minerve* enjoyed a great popularity and cafe owners subscribed to them to attract customers.[48] In 1820, however, under the pressure of new censorship laws, both newspapers ceased publication. In 1839, two short-lived Bonapartist newspapers, *Le Capitole* and *Le Commerce,* the latter formerly a left wing journal, appeared. Despite their common loyalty to the Bonapartist cause, the two newspapers engaged in a bitter controversy, including accusations of duplicity and treason.[49]

Such Bonapartist and Bonapartist-inclined newspapers did not usually appeal to workers as workers. They stressed political propaganda, particularly the emerging belief that Napoleon I had been a liberal and the defender of the principles of the French Revolution against the conspiracy of the crowned heads of Europe and their aristocratic followers. Thus, *Le Capitole* (September 18, 1839) printed an imaginary conversation between the *colonne de Juillet* and the *colonne Impériale,* the symbols respectively of the July Monarchy and the Empire, in which the Imperial column charged that Louis Philippe ruled illegally, since he lacked the sanction of either legitimacy or popular choice.[50] The Imperial column also called for electoral reform

[47]Collins, *The Government and the Newspaper Press,* 8. I have relied heavily on Collins' study for the press before 1848.

[48]Collins, *The Government and the Newspaper Press,* 20.

[49]Delord, *Histoire illustrée du Second Empire,* I, 47.

[50]*Bibliothèque nationale* (hereafter B.N.), Gr. Fol LC². 2851. The B.N. has only a few issues of *Le Capitole.*

and denounced what it called the peace at any price foreign policy of the July Monarchy.

Only occasionally did Bonapartist newspapers exploit the social and economic grievances of *Le peuple*. Thus, the *Capitole* (September 19, 1839) praised Napoleon I's belief in equality: "The Emperor, who refused to believe that low birth was a crime, also refused to believe that the fortunate accident of high birth was a virtue." It also published a statement by the ardent Bonapartist Persigny at his trial for the attempted *coup d'état* at Boulogne in 1840 that revealed that at least some Bonapartists were becoming aware of the social problem. The Napoleonic Idea, said Persigny, "thinks above all of the people, its favorite child; it does not flatter but is ceaselessly concerned with the needs of the people and believes that its greatest glory would be the elimination of need and the organization of labor."[51] In 1829, *Le Peuple* compared the Imperial and the Restoration eras; during the reign of Napoleon I "workers had employment, all the classes were prosperous," while under the Bourbons "France is dissatisfied, industry is ruined, the workers are without bread."[52]

Such infrequent appeals to workers should not, however, be exaggerated. Until 1848 most Bonapartists sought to influence what they regarded as the more influential classes and groups in France. Bonapartists were not very active during the *trois glorieuses*. They posted a few placards in working class neighborhoods praising the son of Napoleon, the Duke of Reichstadt.[53] Two Bonapartist agents, one an officer disguised as a worker, led two or three hundred demonstrating workers "who mingled cries

---

[51]H. Thirria, *Napoléon III avant l'Empire* (Paris, 1895), I, 198-199. Persigny's phrase, *"extinction de la mendicité,"* presages Louis Napoleon's more famous *"extinction du paupérisme,"* and his reference to the organization of labor exploits one of the vague formulas of social reformers of the epoch.

[52]Cited in Ledré, *La presse*, 229.

[53]Lebey, *Les trois coups d'état*, 142-144.

of the Emperor's name with their wishes for liberty."[54] However, such efforts were slight compared to the activities of republicans. Bonapartists also did little to exploit worker disappointment with the July Monarchy. For example, they did not play a significant part in the uprisings of 1831 and 1834.

It is difficult, however, to explain the strong Bonapartist sentiments among workers without the activities of unofficial and unorganized sympathizers, probably workers themselves, who carried the Imperialist message to their fellows. It is, in fact, one of the ironies of history that the class which the Emperor feared most and whose power he sought constantly to limit remained more loyal to him than other classes.[55]

Evidence of pro-Bonapartist feeling among workers is abundant. Shortly after the return of the Bourbons to power a carpenter who had climbed the Vendôme column to insult the statue of the Emperor was ostracized by his fellow workers who also walked off the job whenever he appeared. Despite the efforts of the police, no employer dared hire the carpenter, and he finally had to leave Paris.[56] The stonemason Nadaud, who was a republican member of the legislature during the Second Republic, relates that his father, also a stonemason, believed that his fellow workers who favored either the Bourbon or Orleanist dynasties were misguided. "What we need," he declared, "is the son of the great Napoleon."[57] The three ephemeral workers' newspapers that appeared after the July Revolution (by November 1830 all

[54]Louis Blanc, *Histoire de dix ans 1830-1840*, 6th ed. (Paris, 1846), I, 200.

[55]For Napoleon I and the working class see Georges Bourgin, *Napoleon und seine Zeit* (Stuttgart, 1925), passim.

[56]Levasseur, *Histoire des classes ouvrières*, I, 667. This sympathetic attitude of workers towards Napoleon I also crossed the borders of France. When Louis Napoleon was in London in 1831, English workers often refused payment for services they had performed for the nephew of Napoleon I, Ivor Guest, *Napoleon III in England* (London, 1952), 11-12.

[57]Martin Nadaud, *Mémoires de Léonard ancien garçon maçon* (Bouraneuf, 1895), 44.

three had ceased to publish) frequently printed laudatory poems and anecdotes about the Emperor.[58] In 1834, unemployed silk workers at Lyons believed that Napoleon I would have found work for them.[59]

Although the cult or the legend of Napoleon certainly helped create such loyalty to the memory of the Emperor among many workers, the legend actually included little that was specifically for the worker.[60] The Napoleon of the legend was either the military conqueror, the Little Corporal who had carried France to the heights of glory or the heir to and the defender of the Revolution and its ideals who had saved the Revolution from Royalist conspiracies in *Vendémiaire* and *Fructidor*, only to succumb to them in 1814 and 1815. His government and his laws, continued the legend, had been based upon the revolutionary concepts of equality and liberty. Under Napoleon the great burdens of the state, taxes and military service, had been equitably divided among all Frenchmen. The Emperor had demonstrated his dedication to equality by his policy of the "career open to talent," his encouragement of education, and his abolition of legal privilege. Whatever theoretical or intellectual content the legend inlcuded—and this was far outweighed by its emotional content—was clearly political. Despite frequent remarks about Napoleon's concern with the well-being of the people and praise of

[58]Georges Weill, "Les Journaux ouvriers à Paris (1830-1879)," *Revue d'histoire moderne et contemporaine*, IX (1907), 90-91.

[59]Blanc, *Histoire de dix ans*, I, 422-423; Jules Deschamps, *Sur la légende de Napoléon* (Paris, 1931), 143.

[60]For the Napoleonic legend see, in addition to Deschamps, *Sur la légende de Napoléon*, Albert Guérard, *Reflections on the Napoleonic Legend* (New York, 1929); Philip Gonnard, *Les origines de la légende napoléonienne. L'oeuvre historique de Napoléon à Sainte-Hélène* (Paris, 1900); J. Lucas-Dubreton, *Le culte de Napoléon 1815-1848* (Paris, 1960); A. Tudesq, "La légende napoléonienne en France en 1848," *Revue historique*, vol. CCXVIII (July-September, 1957), 64-85. Most of these works are, however, primarily on the origins and contents of the legend. There is still a need for studies on its dissemination.

Imperial prosperity, the legend had little to say to workers about their economic and social problems.

Moreover, most historians today agree with contemporaries that the legend alone was incapable of creating a Bonapartist movement strong enough to elevate the heir of Napoleon I to the Imperial throne. Thus, Louis Blanc analyzed the failure of the Bonapartists in 1830 in the following way: "It had a flag rather than a principle. That was the insurmountable cause of its weakness."[61] Two years later Heine wrote that the love of the people for the name of Napoleon did not carry over to his heir: "In Napoleon they see the son of the Revolution; in young Reichstadt only the son of an emperor, the recognition of whom would be acknowledging or rendering hommage to the principle of legitimacy which would certainly be ridiculously illogical."[62] Persigny said of the Bonapartist party in the 1830's that it "adored the past more than it believed in the future."[63] And the republican editor Peauger wrote to the imprisoned Louis Napoleon that his Boulogne conspiracy of 1840 had failed because, "You had for you the force of the memories of Napoleon; that was a strong force but not strong enough."[64]

Before Bonapartism could become a potent political force rather than a nostalgia for another and more glorious day, it had to become a doctrine for the century. As Jérôme Bonaparte, the brother of Napoleon I, observed in 1830, a Bonapartist doctrine "capable of adapting itself to modern society" did not yet exist.[65] And in an age in which the problems of the working class could no longer be ignored, Bonapartism had to convince workers that it had a program for them. By the 1840's Louis Napoleon, the

[61]Blanc, *Histoire de dix ans*, II, 195.

[62]Heine, *French Affairs*, 148.

[63]*Mémoires du duc de Persigny* (Paris, 1896), 476-477.

[64]Marc Peauger, "Lettres du Fort de Ham," *La nouvelle revue*, 89 (1894), 446.

[65]Delord, *Histoire illustrée*, I, 22.

de facto heir to the claims of the Bonapartist dynasty, had recognized the need for creating a "Napoleonic idea" and for disseminating it among the entire population, and more than anyone else, he helped shape and propagate such a doctrine. From the 1830's to the fall of the Second Empire, Louis Napoleon was the central figure, the chief inspirer of Bonapartist propaganda.

Between about 1836 and 1840, Louis Napoleon began to think very seriously about economic and social problems and how Bonapartism could profit from the discontent of the working class. This was a common phenomenon of the period. The problem created by industry, particularly the condition of the working class, could no longer be ignored, and economists, reformers, philanthropists, as well as men of letters, began to propose solutions for the poverty which they now began to see all about them. In 1833, a small provincial newspaper, *L'Echo de Vaucluse*, commented:[66]

Journalism in 1833 is no longer what it was in 1829, at the beginning of 1830, nor even the year 1832. New words have appeared in its vocabulary. . . . The words worker, idler, proletarian, credit, bank, material amelioration, which two years ago appeared only in the literature of the economists, today appear in the most backward organs of public opinion.

A contemporary observer stated that in the 1830's a "mania" existed for social, philosophical, and religious innovation.[67] Another contemporary complained that among the upper classes it had become fashionable to criticize the social order.[68]

In addition, however, to the general interest in such questions

[66]Cited in S. Charlety, *La Monarchie de Juillet 1830-1848* (Paris, 1921), 88; in E. Lavisse, *Histoire de France contemporaine depuis la Révolution jusqu'à la paix de 1919.*

[67]Maxime du Camp, *Souvenirs d'un demi-siècle* (Paris, 1949), I, 63.

[68]Du Cellier, *Histoire des classes laborieuses*, 398-400.

prevalent in the decade, Louis Napoleon's personal experiences in the United States and England, the two most advanced industrial countries of the time, also contributed to his growing concern with social and economic problems. After the Strasbourg failure, the Orleanist government hurried Louis Napoleon off to the United States in order to avoid a public trial which, it feared, might embarrass the regime. Although Louis Napoleon spent only a short time in the United States—from March to June 1837—before returning to see his dying mother, his correspondence reveals the impression that the growth of industry in this country made upon him. In a letter to the President of the United States, Louis Napoleon expressed his admiration for the American people who had made greater conquests through commerce and industry than Europeans had made by arms.[69] A letter to Vieillard reveals a new awareness of the importance of social problems.[70] Formerly, he wrote, no great disparity of wealth had existed in the United States, but "now industry and commerce have shattered the equality of wealth. Great towns have appeared where man no longer battles with the soil but with man, his neighbor."

Louis Napoleon was in England several times, briefly in 1831, for almost two years between 1838 and 1840, and again from 1846 to 1848. The accounts of Louis Napoleon's stays in England usually linger upon his social and amatory experiences, his consorting with the English nobility, and such incidents as his participation in the elaborately staged Eglinton tournament (a revival of a medieval tournament). While Louis Napoleon was never adverse to physical comfort and charming women, he also devoted many hours to study and work while in England. He had a private study in the British Museum, and his drawing room

[69]Blanchard Jerrold, *The Life of Napoleon III* (London, 1875), II, 22.
[70]Duval, *Napoléon III*, 202.

was filled with periodicals and the latest books on a wide range of subjects. He also toured the industrial regions of England where, reported an English newspaper, "it was noticed that he was especially interested in the factories and shops, and took copious notes."[71] An American historian has said that on these tours Louis Napoleon first learned about the condition of the working class and of how important it was for him to formulate a Bonapartist social policy.[72]

The product of this new insight into the problems of his own day was *Les Idées napoléoniennes* (1839), a work which revealed both Louis Napoleon's recognition of the need for a Bonapartist social doctrine and for a popular propaganda.[73] Allegedly an exposition of the accomplishments and views of Napoleon I, the *Idées* is actually a platform for the Bonapartist party and another propaganda tract. The parts on politics, diplomacy, and military matters repeat the now familiar gospel of Saint-Helena. The Emperor had always believed in liberty, but war and internal dissension had not permitted him to give the French people the full measure of liberty which he had wished. He had saved the principles of 1789 from both the threat of counter-revolution and their own excesses. In foreign affairs, Napoleon I's great hope had been a European association, and he had never wanted the wars which filled his reign.

However, the importance of the *Idées* rests upon the fact that it added a new dimension to the Emperor—and to Bonapartism. Bonapartism, wrote Louis Napoleon, was not a doctrine of war and glory; it was "a social, industrial, commercial, humanitarian idea."[74] "The amelioration of the needy classes was one of

---

[71] Jerrold, *Life of Napoleon III*, II, 86.

[72] Franklin C. Palm, *England and Napoleon III, a Study of the Rise of a Utopian Dictator* (Durham, North Carolina, 1948), 7.

[73] The text may be found in *Oeuvres de Napoléon III*, v. 1.

[74] *Oeuvres de Napoléon III*, 1, 172.

the Emperor's main concerns," wrote his nephew.[75] To help the lower classes Napoleon I had founded many new charitable institutions and had encouraged the establishment of new industries; his great program of public works had provided jobs for many persons. The Emperor had, moreover, foreseen and warned against the rise of a new industrial feudalism: "Landed property had its vassals and serfs. The Revolution freed the soil. However, the new industrial property, which is increasing daily, passes through the same phases as the first and like it has vassals and serfs."[76] The Emperor had, therefore, sought to aid the working class, without, however, infringing upon the rights of their employers. In fact, the Empire had been a period of well-being and prosperity for workers. Unlike Louis Napoleon's previous works, which were usually for a specific group, the *Idées* was directed at a wide audience, including the *peuple*; a popular edition sold for fifty centimes. Lamartine (probably with poetic license) spoke of "editions of the *Idées napoléoniennes* running to five hundred thousand copies."[77]

At about the same time as *Les idées napoléoniennes*, a second work with a similar title, *L'idée Napoléonienne*, written or inspired by Louis Napoleon, also proclaimed the new doctrine of social Bonapartism.[78] The Napoleonic idea, it said, "goes into the huts of the people not with the sterile declaration of the rights of man but with the means to quench the thirst of the poor, to appease their hunger."[79]

A further sign that Louis Napoleon was now ready to exploit social and economic discontent was the propaganda that he dis-

[75]*Oeuvres de Napoléon III*, I, 68.

[76]*Oeuvres de Napoléon III*, I, 76-77.

[77]F. A. Simpson, *The Rise of Louis Napoleon*, 2nd ed. (London, 1929), 165; Lebey, *Les trois coups d'état*, 238.

[78]Also in *Oeuvres de Napoléon III*, v. I.

[79]*Oeuvres de Napoléon III*, I, 10.

tributed during his second attempt to overthrow the July Monarchy by a *coup d'état*. The plan resembled closely the unsuccessful Strasbourg conspiracy. Landing at Boulogne in 1840, with a small group of followers, Louis Napoleon again placed his hopes on the military, whose adherence he sought as a prelude to a march on Paris. The Boulogne attempt was even a greater disaster for the Bonapartist cause, since the government seized and condemned the Pretender to life imprisonment in the fortress of Ham in northern France.

However, despite Louis Napoleon's continuing reliance upon the army, his proclamations at Boulogne stressed economic discontent far more than did the propaganda at Strasbourg four years earlier.[80] A proclamation to the French people, for example, appealed to the economic interests of the different classes in a way that anticipated Bonapartist propaganda in 1848. Taxes, it charged, were higher in peacetime than during Napoleon I's wars. The tariff policy of the July Monarchy sacrificed the interests of French merchants and industrialists to foreigners. The proclamation charged the Orleanist government with responsibility for the decline of trade, for almost deserted ports and idle ships, and for the condition of the "laboring population which does not have enough to feed its children." And it reminded the lower classes that the Emperor had chosen "his lieutenants, his marshals, his ministers, his princes, his friends from among you."

Louis Napoleon's imprisonment at Ham from October, 1840 until his escape in May, 1846, was in keeping with his position as the nephew of the great Napoleon. He had a valet, received frequent visitors, including a young woman from the town of Ham by whom he had two children, and he joined the commandant of the fortress in friendly games of whist. But the prisoner

[80]The complete text of Louis Napoleon's proclamations may also be found in Lebey, *Les trois coups d'état*, 304-308.

also continued his study of contemporary problems; he later referred to his prison as the University of Ham.[81] A childhood friend, the brilliant Madame Cornu, supplied the prisoner with books and periodicals and encouraged his study of social questions.[82] In February, 1843, Louis Napoleon requested of Madame Cornu, "subscribe me to *L'Atelier*. Purchase the books which you have discussed with me. I have only the one by Louis Blanc. I have read Say but I have forgotten him. I am reading the new edition of Adam Smith."[83] The following month he requested a recent work by Buret on the condition of the working classes in England and France,[84] and wrote that he had read *L'Union ouvrière* by Flora Tristan, a feminist and worker leader.[85]

Louis Napoleon also completed his education as a propagandist at the "University of Ham." He had long insisted that a revival of the Empire depended upon popular support. Without neglecting the political, military, and intellectual leaders to whom he had usually appealed in the past, he now set out to gain and organize that support. For this purpose he wrote numerous newspaper articles and pamphlets for the lower classes, sometimes specifically for workers. He corresponded with and encouraged visits by leading republicans and socialists, including Ledru-Rollin, Edgar Quinet, George Sand, and Louis Blanc.

Many of his articles appeared in republican newspapers, particularly the *Journal du Loiret* and the *Progrès du Pas-de-Calais*.

[81]Lebey, *Les trois coups d'état*, 416-417.

[82]Marcel Emerit, "L'Egerie de Napoléon III, Madame Cornu," *Revue de Paris*, III (1937), 556-557.

[83]Jerrold, *Life of Napoleon III*, II, 421. *L'Atelier* was a workers' newspaper, important in the history of the French working class, which appeared between 1840 and 1850. See, A. Cuvillier, *Un journal d'ouvriers, "L'Atelier," 1840-1850* (Paris, 1914).

[84]Eugène Buret, *De la misère des classes laborieuses en Angleterre et en France* (Paris, 1840), 2 vol.

[85]Marcel Emerit, *Lettres de Napoléon III à Madame Cornu* (Paris, 1937), II, 67-68.

(The editor of the latter newspaper believed that Louis Napoleon had forgotten his dynastic ambitions and had become a sincere democrat.)[86] An article in *Le Progrès* (June 26, 1843) declared that governments had the obligation "to seek by all methods to eliminate poverty."[87] Another article, also in a republican newspaper, condemned the practice of ennoblement as undemocratic and outmoded.[88] The government, he wrote, would do better to ennoble "thirty-five million Frenchmen by offering them the opportunity for an education, a moral life, well-being, blessings which up to now have been the prerogative of a small number and which should be the prerogative of all." A public letter by Louis Napoleon in response to an attack upon Napoleon I by Lamartine, agreed that, "Napoleon made mistakes and had prejudices, but what will mark him off forever in the eyes of the masses is that he was the king of the people while the others were the kings of the nobles and privileged."[89] Louis Napoleon was particularly concerned that his response to Lamartine appear in the worker newspaper, *L'Atelier*.[90]

Louis Napoleon's plan to found a newspaper for workers reveals how important it now seemed to him to influence the working class. In 1844 and 1845, he attempted to found or purchase a newspaper "of the extreme left . . . which combines memories of the Empire with democratic ideas."[91] He hoped to establish a weekly newspaper similar in appearance to *L'Atelier*, since weeklies had in England the largest circulation "among the people."[92]

86Lebey, *Les trois coups d'état*, 424-425.

87*Oeuvres de Napoléon III*, II, 11.

88*Oeuvres de Napoléon III*, II, 55.

89*Oeuvres de Napoléon III*, I, 368.

90Emerit, *Lettres de Napoléon III*, II, 69.

91Peauger, "Lettres du fort de Ham," 664; Louis Napoleon to Peauger, September 30, 1844.

92Peauger, "Lettres du fort de Ham," 670; Louis Napoleon to Peauger, July 16, 1845.

Despite considerable efforts, nothing, however, came of Louis Napoleon's plan, probably because of financial reasons.

From Ham, Louis Napoleon continued his campaign to convince republicans that they could, without violating their beliefs, support Bonapartism. In June 1844, he sought the aid of the republican Ledru-Rollin, "I would be happy to have as a representative a man whose political convictions approach mine so closely."[93] Among the many visitors whom Louis Napoleon received at Ham was the socialist Louis Blanc who spent three days exchanging views with the prisoner.[94] According to Blanc's account, although the two differed on the question of the best form of government for France, their views on social problems were quite similar. Blanc wrote that he was amazed at Louis Napoleon's apparent acceptance of socialist principles. Before Blanc left, the prisoner presented him with an autographed copy of a work that he had just completed, *L'Extinction du paupérisme.*

This short book, published in 1844, was Louis Napoleon's most direct and most striking effort to convince workers that Bonapartism called for basic social reforms.[95] During the Second Republic and the Second Empire, Bonapartists constantly quoted from the *Extinction* and cited it as incontrovertible evidence of Louis Napoleon's early interest in the working class. In the *Extinction*, Louis Napoleon proposed to expropriate uncultivated lands, with compensation to the owners, and convert them into agricultural colonies for the needy and for the unemployed until private industry again required them. The book is, however, ambiguous on a number of points, which Louis Napoleon did not subsequently clarify. This failure is not very significant,

[93]Thirria, *Napoléon III*, I, 212.

[94]For Louis Blanc's own account of these conversations see his *1848, Historical Revelations* (London, 1858), 496-497. See also Leo A. Loubère, *Louis Blanc, His Life and His Contribution to the Rise of French Jacobin-Socialism* (Northwestern U. Press), 1961, 58-59.

[95]It may be found in *Oeuvres de Napoléon III*, v. II.

since the propaganda value of the *Extinction* is based upon its attacks upon social evils rather than the plan for colonies. In fact, in 1848 and during the Second Empire when publicists and officials quoted from or cited the *Extinction du paupérisme*, they usually forgot the colonies (perhaps because Louis Napoleon had also forgotten them). The work attacked the evils of the factory system—a system that forced workers to live in crowded and unhealthy neighborhoods that weakened both body and mind.[96] And, it continued, when industry did not require their services it threw into the streets the workers who had "sacrificed their strength, their youth, and their being to enrichen it." It was, further, a disgrace that in the nineteenth century "at least a tenth of the population is in rags and is dying of hunger in the presence of manufactured products which cannot be sold and millions in products of the soil which cannot be consumed."[97] Like so many socialists of the time, he condemned "a selfish world abandoned to the feudality of money."[98]

From its very conception, Louis Napoleon regarded his work on the social problem as a major piece of propaganda. In February 1843, he wrote Madame Cornu that he was planning to write a book which "cannot fail to help me greatly if I treat the subject adequately; it is on the well-being of the working class."[99] After completing the *Extinction* Louis Napoleon wrote that he hoped to obtain a wide circulation for it, "for I think that nothing else will serve me as well." He expected, of course, that workers would read the *Extinction*, and, in April 1844, he sent a representative to Paris to encourage its circulation "as widely as possible among the working class.[99a] In June 1844, he instructed

[96]*Oeuvres de Napoléon III*, II, 112.
[97]*Oeuvres de Napoléon III*, II, 148.
[98]*Oeuvres de Napoléon III*, II, 126.
[99]Emerit, *Lettres de Napoléon III*, II, 46-48.
[99a]Emerit, *Lettres de Napoléon III*, II, 46-48.

his Parisian representative to deliver copies of the *Extinction* to several persons whom he named, including a M. Zhendre, a resident of the Parisian working class neighborhood, the Villette, who had a "great influence on elections in the quarter."[100] Louis Napoleon also followed closely the impression created by *Extinction* and responded to comments upon it. In August 1844, he complained that few newspapers had discussed his book and that several had expressed unfavorable opinions, including *L'Atelier,* which had "published a not very kind article."[101] When a group of printers thanked Louis Napoleon for his concern with the working class, he replied that a "sign of sympathy from men of the people" was very "precious" to him, and that he would always do his utmost "to merit the praise and to work in the interest of that immense majority of the French people which at the present time has neither political rights nor the assurance of well-being."[102]

The Revolution of 1848 opened a period of unprecedented propaganda. The proclamation of universal manhood suffrage increased the number of eligible voters from less than 300,000 to about 9,000,000. Henceforth, the factions and parties competing for the support of the French electorate had to appeal to millions of voters and not just the *pays légal*. Between February 24 and the end of 1848, some 450 newspapers appeared; most of them consisted of a single page and often disappeared after the first issue.[103] Not satisfied with customary white paper and black type, some newspapers appeared on colored paper—scarlet, pink,

---

[100]Peauger, "Lettres du fort de Ham," 458.

[101]Emerit, *Lettres de Napoléon III*, II, 46-48.

[102]Thirria, *Napoléon III*, I, 265.

[103]For these newspapers, some impossible to find today, see Eugène Hatin, *Bibliographie historique et critique de la presse périodique française* (Paris, 1866). Collins, *The Government and the Newspaper Press*, 102-103, has a vivid account of this sudden blossoming of newspapers.

white with yellow stripes or colored ink. In the enthusiasm for reform that prevailed in Paris in the weeks following the February Revolution, even conservative newspapers adopted radical and democratic titles. Placards and pamphlets also disseminated the message of the rival claimants to leadership in France. (The catalogues of the *Bibliothèque nationale* reveal the enormous number of pamphlets that appeared during 1848.) Much of this propaganda appealed particularly to the working class which had overthrown a monarch and which, until the spring, seemed to control the destiny of France. Typical of this propaganda was an article in the Legitimist *L'Union* praising the Bourbon pretender for his interest in social problems.[104]

Before the June Days, Bonapartist propaganda to the working class resembled that of the radical republicans and socialists. Its promises to the workers matched those of its rivals, and, in addition, it offered the name Napoleon.[105] Bonapartist agents mingled with the workers of Paris who since the Revolution spent much of their time on the streets demonstrating and discussing the issues of the day. They were active among the workers employed in the *Ateliers nationaux*, where they had the cooperation of the director, Emile Thomas.[106] For the June elections to the Constituent Assembly, Bonapartists created an efficient organization for the posting of campaign placards; each evening Persigny and the

[104]L. A. Garnier-Pagès, *Histoire de la Révolution de 1848* (Paris, 1872), X, 85. The Bourbon claimant to the throne, said the article, had read all of the works by the socialist writers and not out of simple curiosity, "mais pour chercher la solution des graves questions aux développements desquelles ils sont consacrés. L'organisation du travail, cette pierre d'échoppement des socialistes, a été l'objet constant de ses études, et j'ose affirmer que personne n'a sur cette matière des notions plus étendues et plus complètes."

[105]For Bonapartist propaganda in 1848 see Robert Pimienta, "La propagande bonapartiste en 1848," *La Révolution de 1848*, VI (1909), VII (1909-1910); also P. Ulin, *Prince Louis Napoléon and the Workers Vote in 1848. A Study in Modern Revolution* (Harvard, 1943), unpublished honors thesis.

[106]Garnier-Pagès, *Histoire de la Révolution de 1848*, II, 315.

banker Aristide Ferrère walked through the streets of Paris to make certain that the placards were in place and to locate advantageous spots for others.[107] Among the specialized newspapers founded by the Bonapartists for the different classes were several for workers: *Le Napoléon républicain, Le Napoléonien,* and *L'Organisation du travail.*

Two men directed Bonapartist propaganda in 1848: Persigny and the banker Ferrère. Shortly before the outbreak of the February Revolution, Persigny, sensing that the July Monarchy was nearing its end, wrote two letters to Louis Napoleon in England (February 17 and 18, 1848) requesting funds for more propaganda and insisting that the Bonapartists must associate themselves with the revolution as soon as it began.[108] Ferrère believed that the Strasbourg and Boulogne attempts had failed "because they were made at an inopportune time and relied upon a military conspiracy without the participation of the people."[109] To remedy this weakness, Ferrère and Persigny prepared a plan, which Louis Napoleon accepted, to exploit universal manhood suffrage for the Bonapartist cause.

Bonapartist propaganda to workers in 1848 was obvious and direct, uncomplicated subtilties. A typical placard cited Louis Napoleon's interest in "the amelioration of the condition of the working classes," and "the extinction of poverty by work."[110] Another placard urged: "Read *L'Extinction du Paupérisme* which he wrote at the prison of Ham. I am certain that you will be able

[107]Aristide Ferrère, *Révélations sur la propagande napoléonienne faite en 1848 et 1849 pour servir à l'histoire secrète des élections du prince Napoléon Louis Bonaparte* (Turin, 1863), 163-165. Ferrère's role in the planning and dissemination of Bonapartist propaganda in 1848 would not be known except for his own account. Much of what we know about the organization of this propaganda is based on Ferrère, who perhaps exaggerated his own part, since he wrote to remind Napoleon III of what he regarded as his unrewarded services.

[108]Paul Chrétien, *Le duc de Persigny* (Toulouse, 1943), 27.

[109]Ferrère, *Révélations,* 27-28.

[110]Pimienta, "La propagande bonapartiste," VII, 93-94.

to judge his heart, his talents, and his love for the people."[111] Improvising on the same theme, a placard told workers that in voting for Louis Napoleon they would show their gratitude to him "for having thought of them while he was in the prison of Ham."[112] The *Napoléon républicain* quoted Napoleon I as saying, "I wished the worker to be happy and to earn his six francs per day."[113]

Until the June Days, Bonapartist attacks upon the wealthy and appeals to class interest were often extremely violent. "The people," said *Le Napoléonien*, "is still under the yoke of the aristocracy of money whose maneuvers precipitated the downfall of Napoleon."[114] Another Bonapartist newspaper, *L'Organisation du travail*, after listing the names of sixty Parisian millionaires, asked, "Is it possible that one can acquire some twenty millions honestly in a period of twenty years?"[115]

Although antisemitism played a part in Bonapartist propaganda, its importance should not be exaggerated; it was not a major theme of Bonapartist propaganda, nor were Louis Napoleon's supporters the only ones to use it. The prominence of Jewish bankers, notably the Rothschilds, had introduced antisemitism among the left and the socialists.[116] After the names of

[111]André Lebey, *Louis-Napoléon Bonaparte et la Révolution de 1848* (Paris, 1907), I, 195-196.

[112]Odette Merlat-Guitard, *Louis-Napoléon Bonaparte de l'exile à l'Elysée* (Paris, 1939), 199.

[113]Lebey, *Louis-Napoléon Bonaparte*, I, 237. A contemporary anti-Bonapartist print shows a worker and his wife gazing with admiration at Ratapoil, a caricature of the Bonapartist adventurer. The caption reads: "Ce bon M. Ratapoil leur a promis qu'après qu'ils auraient signé sa pétition les alouettes leur tomberaient toutes rôties." Georges Renard, *La République de 1848 (1848-1852)* (Paris, 1907), 229; v. IX of *Histoire socialiste*, ed. by Jean Jaurès.

[114]Pimienta, "La propagande bonapartiste," VII, 159-160.

[115]Pimienta, "La Propagande bonapartiste," VII, 160-161.

[116]For this subject see Robert F. Byrnes, *Antisemitism in Modern France. The Prologue to the Dreyfus Affair* (New Brunswick, New Jersey, 1950), Ch. II, particu-

some of the wealthy Parisians listed in the article in *L'Organi-sation du travail* cited above, appeared the epithet, "foreigner and Jew." The *Napoléonien* blamed the ills of France upon the Jews: "Down with the Jews. . . . The usurers and the Jews are re-sponsible for our hardships and miseries."[117]

After the June Days, Bonapartist propaganda among workers was more restrained. Bonapartists, who were believed by many to share in the responsibility for the uprising, had to dissasoci-ate themselves from it. Louis Napoleon, moreover, had been shocked by the violence of the civil war; to Madame Cornu he wrote, "We live in a very terrible time, and I see everywhere only the approaching dissolution of society."[118] Bonapartists still in-sisted upon their sympathy for the working class, but now con-trasted what they called their own practical and realizable re-forms with the Utopian schemes of radical republicans and socialists. A manifesto signed by a group of workers from Lyons and published in several newspapers and as a placard was typical; it stated that Louis Napoleon favored a democratic and prudent-ly progressive government "with respect for the family and for property."[119] However, not all Bonapartist propaganda, after the June Days had this restrained tone. Louis Napoleon's followers

---

larly pp. 114 ff on the antisemitism of the left. Byrnes says (p. 114): "Most antisemi-tism in France before 1880 or 1885 came from the Left not the Right."

During the Second Empire, moreover, Jews occupied an important place in gov-ernment, finance, industry and the press, and I have found few signs of antisemitism by public officials. Most reports that described antisemitic incidents attributed them to outdated prejudices. In Alsace, it is true, some officials shared the popular feel-ing against Jews and attacked them as usurers. Louis Napoleon did not use anti-semitism. In *Des idées napoléoniennes*, he praised Napoleon I for integrating the Jews into the national community: "Les Juifs deviennent citoyens, et les barrières qui les séparaient du reste de la nation disparurent peu à peu," *Oeuvres de Napo-léon III*, I, 52.

[117]Pimienta, "La propagande bonapartiste," VII, 160.

[118]Emerit, *Lettres de Napoléon III*, II, 258.

[119]B.N. Lb54 2218, "Manifeste des ouvriers lyonnais en faveur de la candidature du citoyen Louis-Napoléon Bonaparte" (Paris, 1848). This is a placard.

continued to distribute among workers copies of the *Extinction du paupérisme* with its radical sounding attacks upon the social order. The *Procureur général* at Metz complained that a Bonapartist circular issued during the presidential campaign of 1848 aroused the popular classes "and particularly the working class against the government."[120] A copy of the circular that the *Procureur général* included with the report reveals that he was not exaggerating.

Louis Napoleon himself had a considerable part in the Bonapartist propaganda campaign of 1848.[121] His few public statements were well-chosen and calculated. In October 1848, for example, he made a bid for the favor of the June Day victims and their families. France, he said, needed a strong and wise government that was more concerned with the ills of society than with seeking vengeance.[122] He also found time to write brief notes to workers and to reply to their letters. When workers from the city of Troyes wrote to assure him of their votes in the presidential election, Louis Napoleon replied that he had meditated upon workers' problems in prison and in exile and that he would always continue to be concerned with them.[123]

Louis Napoleon also shared in the planning of Bonapartist propaganda and followed its effects closely. In April 1848, he asked Persigny for more information "concerning the news published by *The Times* that all the boatmen and coal dealers in the Villette voted for me."[124] On September 2, 1848, he wrote

[120]*Archives nationales* (hereafter A.N.) BB[18] 1848, *Procureur général* at Metz to the Minister of Justice, December 1, 1848.

[121]H. N. Boon, *Rêve et réalité dans l'oeuvre économique et sociale de Napoléon III* (The Hague, 1936), 50, underestimates Louis Napoleon's role in 1848. "Il était pour très peu dans toute la bagarre qui se concentrait autour de son nom."

[122]*Oeuvres de Napoléon III*, III, 22.

[123]Lebey, *Louis Napoléon Bonaparte*, II, 287-288.

[124]Paul Duchon, "Les élections de 1848 d'après les correspondances inédites du prince Louis Napoléon et de M. de Persigny," *Revue de Paris* (1936, II), 48.

Persigny, "It is necessary to see to Lille, Metz, and Lyons [all industrial towns]."[125] And a week later he complained of an agent that Persigny had sent to Lille: "He is a fool and the most stupid, most senseless, most tedious man whom I have ever seen. How could you send him to Lille?"[126] The presidential candidate also personally wrote some anonymous Bonapartist propaganda. His letter of August 10, 1848, to Persigny said, "I am busy on a pamphlet that will have great effect; it is not concerned with politics but with political economy."[127] The letter also stated that he was forwarding a completed pamphlet but did not give further details. Louis Napoleon himself changed the statement of principles prepared by his aids for the presidential campaign of 1848 so as to make it more attractive to workers. He added, for example, the sentence, "Whoever says republic also says association."[128] (Association was one of the favorite terms of reformers in 1848; it had almost as many meanings as the persons who used it.)

Just as during the years at Ham, Louis Napoleon sought out and maintained amicable relations with socialist leaders. Louis Blanc relates that soon after he arrived in England following the *journée* of May 15, Louis Napoleon paid him a visit.[129] "He came to me in the most friendly way," wrote Blanc, "expressing how indignant he felt at the iniquitous treatment I had experienced." During their conversation he tried to convince Blanc "that he was heartily devoted to the people; and that, on social questions

[125]Duchon, "Les élections de 1848," 393, 394.

[126]Duchon, "Les élections de 1848," 395.

[127]Duchon, "Les élections de 1848," 390.

[128]Emerit, *Lettres de Napoléon III*, II, 259. Emerit says that the corrections on the printer's proof are in Napoleon's handwriting.

[129]Blanc, *Historical Revelations*, 501-502. Blanc also complained that Louis Napoleon's letters after their discussions at Ham gave him reason to believe that the Pretender "would come to the manly resolution of declaring himself Republican" (p. 500), and that in 1848 Napoleon had published a private letter "with a view to delude the Parisian workingmen into voting for him" (pp. 501-502). Blanc wrote his *Revelations* in English.

especially, his opinions were to a great extent in accordance with my own."

Louis Napoleon also attempted to gain the support of the socialist P.-J. Proudhon. In September, 1848, he arranged a meeting with Proudhon and the republican Joly to discuss the political and social problems faced by France.[130] Although Proudhon and Joly expressed the most radical opinions, wrote Darimon, who was also present, "to their great astonishment they were heard with marked favor and some very significant signs of approval gave them reason to believe that their illustrious colleague agreed with them on almost everything."[131] Louis Napoleon assured Proudhon that he did not oppose the socialists and that he disapproved of Cavaignac's repressive measures against workers. His efforts to convert Proudhon to Bonapartism were not, moreover, entirely wasted; even after the *coup d'état* Proudhon still believed that in order to remain in power a Bonapartist government must be revolutionary.[132]

[130]Alfred Darimon, *A travers une révolution (1847-1855)* (Paris, 1894), 68 ff. Darimon was Proudhon's secretary.

[131]Louis Napoleon had the gift of leaving people with the impression that he agreed with or had been convinced by their arguments, even though subsequent actions revealed his opposition.

[132]This is the message of Proudhon's *La révolution sociale démontrée par le coup d'état du deux décembre* (Paris, 1936), new ed. by C. Bouglé and H. Moysset.

Propaganda Media: The Press

The victory of Louis Napoleon in the presidential elections of 1848 was due primarily to the skill with which Bonapartist propagandists appealed to the recently enfranchised masses. The lessons of the election of 1848 were never forgotten by the men of the Second Empire. From its beginning to the very end the government of Napoleon III was constantly preoccupied with public opinion. The Minister of the Interior Morny was merely voicing a widely accepted view when, in a general circular to the prefects, he wrote that in the age of universal manhood suffrage public opinion was the most powerful force in society.[1]

In order to influence public opinion, the government had to know what the people were thinking. The Second Empire, therefore, organized an elaborate machinery to learn the attitude of Frenchmen towards the regime and on current issues.[2] The *procureurs généraux*, the public prosecutors at the appeals courts, sent regular reports to the Minister of Justice on conditions in their jurisdictions, with particular emphasis on public opinion. The frequency of the *procureurs'* reports varied with the situation in the country, from twice a year during the relatively calm

---

[1]Pierre de la Gorce, *Histoire du Second Empire* (Paris, 1899-1905), I, 53.

[2]For how the Second Empire attempted to keep informed on public opinion see Lynn M. Case, *French Opinion on War and Diplomacy during the Second Empire* (Philadelphia, 1954), 6 ff.

middle 1850's to once a week during the war with Austria. In addition, the prefects regularly prepared similar reports to the Minister of the Interior. To supplement these, the reports of the Prefect of Police described conditions in Paris. The reports, moreover, were carefully studied and summaries were prepared for the Emperor. Frequent reprimands by ministers for inadequate reports further reveal the importance that the government attached to them. In 1853, the Minister of the Interior complained to the Prefect of the Department of the Seine-Inférieure that a report by a sub-prefect dated November 22 "had been copied word for word . . . from that of September 25."[3] Another report the Minister called "superficial."[4] The reports of the sub-prefect at Vienne were so eager to say what they assumed the government wanted to hear that they were of little value.[5] The reports of the Prefect of the Department of the Bouches-du-Rhône, complained the government, did not include sufficient details.[6]

The care with which the Press Bureau examined and analyzed the contents of newspapers also shows the government's concern with ascertaining public opinion. The Press Bureau regularly examined and prepared summaries of the contents of French and foreign newspapers. A memorandum stated that the bureau received 546 departmental newspapers and prepared summaries of the contents of the Parisian press for the Emperor.[7]

The gathering of information was only the beginning; the government also believed that it must form public opinion. "It is in the public interest in France," wrote a government publicist, "that the state speak to the people and not abandon the direction

[3]*Archives Nationales* (hereafter A.N.), F1c III Seine Inférieure 9, December 6, 1853.

[4]A.N. F1c III, Seine-Inférieure 9, 1855 (Summer).

[5]A.N. F1c III, Isère 7, no date but in the 1850's.

[6]A.N. F1c III, Bouches-du-Rhône 7, November 11, 1858.

[7]A.N. F18 310, "Division de la presse," no date.

of opinion to the caprices of chance and the incitements of factious minorities."[8] The editor of a leading pro-government newspaper declared that the press had "the important mission of speaking to the public mind, of instructing, of forming, of correcting it when it has been misled," and of establishing between the state and the public the good relations "without which the government is always weak and liberty always dangerous."[9]

Government propaganda sought, particularly, to shape the thinking of those classes which had, in Persigny's words, "received from Providence the lot of work and poverty."[10] When these classes, said Persigny, have faith in the justice and solicitude of the constituted authorities, society is secure, "for it has to defend it the very forces which aid revolutions." Emile Ollivier relates that at their first meeting (June 27, 1865), Napoleon III was eager to have his estimate of "the state of mind of the working classes."[11] Official reports on public opinion also reflected this preoccupation with worker opinion. In the industrialized departments they devoted more space to the attitudes and activities of the working class than to those of any other class.

In order to direct public opinion, the government utilized most of the available means of communication with the French people. The propaganda media available to the Second Empire were the traditional ones; technological innovations, such as radio and television, which play so large a part in propaganda today, were still far off. What is new, however, is the attitude of the government towards the media that it inherited from the past, its willingness and capacity to use them to mold the thinking of Frenchmen.

[8]Hippolyte Castille, *Le vicomte de la Guéronnière* (Paris, 1860), 52.

[9]*La Patrie*, March 4, 1851.

[10]J. Delaroa, *Le duc de Persigny et les doctrines de l'Empire* (Paris, 1865), 45.

[11]Emile Ollivier, *L'Empire libéral* (Paris, 1895-1910), VII, 405.

The Press

Government use of the press for propaganda purposes was an old French tradition—as old as the articles Cardinal Richelieu wrote for the first French newspaper, *La Gazette.* Following the French Revolution, however, the Restoration and July Monarchies, faced as they were by constant opposition from competing dynasties and the republicans, relied more upon the press to influence public opinion than ever before. The July Monarchy, for example, founded the *Bureau de l'esprit public,* a kind of propaganda agency whose main concern was the press.[12] It also subsidized several important Parisian newspapers and provided financial assistance for cooperative provincial newspapers.

This propaganda, particularly during the July Monarchy, did not, however, seek to influence the attitude of workers, peasants, and the petty bourgeoisie; it was directed primarily at those Frenchmen who paid sufficient taxes to have the right to vote, and then only during electoral campaigns.[13] The pro-government newspaper, the *Débats,* for example, "had nothing to offer to the *petit bourgeois* reader who hoped for extension of the franchise or to the worker who hoped for social reform."[14] Louis Philippe's government ignored the advice of Emile de Girardin, a pioneer of the modern press, who urged it to encourage the founding of "newspapers capable of being understood by the poor and uneducated classes."[15] Girardin also recommended that the government reduce the subscription rate for *Le Moniteur,* and make it a more lively newspaper.

[12]Jean Morienval, *Les créateurs de la grande presse en France* (Paris, 1934), 15.

[13]For the July Monarchy's use of the press during electoral campaigns see, Sherman Kent, *Electoral Procedure under Louis Philippe* (New Haven, Conn., 1937), 119 ff.

[14]Irène Collins, *The Government and the Newspaper Press in France (1814-1881)* (London, 1959), 86-87.

[15]Morienval, *Les créateurs de la grande presse,* 36-37; Hippolyte Castille, *E. de Girardin* (Paris, 1858), 25.

Because of the limited appeal of official newspapers, the opposition parties, particularly the republicans, made far more effective use of the press than the government before the arrival in power of Napoleon III. Newspapers, such as *Le National,* in 1830, and *Le National* and *La Réforme,* in 1848, had key roles in the two revolutions.

However, unlike the regimes which preceded it, the Second Empire believed that newspapers should be used to influence the entire population, and until the last years of Louis Napoleon's reign the press was an instrument in the hands of the government. There was considerable truth in Jules Faure's statement before the *Corps législatif* in 1862, "There is but one journalist in France and that journalist is the Emperor."[16] A bitter satire on the press during the Second Empire by the republican journalist Maurice Joly, despite its exaggerations, also contains much that is true.[17] Machiavelli, who is the spokesman for Bonapartist principles and tactics in Joly's imaginary dialogue, discusses the Imperial press policy. He first describes the repressive features of the Second Empire's press laws. Repression is, however, but the negative aspect of the government's relations with the press. Newspapers, says Machiavelli, can also serve positively to strengthen the regime:

I dare say that until the present no government has had a conception more bold than that which I am going to discuss with you. In parliamentary states, governments almost always fall as the result of the action of the press. Well, I foresee the possibility of neutralizing the

[16]Charles Ledré, *Histoire de la presse* (Paris, 1958), 248.

[17]Maurice Joly, *Dialogues aux enfers entre Machiavel et Montesquieu ou la politique de Machiavel au XIXe siècle* (Brussels, 1864), 139 ff. The publication of this "revolutionary book" gained Joly a sentence of fifteen months in prison, Henri Dabot, *Souvenirs et Impressions d'un bourgeois du quartier latin de Mai 1854 à Mai 1869* (Péronne, 1899), 169. The famous antisemitic tract, *The Protocols of the Elders of Zion,* is a paraphrase of Joly's work. Konrad Heiden, *Der Fuehrer* (New York, 1944), 1 ff.

press by the press itself. Since journalism is such a great force, do you know what my govenment will do? It will become a journalist, it will be journalism incarnate.

Whatever the number of opposition newspapers, continued Machiavelli, the government would have double the number. The government, moreover, would have several categories of newspapers. One category, the avowedly official newspaper, would have a very limited value. Another category of newspapers would be less official, but still frankly pro-government. Machiavelli anticipated, however, that the newspapers in the third category, those without visible ties to the regime, would be most useful. Newspapers of his kind would be published for every shade of opinion. "I will have an aristocratic organ in the aristocratic party," wrote Machiavelli, "a republican organ in the republican party, an anarchist organ, if necessary, in the anarchist party." Machiavelli also prescribed the contents of government newspapers:

Every day my newspapers will be filled with official speeches. . . . They will not forget that I live in an epoch when people believe that all the problems of society can be solved by industry, an epoch which is ceaselessly concerned with the amelioration of the working classes. . . . The well-being of the people will be the sole, unchanging subject of my public announcements.

The Second Empire did not, however, heed all of Machiavelli's advice (nor the advice of some public officials on the matter).[18] Ignoring the lessons of 1848, when Bonapartists had founded newspapers especially for workers, the government failed to organize a workers' press. As a result, government propaganda for workers appeared in the general press, in municipal or regional

[18]See pp. 197-198.

newspapers. This raises, of course, the question whether workers during the Second Empire read newspapers.

In the absence of detailed studies of the reading habits of workers and of how ideas reached them, an entirely satisfactory answer to this question cannot be given.[19] However, there is reason to believe that many workers read newspapers. The sharp increase of newspaper circulation, the appearance for the first time of a mass circulation press, suggests strongly that many workers read newspapers. Before the Second Empire a daily circulation of more than 20,000 was rare. In the 1860's, the popular edition of the official newspaper, *Le Moniteur*, reached a circulation figure of some 200,000,[20] and *Le Petit Journal*, 259,000.[21] And the circulation of other newspapers increased almost as dramatically. Material clearly intended for workers in government (and opposition) newspapers is also evidence that such newspapers believed or hoped that workers read them. In the 1860's, some government newspapers published articles and letters by workers. The considerable increase in the literacy rate of workers and evidence of their enthusiasm for the written word also suggests strongly that workers read newspapers. Tolain, one of the founders of the French section of the First International, commented on "the need to read everything which has seized the worker, the female worker, the apprentice."[22] The reports of the prefects and the *procureurs généraux* frequently complained that workers read opposition newspapers, especially *Le Siècle*; it is

[19]Georges Duveau has studied the "light" and "self-improvement" reading habits of workers, but not how political and social ideas penetrated them. *La vie ouvrière en France sous le Second Empire* (Paris, 1946), 469 ff.

[20]A.N. F12 295, "Tirage des journaux politiques de Paris, 1852-1867." This figure is an average for July, 1867.

[21]Morienval, *Les créateurs de la grande presse*, 228. For a brief time, in 1869, the circulation of *Le Petit journal* went to 467,000, when the newspaper published detailed and lurid accounts of the massacre of a father, mother, and their six children.

[22]Duveau, *La vie ouvrière*, 477.

reasonable to assume that some workers also read pro-government newspapers. A close observer of the working class during the Second Empire described the scene at a restaurant patronized by workers; in one dining room, a frivolous worker read aloud to his fellows the *faits divers* section of the newspaper, while in another dining room, a more serious minded worker read aloud the important articles.[23]

As Machiavelli had said, the pro-government press was numerous and varied. Since 1799 *Le Moniteur universel*, founded ten years before, had been the official voice of the government. However, Napoleon I, too economical to purchase or found an official journal, had permitted it to remain in private hands and subsequent regimes had continued his policy.[24] As a result, this unusual privately owned official newspaper had two sections, *une partie officielle*, under the direction of the Minister of the Interior, and a non-official section edited by the owners of the newspaper. The latter section, like the commercial newspapers with which it competed, included a *faits divers* column, continued stories, and advertisements. And, also like other newspapers of the time, its contributors included leading literary figures: Alfred de Musset, Alexandre Dumas, Théodore de Bainville, Théophile Gautier, Prosper Mérimée, Sainte-Beuve.

At the beginning of the Second Empire the government thoroughly reorganized *Le Moniteur,* in some instances following the suggestions of Emile de Girardin to the July Monarchy. It also reduced the subscription rate from 120 to 40 francs. As a result of these changes, the daily circulation of *Le Moniteur* rose from 2,000 to almost 25,000 in a short time.[25] Moreover, it tended to

---

[23]Denis Poulot, *La Sublime-Question Sociale,* 3rd ed. (Paris, 1887), 40.

[24]A. Périvier, *Napoléon journaliste* (Paris, 1918), 124.

[25]Henri Avenel, *Histoire de la presse française depuis 1789 jusqu'à nos jours* (Paris, 1900), 452-455.

maintain its circulation throughout the Second Empire, even after the popularity of other government newspapers declined.[26] The influence of *Le Moniteur* cannot, however, be measured by circulation figures alone. The entire French press (including opposition newspapers) looked to it for information not otherwise available; provincial newspapers frequently reprinted articles from the official journal. On the debit side, however, as Joly's Machiavelli had pointed out, the official status of *Le Moniteur* limited its value as an instrument of government propaganda.

Since most persons in the lower classes could not afford even the reduced subscription rate for *Le Moniteur*, the government, in 1864, founded a briefer and cheaper edition of the official newspaper, *Le Moniteur universel du soir*, which became popularly known as *Le Petit moniteur*.[27] It sold for six centimes the issue, a price that led to protests from its competitors (including pro-government newspapers) who paid a tax (the *timbre*) of five centimes on every number they published. The government openly stated that the purpose of the cheaper edition of *Le Moniteur* was to give the lower classes an official version of the news:[28]

The low price of this newspaper indicates that it is intended particularly to reach the classes which up to the present time have not had access to an official journal. It will enable the inhabitants of the town and countryside to understand the business of the nation by obtaining their information from an authentic source.

At first *Le Moniteur universel du soir* had only two pages, but later the format was reduced and the number of pages doubled. The evening edition included a section on official news and lighter reading, such as the *Feuilleton du Moniteur du soir*. While it printed much of interest to the lower classes, it was not

[26] A.N. F18, "Tirage des journaux politiques de Paris."
[27] Dabot, *Souvenirs et impressions*, 280.
[28] *Le Moniteur universel*, April 28, 1864.

intended only for them, as is indicated by the *Résumé de la bourse* which the newspaper published regularly. Circulation figures reveal the popularity of the evening edition; while the daily circulation of *Le Moniteur universel* hovered about 20,000 during the 1860's, the cheaper newspaper reached a circulation of 200,000.[29]

During the 1850's the pro-government newspapers with the largest circulations were the Parisian dailies, *Le Constitutionnel, Le Pays,* and *La Patrie.* These newspapers had been founded before the Second Empire but by the time of the *coup d'état,* for various personal and financial reasons, all three supported Louis Napoleon. *Le Constitutionnel,* which had the largest circulation of the three newspapers, appeared during the Restoration period; it then supported the opposition to the Bourbons. During the July Monarchy *Le Constitutionnel* was pro-government. In 1848, Doctor Véron, owner of *Le Constitutionnel,* deserted the Orleanists and favored the candidacy of Louis Napoleon for the presidency of the Second Republic. After the *coup d'état,* declining circulation and difficulties with the press section of the Ministry of the Interior forced Véron to sell his newspaper to the financier Mirès, also a partisan of Louis Napoleon, who already owned *Le Pays.*[30] On December 2, 1852, *Le Constitutionnel* announced an almost official tie to the newly created Second Empire; it added the subtitle, *"Journal de l'Empire,"* explaining that the new title "expressed the alliance between the country and the Empire of which Napoleon III today becomes the glorious head." The *Patrie,* wrote a contemporary journalist, combined accounts of "crimes, catastrophies, and accidents" with

[29]See p. 49 for the circulation of other newspapers.

[30]Somewhat later the Prefect of Police Maupas wrote to Napoleon III that Mirès' acquisition of *Le Constitutionnel* "a mis dans les mains de l'Empereur une publicité assurée de près de 60,000 abonnés, sans aucune charge pour le gouvernement." A.N. AB XIX (dossier 2), "Papiers des Tuileries," February 8, 1853.

"political news that the government wished to reveal to the public."[31]

The government's intervention in the affairs of these newspapers reveal the close ties that existed between them. The administration, for example, intervened regularly in personnel matters, such as the choice of editors and writers.[32] The Emperor himself urged *Le Pays* to reduce its subscription rate.[33] Mirès, owner of *Le Constitutionnel* and *Le Pays*, aptly described the popular belief concerning the relations between the government and his newspapers, "My devotion to the Empire was so absolute that men requested the position of editor-in-chief of my own newspapers from the government, as if they were public offices."[34]

Although the style and contents of these newspapers were often quite different, they all followed a policy of unqualified and uncritical praise of the government and Napoleon III, particularly during the 1850's. An incidental advantage of this common policy was that it facilitated the considerable interchange and sharing of personnel by the pro-government newspapers. Thus, Paulin Limayrac, who joined *Le Constitutionnel* in 1856 and became editor-in-chief in 1861, also wrote for *La Patrie* and *Le Pays*.[35] (In 1868, Limayrac was rewarded for his journalistic labors by being named Prefect of the Department of the Lot.) In 1862, Auguste Chevalier was named *directeur politique* of both *Le Constitutionnel* and *Le Pays*.[36]

During the last decade of the Second Empire the value to the government of the traditional Bonapartist press declined. As a

[31]Taxile Delord, *Histoire illustrée du Second Empire*, nouvelle ed. (Paris, 1880-1883), II, 191.

[32]A.N. F18 329 A, a file on *Le Constitutionnel* reveals many cases of government intervention.

[33]A.N. AB XIX 175 (dossier 21), "Papiers des Tuileries."

[34]Delord, *Histoire illustrée*, VI, 22.

[35]*La Grande Encyclopédie* (Paris, 1885-1902).

[36]A.N. F18329 A, File on *Le Constitutionnel*.

result, in the late 1850's and in the 1860's, the administration and the Emperor encouraged the founding of new newspapers to fill a need unmet by the existing government press. At a time when newspapers began to pride themselves upon their independence, the close ties known to exist between the government and the older newspapers became a handicap. An official report stated the relations between the established Bonapartist newspapers and the government created a "delicate and often compromising" situation and that it was, therefore, desirable for the government to secure "other auxiliaries."[37] Few persons were convinced when, in 1862, *Le Constitutionnel* and *La Patrie* announced that henceforth they would adopt an independent position towards the government, criticizing it when they believed that it was mistaken.[38] The older newspapers were also disconcerted by the government's new policies in the 1860's. Although they tried faithfully to follow Napoleon III along the unfamiliar paths of the Liberal Empire, they were too closely associated with the policies of the Authoritarian Empire to sound very convincing. Circulation figures show the decline in the popularity of the older government newspapers. While the number of issues printed of the moderately republican *Le Siècle* increased from 22,521 in July 1853 to some 52,000 in October 1860, the comparable figures for *Le Constitutionnel* declined from 23,655 to 21,448 and for *Le Pays*, from 13,261 to about 7,000.[39]

Another reason for the appearance of new government journals in the 1860's was the increased activity of the Emperor who frequently subsidized newspapers more directly subservient to him than were the older newspapers, which were often spokes-

[37]A.N. F18 295, May 28, 1866.

[38]Delord, *Histoire illustrée*, III, 287.

[39]A.N. F18 295. By 1867 the figures for *Le Constitutionnel* had fallen to 10,150, and for *Le Pays*, to 3,000. While the number of copies printed is not the same as the number sold, it is unlikely that a newspaper would either overprint or underprint regularly.

men for particular ministers more than for the government. Persigny observed bitterly that Parisian editors "were easily made to understand that to attack a minister was a more serious matter than to vilify the Empire."[40] The newspapers encouraged by Napoleon III, more in touch with the spirit of the Liberal Empire, frequently proclaimed their dedication to liberal principles and their independence, as well as their support of the government.

Most of these new pro-government newspapers were intended for the general public rather than for any particular class of the population, but their statements of policy and contents reveal that the working class was not forgotten. It is possible to cite, as examples, only a few of the new government newspapers. The *Revue de l'Empire*, founded in 1858, received authorization to discuss political and social questions in 1862. The issue that carried the authorization also announced the policy of the journal —a policy, it said, that was summed up in the words on the masthead, "Order and progress."[41] The *Revue de l'Empire* promised to "devote itself to both the defense of the great liberal principles and the maintenance of conservative interests." Its editor-in-chief, Emile Muraour, also served the Empire in other ways; he was the author of a number of works lauding the regime; *Triomphes de l'Empire* (1861), *Les gloires de l'Empire* (1861), *Campagnes glorieuses du règne de Napoléon III* (1863).

In June, 1866, Auguste Vitu, who had worked for *Le Constitutionnel* and *Le Pays*, founded the short lived *L'Etendard*. The first issue of the newspaper announced its support for "the strengthening of the Empire," and criticized both those who praised the regime uncritically and who condemned everything it did; it concluded that it would support the government "in the only way that seems efficacious to us, with liberty and with

[40]*Mémoires du duc de Persigny* (Paris, 1896), 400.
[41]*La Revue de l'Empire*, December 14, 1862.

frankness."[42] One month later a new pro-government newspaper appeared, *L'Etincelle*, with Florian Pharaon, a government publicist as editor-in-chief.[43] The first issue of *L'Etincelle* proclaimed its purpose to be "education by newspaper," and that it had, therefore, assembled "the writers most appreciated by the public and most devoted to the working classes."[44] The *Etincelle* tried hard to become a newspaper for *le peuple*. Its "education by the newspaper" consisted mainly of anecdotes, comic incidents, and accounts of the social activities of the royal couple and Imperial dignitaries. It printed little obvious propaganda, but frequently inserted news items presenting the ruler and the government in a favorable light.

During the last years of the Second Empire the journalist Clément Duvernois, a former foe of the regime (he had once been sentenced to three months imprisonment for violation of the press laws), became one of Napoleon III's favorite publicists. His most important propaganda task seems to have been to dissuade the working class from joining with the political opposition to the Second Empire. In 1867, Duvernois became editor of *L'Epoque*, a newspaper in which the Emperor was especially interested. Napoleon III gave large subsidies to the newspaper's owner and personally reviewed and changed its statement of policy; a journalist on *L'Epoque* said of the Emperor's changes that they were "in the most socialist sense."[45] Two years later Duvernois founded a new newspaper, *Le Peuple français*, which also received large subsidies from the Emperor. The title and the contents of *Le Peuple français* indicate that it was intended for the lower classes, and, more than most pro-government newspapers

---

[42]Avenel, *Histoire de la presse française*, 518-519.

[43]Pharaon wrote laudatory accounts of Imperial tours: *Voyage en Algérie de Sa Majesté Napoléon III* (1865); *Voyage Impérial dans le nord de la France* (1867).

[44]*L'Etincelle*, July 10, 1866.

[45]Hector Pessard, *Mes petits papiers (1860-1870)* (Paris, 1887), I, 232-234.

especially for workers. The *Peuple français* carried on a two-front war: against the bourgeois liberals who were demanding greater power for the *Corps législatif* and against the radicals and socialists. A division of labor existed on the newspaper: while Duvernois defended the Empire against the liberals, his collaborator, Charles Gaumont, attacked the socialists in a kind of daily column, *Les réunions publiques*.

Most of the newspapers that I have been discussing hitherto belonged to a category known as the "political press"; this gave them the right, under the press laws of the Second Empire, to discuss political and social problems. Until 1868 no newspaper without such prior government authorization could discuss political and social issues. And since the government rarely authorized political newspapers (the first new political newspaper was *L'Opinion nationale* in 1859), a host of newspapers were founded, many of them short-lived, which avoided, or claimed to avoid, the forbidden areas of discussion. These non-political newspapers became popularly known as *la petite presse* or *la presse littéraire*, though few of them were actually literary journals; some specialized in business and financial news, others in crimes, scandals, and continued stories, and only a few, in literature, arts, and philosophy. Of the 1,098 newspapers published in France on January 1, 1865, 761 were by law non-political.[46]

The most successful of the "literary" newspapers, *Le Petit journal*, founded in 1863 by the financier Moïse Millaud, sold for one *sou* the issue and reached the unprecedented daily circulation figure of 250,000 to 300,000.[47] The success of Millaud's newspaper encouraged the founding of other low-priced newspapers, such as *La Petite presse*, and *Le Petit national*, and helped

[46]Eugène Hatin, *Bibliographie historique et critique de la presse périodique française* (Paris, 1866), XCII-XCIII.

[47]For Millaud's journalistic career see the chapter, "Millaud, ou le sou qui fourmille," in Morienval, *Les créateurs de la grande presse*.

provide the impetus for the popular edition of *Le Moniteur universel.*

A police report on the press reveals the relationship that existed between the government and some non-political newspapers:[48]

The small literary newspapers should not be neglected. The *Petite presse* and *Le Petit journal* alone have a printing of 700,000 copies per day. Of course, they cannot engage directly in politics, but by the insertion of a certain item, the omission of another, they can in the long run exert an influence which their very large circulation and the very special nature of their readers renders particularly interesting.

The directors of these two sheets are eager to cooperate discreetly with the government.

According to a press official in the Ministry of the Interior, Millaud agreed to print in *Le Petit journal* a number of brief biographies (*"portraits personnels"*) of Napoleon III's ministers and of the leading members of the majority in the *Corps législatif.*[49] "These very ably prepared biographies," said the official, "border on politics without discussing it."

Although *Le Petit journal* (specimen issue) assured the public that it did not intend "to modify the social order or even to give lessons to the government," Millaud's newspaper did, indeed, skirt the borders of politics. Between anecdotes, *faits divers,* and the articles of Timothée Trimm, probably the first popular columnist, *Le Petit journal* inserted brief news items favorable to the government and the Emperor. The specimen issue, for example, reprinted the following item from *Le Moniteur:* "The Emperor has had a new sum of 100,000 francs sent to the prefects

---

[48]*Papiers secrets brûlés dans l'incendie des Tuileries* (Brussels, 1873), 78-79. The report was unsigned and undated.

[49]*Papiers et correspondance de la famille impériale* (Paris, 1870-1872), I, 28.

for aid to needy workers which is an addition to the money which His Majesty has subscribed for the cotton workers of the Seine-Inférieure." Other issues frequently printed news items that revealed the government's and the Emperor's kindness towards and interest in workers: a government appropriation of 5,000,000 francs for workers in the depressed cotton textile industry (February 23, 1863), the inauguration of a new workers' housing project (June 29, 1863), subsidized restaurants for workers (January 11, 1864), awards for excellence to workers attending adult education classes (February 2, 1864). The *Petit journal* frequently praised the generosity of the Imperial family. When, in 1863, the Empress visited the *Hospice des enfants trouvés, Le Petit journal* acclaimed the act: "The Empress is the first princess since 1815 to have visited the institution" (June 14, 1863). After an inspection of the home for convalescent workers at Vincennes which had been founded by Napoleon III, the Prince Napoleon, the Emperor's cousin, reported that it was being administered "in perfect harmony with the generous thought which inspired its founding" (March 11, 1864).

The leading Parisian newspapers both "political" and "literary" also circulated in the provinces. But, in addition, a local and regional press also existed. The provincial press was predominantly pro-government. An official report of January 1, 1867, listed 272 political newspapers in the provinces; of these, 222 were pro-government, 24 Legitimist, 8 Orleanist, 10 liberal, and 8 democratic and republican.[50] Another report on the provincial press stated that, in 1868, 245,240 persons subscribed to government newspapers and 98,200 to opposition newspapers, and that while all but two departments had at least one pro-government

---

[50]A.N. F18 295. A note added: "Parmi les 222 feuilles gouvernementales, 9 échappent le plus ordinairement à l'action administrative et deviennent, dans certaines circonstances, les organes d'une opposition modérée.

newspaper, only 44 departments had an opposition newspaper.[51]

Moreover, as the reports of the prefects show, cooperation between the administration and the press was much closer in the provinces than in Paris. The following are typical of many reports that I have seen: The Prefect of the Bouches-du-Rhône wrote that the press in his department "followed the government line absolutely."[52] The Prefect of the Department of the Seine-Inférieure reported: "The newspapers loyal to the government are always eager to receive the administration's communications."[53] The subservience of the local press was due, in part, to more effective government pressure than was possible in Paris. By granting or denying official announcements the administration often decided the fate of a newspaper. There can be no mistaking the meaning of the *procureur général* at Rouen who, after reporting his dissatisfaction with a local newspaper, observed that it probably could not survive without the income from judicial announcements.[54] The *procureur général* at Toulouse was even more blunt: a newspaper in the town of Castres which had shown signs of independence "did not resist the threat to withdraw legal announcements that the administrative authority had thought it necessary to make."[55]

The government used the press agencies for the dissemination of propaganda and for the suppression or distortion of unfavorable news. Havas, the largest of them, received generous subsidies

[51]Collins, *The Government and the Newspaper Press*, 144-146.

[52]A.N. F1c III, Bouches-du-Rhône 7, prefect to the Minister of Interior, October 19, 1864.

[53]A.N. F1c III, Seine-Inférieure 9, prefect to the Minister of the Interior, October 18, 1864.

[54]A.N. BB30 387, *procureur général* at Rouen to the Minister of Justice, April 12, 1862.

[55]A.N. BB30 388, *procureur général* at Toulouse to the Minister of the Interior, January 5, 1861.

from the government.[56] A letter to the Minister of Justice by Charles and A. Havas revealed how the press agency served the regime: Havas toned down or suppressed news harmful to the government and supplied the local press with news reports slanted in favor of the administration.[57] A report by an official in the press bureau of the Ministry of the Interior, probably towards the end of the Empire, stated that Havas was in daily contact with the Ministry and that "every time a denial, or a rectification, or useful information must be rapidly circulated, Havas condenses it into telegraphic form and distributes it throughout France."[58] Since Havas served 307 newspapers, continued the report, it was, indeed, a useful medium for the dissemination of pro-government information. The same report also described an agreement with a smaller press agency that served twenty-seven newspapers; the manager of the agency had agreed to report to the Ministry of the Interior daily during the electoral campaign (probably 1869) for instructions and to slant its dispatches in favor of the government insofar as he could do so "without revealing his relations to the government."

Far from desiring a uniform press, the government believed in diversity among the newspapers that supported it (Joly's Machiavelli had said that he would have a newspaper for each opinion). Although, in the 1860's, *L'Opinion nationale* vigorously attacked more conservative pro-government newspapers, at the same time it performed valuable services for the Second Empire among workers and liberals. An official report on the press ad-

[56]A.N. F18 310, Press Subventions.

[57]A.N. BB18 1644 (A3 6166), letter to the Minister of Justice, January, 1862: "Nous donnons aux journaux les dépêches télégraphiques que nous faisons venir de tous côtés, les atténuant, les adoucissant, . . . De plus, nous fournissons aux feuilles de province une correspondance politique très complète rédigée dans le sens gouvernemental."

[58]*Papiers et correspondances*, I, 25-26.

vised the government against giving *"une impulsion unique"* to all friendly newspapers, that is, against establishing a rigid party line for them to follow.[59] The *procureur général* at Lyons was not disturbed because one of the two pro-government newspapers in the Department of the Ain was "inclined towards moderate liberalism," while the other had "a rather clerical tone."[60] A police report on the press listed under the rubric, "Newspapers loyal to the government," journals which it said might "criticize the acts or the tendencies of the government on certain secondary questions," but generally supported the administration: "that manner of serving," observed the report, "is today perhaps the most useful."[61]

Even the existence of an opposition press was not necessarily a disadvantage. Relations between the government and opposition newspapers were often most cordial. These relations, it has been said, were marked by "useful silences and secret accommodations."[62] There were even "official" opposition newspapers. Emile Ollivier refused a salary of 40,000 francs to found a newspaper, *"d'opposition dirigée."*[63] Imperial officials accepted, even if sometimes reluctantly, the existence of an opposition press in a country as politically divided as France. "In a large city, in the midst of active parties with such diverse tendencies, I accept and I submit to the necessity of an opposition newspaper," wrote the

[59]A.N. F18 295, May 28, 1866.

[60]A.N. BB30 379, *procureur général* at Lyons to the Minister of Justice, March 26, 1864.

[61]*Papiers secrets brûlés dane l'incendie des Tuileries*, 74-75. This undated report is probably from the late 1860's.

[62]P.-J. Proudhon, *De la capacité politique des classes ouvrières*, new edition under the direction of C. Bouglé and H. Moysset (Paris, 1924), editors introd., 8.

[63]Emile Ollivier, *Journal*, v. I, 1848-1860 (Paris, 1961), preface, XVII; *Journal*, v. II, 1861-1869 (Paris, 1961), 96. Ollivier says that Morny spoke to him of a newspaper that the former wished to found: "J'en parlerai à l'Empereur, m'a-t-il dit. Si vous le voulez nous le fonderons ensemble. Ne vous adressez à personne; je vous donnerai de l'argent." Ollivier says that he refused the help.

procureur général at Lyons.[64] The *procureur général* at Toulouse saw certain advantages in permitting Emile Ollivier, then still an opposition leader, to acquire a newspaper at Toulon; such a newspaper might "render some service to the government" by restraining the ardor of revolutionaries.[65]

The administration also realized that praise or favorable news in opposition newspapers was more convincing than in the newspapers known to be pro-government. A report by an official in the Ministry of the Interior said of the *Journal des débats* that its services to the government had been "all the more precious since it is considered independent."[66] A police report on the press at Lyons derided the government newspaper, *Le Salut public*: "It simulates an independence more harmful than useful which does not deceive anyone."[67] On the other hand, *Le Progrès, Journal de l'union démocratique*, with many working class readers, had a greater influence, and if "radical for the public was amenable to arrangements with the administration."

The ties between the government and the opposition press were sometimes direct, sometimes more subtle. The Prefect of the Department of the Haut-Rhin reported that the editor-in-chief of the *Industriel Alsacien*, "the echo of advanced liberal ideas," had expressed "his desire to live on good terms" with the sub-prefect at Mulhouse.[68] A letter of Napoleon III to his cousin, the Prince Napoleon, urging him to use his influence on republican newspapers to curb their ardor for the Italian cause, sug-

[64]A.N. BB30 379, *procureur général* at Lyons to the Minister of Justice, December 28, 1864.

[65]A.N. BB30 345, Correspondence of the Minister of the Interior, November 18, 1868.

[66]A.N. F18 295, May 28, 1866.

[67]*Pièces saisies aux archives de la police politique de Lyon* (Lyon, 1870), 3-4.

[68]A.N. F1c III, Haut-Rhin 7, prefect to the Minister of the Interior, February, 1868.

gests the often unexpressed ties that existed between the government and the opposition press.[69]

The *Siècle*, a moderate republican newspaper, was by far the
most influential opposition journal; in the 1860's, its circulation
exceeded that of any other political newspaper, either governmental or opposition. Officials frequently expressed their fears
of its influence, particularly upon workers. The Prefect of the
Department of the Calvados denounced "the pernicious influence" of *Le Siècle*.[70] The Prefect of the Department of La Nièvre
reported that *Le Siècle*, very popular with workers, was the "apostle" of ideas that threatened "order and hierarchical discipline";
factory managers, he continued, attributed the "evil" views of
so many workers to their reading of republican newspapers.[71]

Napoleon III and the government at Paris did not, however,
share the alarm of local officials about the "pernicious influence"
of *Le Siècle*. In 1851 and 1859, the question of suspending *Le
Siècle* was raised, but on both occasions the government decided
against the action. In 1859, the Minister of the Interior said that
in view of the newspaper's support of the government's Italian
policy and its praise of the Emperor's conduct on the battlefield
of Solferino, suspension would be "an unpolitical measure."[72]
Havin, the director of *Le Siècle*, was described by a contemporary
journalist as "half Bonapartist,"[73] and by Emile Ollivier as by no
means "irreconcilable with the Empire."[74] When Havin announced his candidacy for the *Conseil général* of his department,
he obtained the endorsement of the prefect of the department,

[69]Ernest d'Hauterive, *Napoléon III et le prince Napoléon correspondance inédite*
(Paris, 1925), 121-123: "Si tu as de l'influence sur la presse [republican] conseille leur
de ne point emboucher la trompette lorsqu'on ne veut pas marcher.

[70]A.N. F18 417, file on *Le Siècle*, April 13, 1858.

[71]A.N. F18 417, April 13, 1856.

[72]A.N. F18 417, July 2, 1859.

[73]Pessard, *Mes petits papiers*, I, 37.

[74]Ollivier, *L'Empire libéral*, IV, 17.

the Minister of the Interior Persigny and Napoleon III himself—support which Havin proudly listed in his campaign literature.[75] Pierre de la Gorce, an historian not unsympathetic to the Second Empire, concluded from the relations between the government and *Le Siècle* that, "Napoleon had accomplished the miracle of becoming the regulator of the opposition itself."[76]

Why did most newspapers during the Second Empire, including the opposition press, arrive at an understanding with the government? A basic reason was that newspapers during the Second Empire were commercial ventures interested above all in providing a profit for their owners, and the favor or disfavor of the government often made a great difference. The owners of the great Parisian dailies, publishers like Mirès and Millaud, were also financiers, speculators, and entrepreneurs for whom relations with the government were often vital. Mirès placed his two newspapers, *Le Constitutionnel* and *Le Pays*, at the disposal of the government without receiving any immediate or direct reward, but certainly with the hope that the government would look upon his enterprises favorably. The award of judicial announcements was, we have seen, vital to some provincial newspapers; it was significant that in 1860 and 1864, official reports listed the names of newspapers whose existence probably depended upon judicial announcements.[77]

The Second Empire did not invent the practice of subsidizing newspapers, but as the contemporary journalist Taxile Delord stated, "No sovereign had ever spent more money for newspapers and for journalists" than Napoleon III.[78] This was especially

[75]Ollivier, *L'Empire libéral*, V, 310.
[76]La Gorce, *Histoire du Second Empire*, II, 82-83.
[77]Collins, *The Government and the Newspaper Press*, 132-133.
[78]Delord, *Histoire illustrée*, VI, 21-22.

true during the 1860's when opposition to the Empire increased.[79] Thus, a considerable portion of the *fonds secrets* went to the *service de la presse*.[80] According to a report by a press official, government subsidies had four purposes: to gain the support of newspapers whose precarious financial situation made it tempting for them to accept help from any source, to found new government newspapers and to assist existing ones, to enable government newspapers to distribute free issues and to purchase the secret cooperation of opposition newspapers.[81] The following examples are typical of the way in which government funds were distributed and used. An undated letter placed a sum of 5,000 francs at the disposition of the Prefect of the Bouches-du-Rhône for the needs of the press in his department.[82] On January 7, 1862, the Minister of the Interior sent to the Prefect of the Basses-Alpes "a sum of 150 francs for the editor-in-chief of *Le Journal des Basses Alpes*."[82a] The Prefect of the Department of the Allier received 1,000 francs to assist the government press in combatting "the evil influence of the journal the *Hebdomadaire de Vichy*."[83] In addition to the regular budget, the Emperor also drew upon his civil list to subsidize newspapers in which he had a special interest.[84] Between December 1867 and April 1868, Dusautoy,

[79]Although there is not a full record of government press subsidies, the published and archival sources are abundant. For example, I have seen an itemized list of press subsidies for the years 1862-1863, A.N. F18 306.

[80]*Papiers et correspondance*, I, 121. Though it was well known that the government aided friendly newspapers, the administration tried to keep the details secret. Thus, letters from the Minister of the Interior to the prefects authorizing subsidies for particular newspapers were regularly labelled "*confidentielle*," A.N. F18 367, "Presses départmentales subventions."

[81]Collins, *The Government and the Newspaper Press*, 153-154; letter to the Minister of the Interior, January, 1869.

[82]A.N. F18 306.

[82a]A.N. F18 306.

[83]A.N. F18 307, April, 1869.

[84]See pp. 51-52.

founder of *L'Epoque,* received 275,000 francs from Napoleon III, and in 1869-1870, 80,000 francs more.[85] The *Peuple français* received 1,417,000 francs from the royal purse between March 1, 1869 and July 30, 1870.[86] Napoleon III extended generous aid to Florian Pharaon and his newspaper *L'Etincelle*; in 1867-1868, the Emperor gave Pharaon 24,000 francs at the rate of 2,000 francs per month for his own use, and 150,000 francs for *L'Etincelle.*[87] In the late 1860's, Granier de Cassaignac, director of *Le Pays* and member of the *Corps législatif*, received 176,000 francs from Napoleon III.[88]

In addition to assisting loyal newspapers with subsidies, the government tried to help them improve their competitive position. The careful statistics compiled on circulation indicate the interest of the government in the popularity of the various newspapers. Public officials intervened constantly in the affairs of pro-government newspapers. A change in the subscription rate or the daily price of a government newspaper was a matter which interested the administration. The Prefect of the Bouches-du-Rhône reported that he had persuaded the only government newspaper in Marseilles "to enlarge its format, improve its commercial and political coverage, and to print two editions per day."[89] A confidential note from the Ministry of the Interior to the prefects (August 29, 1859) stated: "It is to be hoped that the departmental administration can help to increase the circulation of the *Revue contemporaine.*"[90]

The government frequently encouraged the establishment of

[85]*Papiers et correspondance*, II, 131.

[86]*Papiers et correspondance*, II, 171-172.

[87]*Papiers et correspondance*, II, 154-155.

[88]*Papiers et correspondance*, II, 138.

[89]A.N. F1c III, Bouches-du-Rhône 7, prefect to the Minister of the Interior, November, 1867.

[90]Lynn M. Case, *French Opinion on War and Diplomacy* (Philadelphia, 1954), 4.

new newspapers when it was dissatisfied with the existing press. In 1852, after failing to win over existing newspapers in Bordeaux, the Prefect Haussmann helped to found *La Gironde*, a new pro-government journal.[91] The *procureur général* at Douai reported, in 1837, that "the administration has founded a newspaper at Lille which seems destined to progress."[92] In 1860, the *procureur général* at Poitiers urged the Minister of Justice on three different occasions to found a newspaper favorable to the government in that city.[93] A contemporary journalist wrote that the administration had founded forty-six new provincial newspapers to aid government candidates in the 1869 electoral campaign for the *Corps législatif*.[94] The *Phare de Marseilles* was created to support the government candidate, De Lesseps, in 1869; it ceased publication after the elections.[95] The *Petit Marseillais*, founded on March 22, 1868 as a "literary" journal, became a political newspaper a month later in order, it said, to inform the working class concerning the approaching elections.[96] Although the *Petit Marseillais* supported government candidates, it is not entirely clear whether the administration was responsible for the change from a "literary" to a political newspaper.

How did the government give direction to its formidable array of official, friendly, and accommodating opposition newspapers? The influence of the administration on the press was both direct and indirect. The decree of February 7, 1852, that estab-

[91]Georges Eugène Haussmann, *Mémoires du Baron Haussmann* (Paris, 1890-1893), I, 536-537.

[92]A.N. BB30 377, *procureur général* at Douai to the Minister of Justice, July 22, 1857.

[93]A.N. BB30 423, No. 1802 bis P, "Série politique (1850-1866)."

[94]Pessard, *Mes petits papiers*, I, 264-265.

[95]*Les élections de 1869. Bibliothèque de la révolution de 1848*, Tome XXI (Paris, 1960), 86.

[96]*Les élections de 1869*, 85-86.

lished the press regulations which remained in effect for almost
the entire Second Empire provided one direct means by which
the government could impose its views on newspapers. Article
19 of the decree required newspapers, including the opposition
press, to insert without change all notices, corrections, and comments on articles that they had printed submitted by the administration.[97] The government's *communiqué* appeared at the head
of the first column of the first page. These official corrections and
rebuttals were usually anonymous and often sharp and insult-
ing. The *communiqué* was sometimes an article from a government newspaper.[98] In reply to a query from a local official, the
Minister of Justice ruled that Article 19 applied to non-political
as well as political newspapers.[99] The administration urged prefects to make wide use of the *communiqué*, and this advice was
followed.[100] As a consequence, the official *communiqué* was as
much a part of newspapers during the Second Empire as the
comics and sports sections today. During the electoral periods all
newspapers also had to print the names of the official candidates
in their first column.

The government had, in addition, less overt ways of influenc-
ing the contents of the press than the official *communiqué*. The
Press Bureau of the Ministry of the Interior bore the main responsibility for the shaping and dissemination of government
information. It would be an exaggeration to compare the Press
Bureau to twentieth century propaganda agencies; nevertheless,

97Collins, *The Government and the Newspaper Press*, 133. A better known feature of the decree of February 7, 1852 was the original method of self censorship of
the press that it provided.

98A.N. F1c III, Seine-Inférieure 9, prefect to the Minister of the Interior, November, 1866; Delord, *Histoire illustrée*, II, 207-208.

99A.N. BB30 429, "Elections," May 18, 1863.

100Collins, *The Government and the Newspaper Press*, 150. In 1869, Rouher's
under-secretary called for "le concours de chaque administration à la défense commune contre les attaques de la presse, à la rectification des erreurs de celles-ci, au
redressement de l'opinion égarée."

it performed some of the tasks of the latter. A memorandum of 1859 in the Ministry of the Interior described the two objectives of the Press Bureau: "to exercise an active and incessant surveillance over newspapers and all manifestations of thought"; and "to give direction to the newspapers which come to it every day for ideas and news."[101] Nor was this wishful thinking. Persigny, who had been Minister of the Interior and, therefore, knew of the activities of the Press Bureau, said that the editors of Parisian newspapers appeared daily at the Bureau to receive instructions (*"le mot d'ordre"*).[102] During electoral periods, wrote a high official of the Press Bureau, "eight or ten editors come to the Ministry of the Interior for instructions."[103] The Press Bureau also provided the prefects with daily summaries of the news to aid them in guiding "newspapers . . . that followed the government's direction."[104] To supplement these, the Press Bureau also sent special communications to the prefects outlining the government's position on important questions. Despite all this guidance, a memorandum by a press official stated that the administration failed to provide sufficient direction to its newspaper; it should "give the line on every question."[104a]

The Press Bureau attempted to improve the competence of public officials in the area of propaganda. In 1859, a circular from the Press Bureau to the prefects described a new service it was inaugurating, a *"Résumé quotidien des journaux de l'Etranger, de Paris et des départements"*; precise instructions on how to use the *Résumé* would accompany the daily summary (*"des nouvelles à accepter, à dementir ou à rectifier."*)[105] The circular insisted

101A.N. F18 310, "Division de la presse," December 7, 1859.
102*Mémoires*, 400.
103*Papiers et correspondance*, I, 31.
104A.N. F18 310, December 7, 1859.
104aA.N. F18 310, December 7, 1859.
105A.N. F18 310, January 8, 1859.

that the resumé must remain confidential and never leave the hands of the prefect. The summaries were to be used with great caution and the texts must never be given to the press, lest the same text in several newspapers reveal their "official inspiration."[106] Another ministerial circular to the prefects instructed them to reprint in local newspapers the articles or extracts of articles from Parisian newspapers which they received from the Press Bureau when they believed that this would be useful.[107] Although the circular permitted the prefects to determine whether a particular article or extract should be reprinted in local newspapers, it insisted that once a prefect decided that an article was worth reprinting he must use all of his influence to see that it was. The circular added that a study had shown that the number of articles reprinted in provincial newspapers varied with the zeal of the prefect, and, to stimulate this zeal, the Minister asked the prefects to report on articles or extracts of articles reprinted in the newspapers within their jurisdiction.

A voluminous correspondence exists between the Ministry of the Interior and the prefects concerning the details of government press propaganda. The following examples are typical of the subject matter of this correspondence. The Prefect of the Department of the Saône et Loire requested by telegram whether a local newspaper scheduled to appear the following day should be delayed so that it could carry a speech to be delivered by the Emperor.[108] The Prefect of the Isère forwarded to the Ministry

[106]The efforts of the government to conceal its relations with the press were not, however, successful. *The Times* (London) (September 27, 1866) wrote: "The means employed in France to influence public opinion in a sense favorable to the government are a secret to nobody. It is well known that, besides the semi-official papers and several other Parisian journals which, while professing independence, are in reality more or less at the orders or in the pay of the Minister of the Interior, there are bureaux in which a regular manufactory of leading articles is established, and whence these productions carefully lithographed, are dispatched to numbers of provincial papers."

[107]A.N. F18 307, no date but probably late in the Empire.

[108]A.N. F18 309, "Dépêches télégraphiques, ler semestre 1870," May 20, 1870.

of the Interior a copy of the *Courrier de l'Isère* containing an account of Napoleon III's visit to the department; the article, said the Prefect, had been prepared under his supervision, "and you may regard it as being entirely official."[109] An unsigned and undated letter to the Press Bureau, but undoubtedly from a high source, requested the agency to call the attention "of writers loyal to the government" to a pamphlet defending the administration's policy and to see to it that the departmental press also make use of the pamphlet.[110] A note in the Ministry of the Interior stated that *Le Moniteur* would reply to a criticism of administration's public welfare program that had appeared in *Le Siècle.*[111]

Napoleon III, ministers, and government officials also gave verbal instructions and guidance to journalists. Granier de Cassagnac relates that the Emperor requested him to write an article for *Le Moniteur* defending the government's Italian policy.[112] A journalist, Charles de Guigny, wrote to Rouher that he had prepared an article on the subject "that you had the goodness to indicate to me"; the article would appear in *La Patrie.*[113] Paulin Limayrac, editor of *Le Constitutionnel*, sent Rouher a draft of an article and assured the Minister that he was prepared to rewrite it if necessary.[114] The Prefect of the Seine-Inférieure reported that he had delivered an *"officieuse et verbale"* communication to the press on the subject of armaments.[115]

[109]A.N. F1c III Isère 7, prefect to the Minister of the Interior, September 25, 1852.

[110]A.N. F18 310, "Division de la presse."

[111]A.N. F18 417, "Le Siècle," September 22, 1858.

[112]A. Granier de Cassagnac, *Souvenirs du Second Empire* (Paris, 1881-1884), III, 154-155.

[113]A.N. 45 AP III, "Papiers de Rouher," no date.

[114]A.N. 45 AP III, no date but probably in the 1860's.

[115]A.N. F1c III, Seine-Inférieure 9, prefect to the Minister of the Interior, in the 1860's.

The close relations and the understanding that prevailed between the government and the press is suggested by the fact that it was not even necessary, in most cases, to communicate the official "line" to newspapers. Statements by the Emperor, ministers, and leading officials, articles in *Le Moniteur* or other important government newspapers were usually sufficient. Newspaper editors had already developed an ear for the official propaganda "line" and before long were repeating the government's message, often in the very words used by Napoleon III or other Imperial spokesmen.

III

Other Propaganda Media

Royal Tours

The use of the press for propaganda was a practice as old as the newspaper itself. Nor was the royal tour an invention of the nineteenth century. Heads of state have always visited parts of their country, often troubled areas, in order to keep or gain the loyalty of the inhabitants. During the Old Regime the king's entry into one of his towns, often for propaganda reasons, was a great event for the community. However, Louis Napoleon's use of the royal tour was so different from that of his predecessors that it became a new and original propaganda technique. No previous ruler had made such a planned and conscious effort to enter into personal contact with and to speak directly to his subjects.

Louis Napoleon discovered the new propaganda technique during the Second Republic; it was apparently his own idea. The first of the Prince-President's "whistle stop tours" about France occurred in the summer and fall of 1850; its objective was to rally popular support behind the ruler in his conflict with the royalist controlled legislature.[1] Again, in 1852, as the campaign for the reestablishment of the Empire reached a climax, Louis Napoleon made another tour, "a mark of interrogation," he called

[1]Emile Ollivier said of this first tour: "No chief of state ever took greater trouble to present his views," *L'Empire libéral* (Paris, 1895-1915), II, 30.

it, to discover the popular will on the question.[2] After the founding of the Second Empire, Napoleon III's (and Eugenie's) frequent and well-advertised tours became a characteristic feature
of the regime.[3]

The official explanation for the tours was that the chief of
state hoped to inform himself of the needs and desires of his people by visiting and talking with them. In the words of *Le Moniteur*, Louis Napoleon wished "to enter into contact with the populations whom he had not yet been able to visit, to study their
interests on the spot, and to come to an understanding with them
concerning all possible ameliorations."[4] In September 1852, the
Prince-President told a workers' delegation at Lyons that the
principal purpose of his visit to their city was to study intensively
the problems of the working class.[5] A placard describing a royal
tour developed this idea more fully: The ruler desired "to learn
for himself what were the needs and desires of the country. . . .
Until the present he had studied and meditated theory in his
study, but now he wished to investigate on the very ground, on
the soil, in the midst of the population which had placed him at
the head of the nation."[6] Louis Napoleon, said the placard,
thought of his visits to different parts of France as similar to the
tours de France made by journeymen in some of the crafts to
improve their skill. On his visit to the town of Thiers in 1864,
Napoleon III stated that he wished to see for himself why this
town was able to produce cutlery fine enough to compete with
the products of Sheffield.[7]

[2]F. A. Simpson, *Louis Napoleon and the Recovery of France*, 3rd ed. (London,
1951), 143.

[3]*Le Moniteur universel* and other government newspapers published the itinerary and detailed accounts of the tours.

[4]*Le Moniteur*, August 28, 1852.

[5]*Le Moniteur*, September 21, 1852.

[6]B.N. Lb[55] 334, "Voyage de Louis Napoléon en France" (Paris, 1849).

[7]*Le Moniteur universel du soir*, July 25, 1864.

Louis Napoleon's tours took him to all parts of France. Usually he remained for a day or two in the larger towns and stopped or moved slowly through smaller towns and villages. He made a special effort to visit regions where opposition to the regime, either Legitimist or republican, was strongest. He frequently toured industrial regions like the Department of the Nord and towns with a large worker population. Napoleon III probably visited Lyons more frequently than any other town; he also remained there longer and seemed to make a particular effort to impress the inhabitants. The correspondence of Imperial officials often gives the impression that they believed that if the Emperor could gain the loyalty of the workers at Lyons, the battle for the working class was won.

Government officials had great faith in royal tours as a particularly effective device for increasing loyalty to the regime. The reports of the *procureurs généraux* and the prefects frequently commented upon the favorable impression created by royal visits. Thus, in 1852, the *procureur général* at Aix reported, "The passage of the Prince through our departments was an event of great political significance."[8] The following year the Prefect of the Department of the Nord wrote that the visit of the Emperor and Empress to his department had so impressed workers that "the fomenters of disorder" were discouraged.[9] "The Emperor's visits in the flooded departments," reported the *procureur général* at Douai, "have had a great effect here; they have resulted in new conquests, particularly among the popular classes."[10] And, in 1866, the same *procureur général* assured the Minister of Justice that "the visit of Her Majesty to the cholera victims at Amiens

[8] A.N. BB30 404, *procureur général* at Aix to the Minister of Justice, October 14, 1852.

[9] A.N. F1c III, Nord 8, prefect to the Minister of the Interior, November 11, 1853.

[10] A.N. BB30 377, *procureur général* at Douai to the Minister of Justice, July 29, 1856.

is worth a victory of our arms for the consolidation of the Napoleonic dynasty in the hearts of the people."[11] The detailed reports of prefects, *procureurs*, police officials, and *maires* on the planning, the itinerary, the progress, and the success of royal tours also indicate their value in the eyes of the government. Royal tours were, therefore, planned carefully and long in advance, with as little left to chance as possible.

The success of Louis Napoleon's tours as propaganda depended, in large part, upon the enthusiasm of the populations on the itinerary. Public officials strived, therefore, to stimulate zeal for the ruler; a hostile or unenthusiastic reception was a reflection upon the local authorities. The Prefect of the Department of the Rhône, for example, attempted to create the right mood for a forthcoming visit by announcing that a number of gifts and awards would be distributed during the ruler's stay at Lyons: 30,000 francs for charitable agencies, 25,000 francs for workers designated by the Chamber of Commerce and 40,000 francs for "workers who will be named subsequently, and his Imperial Highness will be asked to announce the distribution."[12] The Prefect of the Department of the Nord reported that the Municipal Council of Lille had appropriated 150,000 francs for the welcome of the Emperor to the town; "of that sum, 25,000 is to be distributed to the needy on the day that His Majesty enters Lille."[13] The *maire* of Roanne proudly announced a visit by the ruler, and, reminding his constituents of all that Napoleon III had done for the area, called upon them to show their appreciation.[14] The *maire* of Valence, more arbitrarily, decreed that a fine

[11]A.N. BB30 377, October 5, 1866.

[12]B.N. Lb55 2549, "Séjour à Lyon du Prince-Président. Cérémonie et fêtes" (Lyon, 1852). This is a four-page *arrêt*.

[13]A.N. F1c III Nord 14, prefect to the Minister of the Interior, April 19, 1853.

[14]J. Albiot, *Annales du Second Empire. Les campagnes électorales (1851-1869)* (Paris, 1869), 154-155.

would be assessed against business houses and property owners who failed to display flags and illuminate their premises during the ruler's visit.[15] Persigny relates that in the fall of 1852 he instructed the prefects of the departments on Louis Napoleon's itinerary to distribute banners with the slogans *"Vive l'Empereur"* and *"Vive Napoléon"* and to see to it that the touring Prince-President was welcomed with similar shouts.[16]

It was common knowledge that the government did not always have confidence in the spontaneous enthusiasm of the population and sometimes employed claques. The *London Times* referred to "the official shouters in the service of the police,"[17] and Emile Ollivier, to the *"claqueurs"* who applauded the Emperor and Empress on February 22, 1853.[18] A memorandum, *"Quelques frais occasionnés par le passage de l'Empereur à Lyon, les 29 et 30 Avril 1865,"* consists of an itemized account of the cost of the reception; the final item reads: *"aux zélateurs (pour crier: Vive l'Empereur) 229 francs."*[19]

For security reasons and to avoid unfavorable incidents, public officials kept a close eye on, and frequently arrested, opponents to the regime and potential trouble makers on the royal itinerary. The *procureur général* at Rennes assured the Minister of Justice (July 23, 1858) that the members of the opposition would be closely observed during a royal visit to Brittany, and two days later he instructed his assistants, the *procureurs impériaux*, to imprison "the dangerous men" in their jurisdiction until the

---

[15]Pierre de la Gorce, *Histoire du Second Empire* (Paris, 1899-1905), I, 94.

[16]*Mémoires du duc de Persigny* (Paris, 1896), 177 ff. Louis Napoleon was not, however, aware of Persigny's arrangements.

[17]Lynn C. Case, *French Opinion on War and Diplomacy during the Second Empire* (Philadelphia, 1954), 57.

[18]Emile Ollivier, *Journal, 1846-1849* (Paris, 1961), I, 145-146.

[19]B.N. Lb⁵⁶ 471, *Pièces saisies aux archives de la police politique de Lyon* (Lyons, 1870), 25-26.

Emperor had completed his visit.[20] And a number of persons were actually arrested for political reasons before and during Napoleon III's visit. Often such persons were released when the Emperor left.

On his tours, Louis Napoleon, and later the Empress Eugenie, paid his respects to all classes and interests—industrialists, landowners, peasants, local dignitaries, the army, the clergy,[21] and, particularly, workers. Rarely did the royal couple visit or pass through an industrial town without, in some way, ingratiating themselves to the worker population.

The Emperor frequently visited institutions for workers in the towns along his route. At Roubaix, Napoleon III (and Eugenie) inspected a model and plans for a workers' housing project.[22] Both showed a keen interest in the project, says a brochure describing the incident, and questioned the architect closely: What was the cost of a building and how many families would each building lodge? Why did the plans call for wood for certain purposes rather than brick? How would the apartments be heated? The Empress objected that the plans did not provide for basements. Napoleon III also often visited factories. A common division of labor on Imperial tours was for the Empress to inspect charitable institutions, "establishments whose character particularly interested her,"[23] while the Emperor inspected factories and workshops.

[20]A.N. BB[30] 421, No. 1618, "*Série politique.*"

[21]For Louis Napoleon's attempt to woo the clergy, see Jean Maurain, *La politique éclésiastique du Second Empire de 1852 à 1869* (Paris, 1930), 40-41. On the 1852 tour, "dans tous les évêchés où il passa, Louis Napoléon se rendit à la cathédrale où il fut reçu en souverain par l'évêque entouré d'un nombreux clergé. Aux discours de bienvenue des prélats, il répondit en témoignant sa déférence pour la religion."

[22]B.N. Lb[56] 1809, *Voyage de leurs Majestés l'Empereur et l'Impératrice dans les Départements du Nord (Août, 1867)* (Paris, 1867), 13-14.

[23]B.N. Lb[56] 1807, Théophile Denis, *Voyage de Leur Majestés Impériales dans le nord de la France en Aout 1867* (Douai, 1867). This is a twenty-four page pamphlet based on accounts in *Le Moniteur.*

Almost always the ruler left a sum of money for workers and the needy or conferred other favors upon them—gestures which government spokesmen never neglected to mention. Before leaving Toul, Louis Napoleon left 500 francs for a workman who had been injured during the preparation for the reception for the ruler.[24] After observing the molding of a cannon at an Alsatian foundry, "the prince sent a sum of 600 francs to be distributed among the workers."[25] During the course of a lengthy tour of northern France in 1867, the Emperor visited a printing establishment where he left for the workers "proof of his bounty."[26] At St. Etienne, the Prince-President conferred the cross of the Legion of Honor upon "the oldest worker in the mines."[27] Louis Napoleon also decorated two workers. At the Croix-Rousse, a workers suburb of Lyons,[28] and at Roubaix, in 1867, the Emperor pardoned several workers convicted for illegal activities during a strike.[29]

The propaganda value of Imperial tours was not, moreover, confined to the towns and regions visited by the rulers. Newspapers, pamphlets and placards described the wanderings of the chief-of-state in full detail. Government newspapers either assigned correspondents to the royal party or reprinted accounts from *Le Moniteur* or from local newspapers. It is surprising, in fact, how much space newspapers devoted to Imperial tours. Thus, the *Courrier de l'Isère*, on September 23, 1852, devoted almost three of its four pages to Louis Napoleon's visit and two

[24]B.N. Lb⁵⁵ 2523, *Relation du passage de Louis Napoléon dans la Meurthe* (Nancy, 1852), 9.

[25]*Le Moniteur*, July 24, 1852.

[26]B.N. Lb⁵⁶ 1809, *Voyage de leurs Majestés*, 6.

[27]A.N. BB³⁰ 404, pièce 768, *procureur général* at Lyons to the Minister of Justice, September 19, 1852.

[28]B.N. Fol Lb⁵⁵ 2555, "Relation du voyage de Son Altesse Impériale monseigneur le prince Louis-Napoléon, dans le midi de la France (Paris, n.d.), a placard.

[29]B.N. Lb⁵⁶ 1809, *Voyage de leurs Majestés*, 13-14.

days later more than two pages.[30] The *Etincelle*, which claimed to be especially interested in workers, started on July 16, 1866, a series of lengthy letters on a royal tour. Napoleon III's visits were also a favorite subject for government placards. A sub-prefect at Saint-Pol in the Department of the Pas-de-Calais reported that he posted a daily bulletin on a particular royal tour.[31] Frequently several different placards described the same visit.[32]

Placards and Pamphlets

The propaganda placard has been an historic device for the shaping of public opinion. In modern times every great religious, political, and social conflict has seen a war of placards. However, from the nineteenth century, the age in which the concept of popular sovereignty became a powerful force in society, the placard has become, to quote a student of contemporary propaganda, the "queen of the walls and of every vertical surface."[33]

Most Bonapartist propaganda before the arrival in power of Louis Napoleon had appeared on placards, a relatively economical medium. After the presidential election of 1848 and the founding of the Second Empire, the placard was somewhat eclipsed by the press, now that most newspapers had become spokesmen for the government. However, the considerable correspondence between Paris and local officials on the contents, posting, and the impact upon the population of placards shows that the government still believed them to be a valuable propaganda medium. The Ministry of the Interior, for example, often forwarded the texts or excerpts from Napoleon III's speeches and

[30]A.N. F1c III Isère 7, prefect to the Minister of the Interior. This report included the two issues of the *Courrier de l'Isère*, revealing, incidentally, the government's interest in the press coverage of the visit.

[31]A.N. F1c III, Pas-de-Calais 9, sub-prefect to prefect, November 1, 1852.

[32]B.N. Lb55 2549, this file includes four different placards describing a visit to Lyons.

[33]Jacques Driencourt, *La propagande nouvelle force politique* (Paris, 1950), 136.

statements to the prefects for posting.[34] And the prefects were expected to report on their compliance and the effect of the placards on the population. The Prince-President's speech at Bordeaux, reported the prefect, had been posted in the Lyons area, where it had been "favorably received by the working class."[35] The Prefect of the Department of the Nord wrote that Napoleon III's address at the opening session of the legislature in 1857 had been posted on the walls of Lille and was read by workers as they left their factories.[36] The *procureur général* at Aix reported that a statement by Napoleon III showed "the generous concern of His Majesty for the working classes" had been posted throughout his jurisdiction.[37] His colleague at Rouen said that he had posted the same speech, one which "discussed with great felicity questions of concern to workers," in every commune in his jurisdiction.[38] Towards the end of the Second Empire government officials and publicists made much of Napoleon III's proposal to repeal the law requiring workers to carry a kind of internal passport, the *livret*. The Prefect of the Isère reported, for example, that the Emperor's speech urging abolition of the *livret* appeared on placards in all the communes of his department and was producing an "excellent effect."[39]

Most of the placards I have seen were clearly intended for the *peuple*, the peasants, artisans, and workers. The titles, usually in large print, and not always descriptive of the contents of the pla-

[34]A.N. F1c III, Bouches-du-Rhône 7, prefect to the Minister of the Interior, July 2, 1852; A.N. F1c III, Pas-de-Calais 9, prefect to the Minister of the Interior, January 26, 1853; A.N. F1c III, Nord 14, prefect to the Minister of the Interior, February 15, 1853.

[35]A.N. F1c III, Rhône 5, prefect to the Minister of the Interior, October 14, 1852.

[36]A.N. F1c III, Nord 8, prefect to the Minister of the Interior, April 10, 1857.

[37]A.N. BB30 370, *procureur général* at Aix to the Minister of Justice, January 9, 1863.

[38]A.N. BB30 307, *procureur général* at Rouen to the Minister of Justice, January 10, 1863.

[39]A.N. F1c III, Isère 7, prefect to the Minister of the Interior, March, 1869.

card, indicated the belief that some persons might not read beyond the title.[40] The titles or subtitles of placards were often statements by the ruler already made famous by government propaganda. The illustrations on many placards also suggest the kind of audience that the government hoped to reach: Louis Napoleon performing some generous act was a common artistic theme; for example, a visit to the sick at a hospital, or the dedication of a charitable institution.

The subject matter of the placards consisted largely of statements and quotations from Napoleon III (often from *L'Extinction du paupérisme*), and items from *Le Moniteur* on the aid provided by the ruler and the administration for workers and the needy. A placard with the title, "Idées sociales de Louis Napoléon," included excerpts from two speeches and quotations from the *Idées napoléoniennes,* the *Rêveries politiques,* and *L'Extinction du paupérisme.*[41] Another placard, "Louis Napoleon visitant les pauvres malades de l'Hôtel Dieu," described the visit, referred to in the title, and told of the ruler's aid for a workers' housing project, and concluded with a poem praising the generosity of Louis Napoleon.[42] Placards frequently described or included incidents from the royal tours that became so common during the Second Empire, usually "human interest" stories that showed the ruler's generosity and sympathy for the suffering, and

[40]The following titles are typical: B.N. LB[55] 58, "Idées sociales de Louis Napoléon"; B.N. LB [55] 174, "Louis-Napoléon Bonaparte, visitant les Pauvres malades de l'Hôtel-Dieu"; B.N. Fol LB[55] 2677, "Visite de Louis Napoléon Bonaparte aux Hospices, Les Paroles qu'il a prononcées, Les Secours qu'il a accordés aux ouvriers . . ."; B.N. Fol LB[55] 1893, "Discours de M. le Président de la République sur les améliorations à apporter aux bien-être des classes ouvrières"; B.N. LB[56] 256 "Pose de la première pierre de l'asile impérial de Vincennes pour les ouvriers convalescents"; B.N. LB[55] 3096, "Fondation d'une caisse de retraite en faveur des ouvriers des Manufactures nationales, telles que Sèvres, les Gobelins et Beauvais."

[41]B.N. LB[53] 58, (Paris, n.d.).

[42]B.N. LB[55] 174, (Paris, n.d.). The concluding lines of the poem were:
"Faire le bien, soulager la misère,
Napoléon, est-il rôle plus beau?"

descriptions of the enthusiasm of the welcoming crowds. A typical placard on these themes, "Entrée à Lille de Leurs Majestés Impériales" (1853), provides details of the royal couple's arrival in Lille, the welcoming speeches by public officials, Napoleon III's response, a notice that the Emperor had left 50,000 francs of his own money "for the poor and workers," and concludes with two poems attacking the opposition to the Empire, particularly the reformers of the Second Republic.[43] Placards sometimes also simply reproduced legislation and decrees that aided workers. One large placard, for example, printed the text of a decree granting an amnesty to persons condemned for political activity and listed the names of the amnestied in the departments about Paris.[44] Another placard consisted entirely of official announcements, most of them dealing with the confiscation of the property of the Orleanist family and indicating that the proceeds from their sale were to be used primarily for the needy and workers.[45]

On February 15, 1852, the administration founded a regular and official placard, the *Moniteur des Communes*. The announced purpose of this one-page bulletin was to provide the population with "a complete knowledge of the official acts of the government."[46] However, a circular of December 13, 1856, from the Ministry of the Interior to the prefects indicated another motive: "The Emperor desired that the actions of his govern-

[43]B.N. Lb[56] 100. Following are some lines from the poems:
> "Des partis voulaient dans leur râge,
> Le rendre à jamais odieux;
> Mais le pays par son suffrage,
> A su le venger à nos yeux."
and
> "Par sa prudence et la parole
> Il a démasqué ces faux dieux
> Qui chez nous voulaient faire école,
> Par maint système insidieux."

[44]B.N. LB[56] 69 (1853).
[45]B.N. LB[55] 2435 (n.d.).
[46]A.N. F[18] 10c, "*Moniteur des communes*," May 28, 1852.

ment be known throughout the Empire, so that, in a way, the entire country witness what his concern for its well-being and glory has led him to attempt and to execute, both domestically and externally."[47] And the Prefect of the Department of the Rhône observed that the *Moniteur des communes* performed the valuable service of informing the masses of "the acts of the government and their sane interpretation."[48] A *maire* in the Lyons area requested additional copies for posting, explaining that it would be useful among the silk workers who lived in his commune.[49] The importance which the administration attached to the *Moniteur des communes* is suggested by the frequent letters to local authorities insisting that they post the bulletin regularly.

In order to make the official bulletin a more effective instrument of propaganda, the Minister of the Interior invited his colleagues to submit material for it that showed the achievements of the regime.[50] Typical of the way in which the bulletin was used was a request from the Minister of Finance to publish in the *Moniteur des communes* "as soon as possible" a defense of the government's fiscal policy, "in order to enlighten the ignorant."[51]

Before the discovery of such pervasive media of communication as radio and television and the firm establishment of the custom of the daily newspaper, the pamphlet was used far more extensively for propaganda than it is today. And the nineteenth century, with its considerable increase in literacy, was the great age of the pamphlet. All political factions, all schools of social and economic thought had their pamphleteers, and editions of

[47]A.N. F18 10c.

[48]A.N. F18 10c, prefect to the Minister of the Interior, July 3, 1852.

[49]A.N. F18 10c, July 3, 1852.

[50]A.N. F18 10c, October 21, 1853.

[51]A.N. F18 10c, March 22, 1852.

pamphlets that ran into the hundreds of thousands were not unusual.

Pro-government pamphlets and leaflets were, of course, most common. It is, however, impossible to determine in every case the source and the motive for this flood of literature praising the regime. Some pamphlets were probably the unsolicited contributions of admirers of the Second Empire or of Napoleon III and of seekers after favors. Others, often profusely illustrated and at a price far above the means of the average worker, were undoubtedly commercial ventures.

There is no doubt, however, that the Emperor, ministers, and public officials commissioned pamphlets and compensated their authors. The government had a "stable" of writers at its call, and public officials carefully considered which of them was most qualified to execute a particular pamphlet. We have seen that Muraour and Pharaon, editors of government newspapers and recipients of generous subsidies, also wrote pamphlets and longer works praising the Empire.[52] Hippolyte Castille, a prolific Imperial publicist, was well rewarded for his literary efforts; in 1867, he was paid 5,000 francs for a seventeen-page pamphlet and for several years received an annual retainer of 6,000 francs.[53] In 1851, Granier de Cassagnac received 2,000 francs for a pamphlet.[54] Eugène de Stadler, *"homme de lettres,"* earned 5,000 francs for an unnamed literary task, and, on another occasion, 2,000 francs for a work requested by Persigny.[55] Madame Mélanie Walder received 5,000 francs for her pamphlet, *Voyage de l'Empereur.* (This figure seems to have been the prevailing rate for such work.)[56] A letter from the *Cabinet de l'Empereur* thanked Eu-

[52]See p. 50.

[53]*Papiers et correspondance de la famille impériale* (Paris, 1870-1872), II, 127.

[54]*Papiers et correspondance,* II, 127.

[55]*Papiers et correspondance,* II, 161.

[56]*Papiers et correspondance,* II, 166.

gène de Mirecourt for his biography of Napoleon III—it does not say whether the biography was commissioned—and assured him that "by order of His Majesty and in his name, I have written, as you desired, to the Minister of Finance to call his attention to you."[57]

The thought and planning that often preceded the publication of a pamphlet is suggested by the lengthy correspondence between Napoleon III and his cousin Jerôme about a work defending the government's nationalities policy.[58] The Emperor, who had the idea for the pamphlet, also assisted with the planning of its content and the selection and compensation of the author. The same kind of calculation is revealed in a letter from Rouher to the Emperor (September 1867) on a projected pamphlet absolving the government from responsibility for rising prices.[59] Rouher stated that the author he had selected for the task was on the staff of *Le Siècle*, and, therefore, "will not seem to be an agent of the government."

Most government pamphlets were published by commercial printing houses. During the Second Republic, the *Imprimerie Centrale de Napoléon Chaix et Cie*, printed many of them, and during the Second Empire, the printer Dentu. Occasionally, however, the official printing office, the *Imprimerie Impériale*, also published pamphlets, particularly the texts of Napoleon III's addresses to the legislature.[60] I have been unable, however, to ob-

[57]A.N. AB XIX 174 (dossier B), "Papiers des Tuileries," April 13, 1870.

[58]Ernest d'Hauterive, *Napoléon III et le prince Napoléon, correspondance inédite* (Paris, 1925), passim. References to the pamphlet appear in the correspondence between November 1857 and July 1858. In the last reference to the pamphlet (July 6, 1858), Napoleon III approved of it and assured Jerôme that he "would give Peyrat whatever he requested if the pamphlet were good."

[59]*Papiers et correspondance*, I, 372.

[60]The *Catalogue général des livres imprimés* of the B.N. shows that nine printings of Napoleon III's address to the opening session of the legislature in 1860 were published by the *Imprimerie Impériale*; eight printings of the 1865 address; fourteen printings of the 1867 address.

tain figures for the number of pamphlets printed by either commercial houses or the *Imprimerie Impériale*.[61] The postal service often helped with the distribution of pro-government pamphlets. For example, 170,000 copies of the pro-Bonapartist, *Titres de la Dynastie Napoléonienne*, were distributed through the mail.[62]

Unlike placards, which were primarily for the *peuple*, government pamphlets were for all classes. Some were quite sophisticated and obviously written for an educated and informed public. There were catch-all pamphlets with something for the different classes in France. However, the titles, the contents, the simple anecdotal style of many pamphlets show that the lower classes were not neglected.[63] Such pamphlets often included the same kind of material as that to be found in placards. One pamphlet, for example, *Clémence et bienfaits de S.M. Napoléon III* (probably 1853) consisted of excerpts from *Le Moniteur* showing the generosity of the Emperor; a story relating how Napoleon III had given money from his own purse to two construction workers who had been injured when their scaffold fell to the ground was typical.[64] An eight-page pamphlet for workers recounted several incidents that revealed the concern of the royal family for workers and the unfortunate: Napoleon III's plan for an insur-

[61]Madame Willemetz, archivist of the *Imprimerie nationale,* very kindly spent an entire morning in an unsuccessful effort to find statistics on the number of pamphlets printed by the public press during the Second Empire. She thought that the records had been destroyed during one of the moves of the national printing office.

[62]A.N. AB XIX 174 (dossier 165), letter of the *Directeur général des postes,* April 2, 1863.

[63]Following are some typical titles of pamphlets for workers: B.N. Lb55 2471, *Visite du Prince Louis Napoléon faite aux métiers de tissage à Elboeuf* (1852); B.N. LB56 672, *Distribution solennelle des prix-Napoléon aux ouvriers les plus méritants de l'agriculture et de l'industrie de la Loire* (1857); B.N. Lb56 402, *Histoire et bienfaits de Sa Majesté Napoléon III Empereur des Français* (1859); B.N. Lb56 1636, *Lettre adressée par Sa Majesté l'Empereur Napoléon III à son Ministre d'Etat en faveur de la classe ouvrière* (1866); B.N. Lb56 2213, *Discours de S.M. l'Empereur prononcé au Conseil d'Etat en faveur de la classe ouvrière , pour la suppression des Livrets d'Ouvriers* (1869).

[64]B.N. Lb56 37.

ance fund to assist workers injured on the job; a visit by the Empress to the hospitals of Paris and to a prison.[65] In the 1860's, however, pamphlets for workers were often more sophisticated and discussed the real problems of the working class.[66]

Workers Organizations. Employer Propaganda.

With memories of 1848, and particularly the "June Days," still fresh, the usual reaction of the government to workers' meetings and organizations was suspicion and repression. The mere fact that workers assembled outside of their place of employment aroused concern. The government realized, however, that meetings and institutions organized by or under the surveillance of public officials or persons trusted by the Empire offered an excellent environment in which to disseminate its message.

As a result, officials and friends of the Empire founded and participated in workers' organizations, meetings, and fêtes. The program at a workers' banquet to celebrate the birthday of Louis Napoleon in 1852 was typical of what occurred on numerous other occasions during the Second Empire.[67] The banquet was honored by the presence of the sub-prefect, the deputy to the *Corps législatif* representing the district, the area military commander, the mayor, and mayors and municipal councilors from neighboring communities. In the principal address, the sub-prefect praised the contribution of the chief of state to the well-being of the working class; by restoring security and prosperity, "he had proven, more than by words, that he honored labor and that the condition and the happiness of the workers was the object of his constant concern." At the dedication of a bust of Louis

[65]B.N. 8⁰ Lb⁵⁶ 1636, *Soirées populaires. Lettre adressée par Sa Majesté l'Empereur Napoléon III à son Ministre d'état en faveur de la classe ouvrière* (Paris, n.d. but probably 1860).

[66] See Ch. IV.

[67]*Le Moniteur*, April 23, 1852.

Napoleon for the Saint-Germain market place, a public official lauded the Prince-President's dedication to "the popular interests."[68] In 1858, the Marshal Canrobert assured a meeting of crystal workers at Baccarat that the Emperor labored tirelessly for the happiness of all.[69]

Government officials frequently organized local festivals to honor workers for their achievements or for loyalty to their employers. These meetings, whose main purpose was to inspire workers to greater efforts and to encourage the reconciliation of the classes, also provided the opportunity for government propaganda. At a meeting, in 1854, to honor a number of workers for their services to local industry, the Prefect of the Department of the Somme assured his worker audience (*"braves ouvriers, braves soldats de l'industrie"*) of the Emperor's concern with their welfare, and concluded with the assurance, "The Emperor loves you. . . . *Vive l'Empéreur."*[70] On a similar occasion at Saint-Etienne, the prefect announced that in honoring workers who had distinguished themselves he was acting in accordance with the wishes of the Emperor who had a "very profound and genuine sympathy for those who work and suffer."[71]

The only form of workers' organizations encouraged by the Second Empire were the mutual aid societies that existed to assist members during periods of illness and incapacity.[72] The basic legislation of the Second Empire on mutual aid societies, a decree

[68]*Le Moniteur,* June 23, 1852.

[69]*Le Moniteur,* April 25, 1858.

[70]*Le Moniteur,* January 8, 1854.

[71]B.N. Lb[56] 672, *Distribution solennelle des prix Napoléon aux ouvriers les plus méritants de l'agriculture et de l'industrie de la Loire* (Saint-Etienne, 1857), 7-8. This pamphlet was published by the Prefecture of the Loire.

[72]Mutual aid societies for peasants and the petty bourgeoisie also existed. The number of mutual aid societies and their membership increased significantly during the Second Empire. At the end of 1852, there were 2,438 societies with 271,077 members; in 1869, 6,139 societies with 916,633 members. J.-B. Duroselle, *Les débuts du Catholicisme social en France (1822-1870).* (Paris, 1951), 509.

of March 26, 1852, provided for two categories of societies, the authorized and the approved. The latter form of mutual aid society enjoyed certain privileges, such as the right to own property, receive gifts and legacies, and a meeting place provided without charge by the commune. In return for these advantages, the government exercised a closer surveillance over the approved mutual aid society, and the chief of state named the president. The decree also required approved mutual aid societies to admit honorary members, persons of means who paid dues and participated in the administration of the society but who did not share in its benefits. The primary purpose of the appointed president, who was usually a public official or a notable, was to guard against the mutual aid society becoming a center of revolutionary activity or a facade for an illegal trade union.[73] In addition, however, appointed presidents and honorary members also served as government spokesmen within the societies. The appointed president of a mutual aid society for clerical workers concluded a speech on the services of the organization with an appeal to the members to show their gratitude to the Emperor for his concern with the "raising of the moral and material condition of the working classes."[74]

Moreover, the Emperor himself, ministers, prefects, *procureurs*, and lesser officials often sent messages to or addressed mutual aid societies, and regularly participated in the ceremonies that accompanied the organization of new societies. Although the audience was larger than usual—2,000 members of mutual aid

[73]A circular by the Minister of the Interior Persigny to the prefects urged that in large towns mutual aid societies be based on districts rather than on trades, since this would discourage strikes. For the same reasons and to discourage laziness, mutual aid societies were not permitted to assist members in case of unemployment. *Le Moniteur*, May 30, 1852. In the 1855, *procureur général* at Paris warned: "L'autorité doit veiller avec persévérance et résolution, à ce que les associations de secours entre les ouvriers ne deviennent pas, dans la main des agitateurs, de puissants instruments de désordre." A.N. BB[30] 383.

[74]*Le Moniteur universel du soir*, January 19, 1867.

societies from Paris and the Department of the Seine—the Minister of the Interior's praise of the efforts of the government to aid the people was typical of the statements of public officials.[75] At a meeting of mutual aid societies of the first arrondissement of Paris, the *procureur général* cited the assistance which the Emperor had given to such societies, aid far more useful than the "systems" offered to the workers before 1852.[76] And, improvising on the same theme, the sub-prefect at Charolles declared before a local mutual aid society that workers, disillusioned with the schemes which had once attracted them, now realized that order, peace, and confidence were more likely to help them than fallicious theories.[77] Napoleon III also frequently offered well-publicized sums of money to mutual aid societies.

During the Second Empire the number of workers attending evening courses, either to improve their general culture, or for vocational reasons, increased considerably. The government did not neglect the opportunity to propagandize workers taking adult education courses. At Paris, the *Association polytechnique* and the *Association philotechnique*, institutions founded during the July Monarchy for adult education, offered a great variety of evening courses for thousands of persons.[78] Not only did government propaganda often find its way into courses offered at these schools, but at every award of prizes and honors to students, public officials, frequently ministers, were present to praise both the zeal of the students and the concern of the government with the problems of the working class. In 1858, the Minister of the Interior told an audience of 5,000 students and their friends and

<hr />

[75]*Le Moniteur*, March 22, 1858.

[76]Charles Robert, *Les améliorations sociales du Second Empire* (Paris, 1868), I, 56-57. This is a pamphlet for workers.

[77]*Le Moniteur*, April 6, 1852.

[78]Branch schools were also established in other parts of France. For these institutions, see pp. 182 ff.

relatives from the two schools that he addressed them at "the express order of the Emperor," an order which demonstrated the ruler's interest in these institutions and in the working classes.[79] The following year the Minister of Public Instruction, who gave the principal address at a distribution of prizes by the two schools, also concluded with praise of the Emperor's aid for the working class.[80] Much the same thing went on at a home for convalescent workers at Vincennes, where distinguished lecturers offered both instruction and propaganda for the ailing workers.[81]

Relations between the government and industry during the Second Empire were usually cordial. This was particularly true in the 1850's when the bourgeoisie still retained vivid memories of the Revolution of 1848. For many of the bourgeoisie Napoleon III always remained the man whom they believed had not only saved France from socialism, but had also established the political conditions for the prosperity that generally prevailed during the Second Empire. Although many of Napoleon III's contemporaries regarded him as a radical and even a socialist, the Emperor's "socialism" did not seem to frighten most industrialists. The factory owner Seydoux praised the Emperor before an applauding *Corps législatif*, that included many industrialists, for his interest in the "laboring classes" and approved of the government's measures in behalf of workers.[82]

The tariff treaty with England strained the relations between some industrialists and the regime, but not to the extent of causing those adversely affected by lower tariffs to become uncompromising foes of the Second Empire. Nor did legislation, in 1864,

[79]*Le Moniteur*, February 1, 1858.

[80]*Le Moniteur*, January 24, 1859.

[81]For the courses offered at Vincennes, see pp. 186 ff.

[82]E. Levasseur, *Histoire des classes ouvrières et de l'industrie en France de 1789 à 1870*, 2nd ed. (Paris, 1904), II, 685.

legalizing strikes alienate industrialists. There were warnings, it is true, that the door was now open to a wave of strikes.

Many employers, therefore, became willing and even eager disseminators of the government's message. For this purpose they took advantage of workers' meetings and fêtes. When, in 1852, an employer at Saint-Ouen offered an open-air banquet for his workers, he placed a bust of Louis Napoleon at one end of the banquet grounds and concluded a speech to the diners with the cry, *"Vive Louis-Napoléon."*[83] At a meeting called by workers to honor their employer, who had just been named *Chevalier* of the Legion of Honor, the latter concluded his remarks by calling for a toast to "the courageous prince who protects the workers."[84]

Cooperation between Imperial officials and employers was particularly close during electoral campaigns and before plebiscites. In 1852, the principal industrialists of the Loire basin agreed to distribute 50,000 copies of the Prince-President's address among their workers. (This was the famous *"L'Empire c'est la paix"* speech.)[85] During the campaign of 1857 for the *Corps législatif,* the *procureur général* at Besançon reported that "everywhere factory directors promise absolute cooperation with the government."[86] The same year the *procureur général* at Douai praised the efforts of employers at Lille "to direct the workers in the right direction."[87] During an electoral campaign, in 1858, the *procureur général* at Colmar reported that most employers supported "the intentions of the government."[88]

Employers frequently posted placards and distributed hand-

[83]*Le Moniteur,* September 10, 1852.

[84]*Le Moniteur,* January 23, 1853.

[85]*Le Moniteur,* October 21, 1852.

[86]A.N. BB18 1567, "Elections législatives de 1857," *procureur général* at Besançon to the Minister of Justice, June 20, 1857.

[87]A.N. BB18 1567, *procureur général* at Douai to the Minister of Justice, June 20, 1857.

[88]A.N. BB30 1567, *procureur général* at Colmar to the Minister of Justice, May 14, 1858.

bills among their workers urging support for official candidates and the government position in plebiscites. Such propaganda to workers often adopted a tone of one worker giving useful advice to another worker; placards and handbills opened with salutations like, *"mes amis,"* *"mes chers camarades,"* *"Ouvriers, mes chers concitoyens."* Sometimes employer electoral propaganda assumed a fatherly tone. One employer who offered electoral advice to his workers emphasized his responsibility as "head of the family."[89] A circular to workers on the approaching elections to the *Corps législatif* (probably 1863), *"Aux ouvriers de la Maison Guérin et Jouault,"* was typical of many that I have seen.[90] The spokesman for the firm assured his "friends" that he did not wish to discuss politics with them, only their "interests." "We think," he observed, "that a change in the present condition of things will be contrary to your interests, and, therefore, without attempting in the least to influence your opinion, we believe that we are offering you the advice of your employer in urging you to vote for the government candidate, M. Seydoux." A circular by the director of a quarry near Dornecy urged the workers to vote "yes" in the plebiscite of 1870 on the question of the liberal reforms of the Empire.[91] The author insisted upon his devotion to the working class "to which I am proud to belong," and declared that it was his duty to enlighten his "faithful collaborators"; therefore, "I come in the name of public tranquillity, in the name of social progress . . . to invite you, even to implore you to vote yes in the plebiscite of May 8."

The Emperor's Hand

This vast propaganda machine existed because the ruler believed that the state should seek to shape public opinion. Con-

[89]B.N. LB⁵⁵ 2367, F. Revilliod, "A nos ouvriers de la fabrique de Vizille" (Grenoble, 1851).

[90]B.N. Le⁷⁷ 2221.

[91]A.N. BB³⁰ 455.

vinced that only a popular regime could survive in France, Napoleon III also participated personally in the propaganda effort of his government. His speeches before the *Corps législatif*, his statements, dedications, tours, visits to factories and charitable institutions were all studied for their effect upon public opinion. In addition to these public activities, the Emperor also played an important role in the planning and execution of government propaganda—a part that, because of the secrecy surrounding propaganda activities, can only be incompletely known. Even questions of details were referred to the Emperor for decision. The Minister of Police Maupas, for example, stated that Napoleon III found "very advantageous" a suggestion to reduce the subscription rate of *Le Pays*.[92] The Emperor made the decision that all official information for the press should be released through the Ministry of the Interior.[93] We have seen that Napoleon III "corrected and considerably augmented in the most socialist sense" the policy statement of a government newspaper, *L'Epoque*."[94] A letter from Napoleon III's secretary Conti to Rouher (probably in 1865) reveals strikingly the Emperor's interest in the details of propaganda:[95] The Emperor requested that an article intended for *Le Moniteur* be returned to him (did Napoleon III write the article?); his Majesty had another use for it. What did Rouher know of a M. Charles whom the Emperor wished to write a history of the *coup d'état*? What did Rouher think of the idea of reprinting several articles from *Le Dix décembre* in *Le Petit Moniteur*? Napoleon III also followed the foreign press closely, including American newspapers. He wrote a letter of thanks to the *New York Times* for opposing the "calum-

[92]A.N. AB XIX, 175 (dossier 2), n.d.
[93]A.N. BB30 345, December 2, 1853.
[94]See p. 51.
[95]A.N. 45 APIII, "Papiers de Rouher."

nies of Marx" that were appearing in the *New York Tribune*.[96] On another occasion, Napoleon III personally had a favorable article inserted in *Le Moniteur* to counteract unfavorable news from the Crimean front.[97] Napoleon III participated personally in the preparation of propaganda pamphlets. Correspondence between the ruler and his cousin, the Prince Napoleon, on a pamphlet, *Les turcs en Europe*, reveals that the Emperor helped select the author of this propaganda tract, and corrected and approved the text.[98] He also worked closely with his propagandists on the preparation of the pamphlet, *L'Empereur Napoléon III et l'Italie*.[99]

Napoleon III also wrote anonymous letters and articles or under pseudonyms, especially for the newspapers *Le Peuple, Le Dix décembre,* and *L'Epoque,* three journals particularly close to him."[100] An article praising the Empress that appeared in *Le Dix décembre* of December 15, 1868, signed by an A. Grenier, was apparently the work of Napoleon III.[101] The article commended Eugénie's charitable activities and her concern with "the condition of the unfortunate classes"; "one still finds in her a little of the young phalansterian."[102] Anonymous communications from the Emperor also appeared in the *London Times*.[103]

[96]Maximilien Rubel, *Karl Marx, devant le bonapartisme* (Paris, 1960), 10.

[97]Comte de Hubner, *Neuf ans de souvenirs d'un ambassadeur d'Autriche à Paris sous le Second Empire* (Paris, 1904), 269-270.

[98]Hauterive, *Correspondance de Napoléon III*, 94; 97; 111; 112.

[99]Case, *French Opinion on War and Diplomacy*, 58-59. Case says of this collaboration between the Emperor and his publicists: "Here, then, we are able to see in details how methodically and deliberately the Emperor prepared propaganda for the public, weighed its words, and timed its appearance. . . ."

[100]*Papiers et correspondance*, I, 385-388.

[101]G. Lacour-Gayet, "Les idées libérales et sociales de l'Impératrice," *La Revue du XIXe siècle.* (1926), 177.

[102]In her youth Eugénie had for a time been an ardent Fourierist. She once told Emile Ollivier, "A seize ans j'étais Fourièriste." Emile Ollivier, *Journal, 1846-1869* v. II, 1861-1869 (Paris, 1961), 193.

[103]Lucy M. Salmon, *The Newspaper and the Historian* (New York, 1923), 188.

Napoleon III or his office more than once prepared propaganda novels. A report on the press in 1869 stated that *Le Petit journal* was planning to publish a propaganda novel on the First Empire from "the Emperor's office."[104] The *Papiers et correspondance* published the outline of a propaganda novel which the editors say was in the Emperor's handwriting.[105] The "upright grocer," M. Benoit, who had quit France for America in 1847, returned in 1868. He had heard from refugees that France is ruled by a despot and is a poverty-stricken land. Imagine, therefore, his astonishment at what he sees: the new iron vessels, railroads, the new and beautiful Paris, universal suffrage, low prices, political freedom (*"point de détenus politiques; point d'éxilés"*), an old-age retirement fund, the home for convalescent workers at Vincennes, the right to strike, etc, etc.

Newspapers and other media of communication served to disseminate the government's message, or rather messages, to the French people. What was the message of the Second Empire to the working class?

[104]*Papiers et correspondance*, I, 28.

[105]I, 218-219. For a discussion of the authorship of this plan for a novel, the original of which has disappeared, see H. N. Boon, *Rêve et réalité dans l'oeuvre économique et sociale de Napoléon III* (The Hague, 1934), 154.

IV

The Imperial Message to the Working Class

After the election of Louis Napoleon to the presidency of the Second Republic in December 1848, and the formation on October 31, 1849, of a ministry that included such future leaders of the Second Empire as Rouher, Baroche, Fould, and Magne, Bonapartist propaganda became government propaganda. The result was a change in the tone and message of this propaganda. With Louis Napoleon at the head of the government it could no longer call for a radical transformation of society or disseminate as irresponsible a message as when the party was in opposition. Nor was the Prince-President's new entourage, with its Orleanist background and bourgeois mentality, capable of the demagogery of fanatics and adventurers like Persigny, Laity, Ferrère, and the small merchants and artisans who had been Louis Napoleon's mainstays before his election.

However, like Bonapartist propaganda before the arrival in power of Louis Napoleon, the government's message to the working class was usually obvious and unsophisticated, particularly during the 1850's. It consisted of a few simple affirmations and slogans which, constantly repeated and cited as truths beyond dispute, became formulas.[1] The historian, Pierre de la Gorce, wrote

[1] A recent student of propaganda says of the effectiveness of the slogan: "Il répond à cette exigence du cerveau humain, paresseux et incapable d'une activité réfléchie, pour des titres courts et typiques. Il concentre tout le contenu, psychologique et sentimental, de l'idée qui cherche des adhérents. Son caractère est impératif." Jacques Driencourt, *La propagande nouvelle force politique* (Paris, 1950), 112.

ironically that the term "laboring classes" occurred so frequently in official statements that one had the impression that the Second Empire had invented it.[2]

Government propaganda among workers was not only very elementary, but it also appealed primarily to the emotions, a policy that probably owed much to the Emperor's advice and example. Before he became ruler and therefore could be more frank about such questions, Louis Napoleon frequently stated that the people responded more readily to appeals to their emotions than to their reason. "Among the people," he wrote, "sentiment comes before reason . . . the heart feels before the mind conceives."[3] And, in 1842, "One always moves the masses through their hearts, never by cold reason."[4]

Basic to Imperial propaganda was the claim, constantly repeated, that Napoleon III and his government labored tirelessly to ameliorate the condition of workers and the needy. "There is not a country," wrote the Councilor of State Bavoux in *Le Pays* (May 1, 1855), "There is not a government, we say it with pride, which shows more sympathy than ours for misfortune, for suffering, for misery."[5] The pro-government *Le Constitutionnel* (January 22, 1863) seconded *Le Pays*, "The government of the Emperor has shown more solicitude for the working classes than any other government." In 1866, *Le Moniteur* stated that it was common knowledge that history had never seen a government more interested in the needy than the Second Empire.[6] When, in 1869, Napoleon III urged repeal of the law requiring workers to carry

[2]Pierre de la Gorce, *Histoire du Second Empire* (Paris, 1899-1905), II, 3-4.

[3]*L'idée napoléonienne, Oeuvres de Napoléon III* (hereafter *Oeuvres*) (Paris, 1856-1869), I, 12-13.

[4]Georges Duval, *Napoléon III, enfance, jeunesse* (Paris, 1894), letter to Vieillard.

[5]Cited in Evariste Bavoux, *La France sous Napoléon III* (Paris, 1870-1872), I, 31.

[6]Emile Levasseur, *Histoire des classes ouvrières et de l'industrie en France de 1789 à 1870*, 2nd ed. (Paris, 1904), II, 662.

a *livret,* Granier de Cassagnac cited it as another example of the Emperor's lifelong sympathy for the people: "At the Tuileries, just as in the prison of Ham, his thoughts are turned towards those who suffer."[7] An electoral placard in 1863 praised the "sympathy" of the Emperor for the working classes—a sympathy "demonstrated by all the acts of his reign."[8]

Government spokesmen not only openly affirmed this "truth," but they also insinuated it on every possible occasion—in the press, in pamphlets, in speeches, in the published reports of ministers and officials: "the profound concern of the President of the Republic for the interests of the workers";[9] the constant efforts of the government to raise "the standard of well-being of the working population";[10] "We are all aware of His Majesty the Emperor's profound concern for the laboring classes";[11] "the government of the Emperor has given new and clear proof of its constant concern with the interests of the majority";[12] the warm affection which the Emperor "like Henry IV has for the working classes."[13] A published report by the Minister of the Interior on nurseries for workers' children did not neglect to mention Napoleon III's "august solicitude for the poor and working populations."[14] Another published report to Napoleon III on the status of an old-age retirement fund repeated what had become a ritual:

[7]*Le Pays,* March 25, 1869.

[8]*Bibliothèque nationale* (hereafter B.N.) Le⁷⁷ 1053, "Le maire de Merville à ses administrés" (Merville, 1863).

[9]*Le Constitutionnel,* January 9, 1852.

[10]*Le Constitutionnel,* June 12, 1857.

[11]B.N. Le⁷⁷ 325, "Aux Electeurs de la 6ème Circonscription du Département de la Seine" (1857).

[12]B.N. Le⁷⁷ 1235 A, "A Messieurs les Electeurs de la Huitième Circonscription électorale du Département de la Seine," an electoral placard (probably 1863) in support of the official candidate, Maximilien Koenigswarter.

[13]Isaac Péreire, *Discours prononcé à l'occasion de l'inauguration de la statue de François Arago à Estagel* (Paris, 1865), 7.

[14]*Le Moniteur universel,* March 3, 1862.

"We know that your enlightened solicitude is never wanting for interests affecting the poor and working classes."[15]

Napoleon III also contributed to this concerted attempt to convince workers of the government's interest in their well-being. At the very beginning of the Empire he assured a workers' delegation, "Those who work and those who suffer can count on me."[16] And after the disaster of Sedan and the fall of the Empire, Napoleon III, still eager to gain the support of workers for his dynasty, repeated the familiar theme: "Who, then, on a throne or in sovereign council has ever been interested in the worker? I alone, and if I return to power it will continue to be the question which interests me most."[17]

Not only was it the main preoccupation of the government to improve the condition of workers, but the Second Empire, unlike other regimes, acted rather than talked. Frequently the activities and creations of the Second Empire were contrasted with the *"idées démagogiques"* and *"utopiques"* of socialists and radical reformers. "While the opposition protests and promises," wrote a government newspaper, "the Imperial government acts and realizes," and replies to "utopian dreams" with positive and practical reforms.[18] Isaac Péreire contrasted the economic progress achieved during the Second Empire with the "sterile" battles of other days.[19]

I do not intend to describe here the legislation and the activities of the Second Empire to aid workers, but only how such efforts were exploited by government propaganda. Like the Restoration and July Monarchies that preceded it, the Second Em-

[15]*Le Moniteur*, July 7, 1862.
[16]B.N. Lb56 41, "Comité des ouvriers de Paris et de la banlieue," December 7, 1852.
[17]Paul Guériot, *La captivité de Napoléon III en Allemagne*, 3rd ed. (Paris, 1926), 108.
[18]*Le Peuple*, April 23, 1869.
[19]Péreire, *Discours prononcé*, 22-23.

pire believed that private charity was the most effective and sound means of aiding the needy. In addition, during periods of economic crises, when private charity could not cope with the greatly increased demands for aid by the lower classes, the government also appropriated funds for relief and public works. Belief in charity and paternalism as the solution to the social problem led to the founding of a variety of institutions for workers and the needy: societies to aid expectant mothers, nurseries, subsidies for the apprenticeship of orphans, homes for convalescent workers, loans at low interest rates, mutual aid societies, public baths, low cost workers' housing. And well advertised charity by the royal couple, drawn from a civil list which increased from 18,000,000 francs under Louis Philippe to 25,000,000 francs, became almost an institution. Royal bounty was, of course, no innovation, but during the Second Empire it became more lavish than under previous regimes. Moreover, while the Emperor continued to aid the victims of floods, fever, storms, crop failures, cholera—the traditional recipients of royal largess—Imperial charity more than ever before went for the relief of the unemployed, to the victims of industrial accidents, to workers hard pressed by high prices or rents.

Imperial spokesmen exploited fully all these efforts to aid the lower classes. Every time that the Emperor awarded a sum of money to the indigent, every time that the government founded a new institution for workers, they cited it as additional evidence of the regime's desire to aid the people.[20] Government newspapers, in fact, devoted more space to accounts of the aid provided for workers and the needy than to any other subject except foreign affairs. (Joly's Machiavelli had said that his newspapers

[20]The republican deputy Alfred Darimon, who later rallied to the Empire, complained that "on endormait le prolétariat au moyen d'institutions philanthropiques, qu'on lui vantait comme les seuls propres à améliorer son sort." *Histoire de douze ans (1857-1869)* (Paris, 1883), 13.

would never tire of writing about the amelioration of the condition of the working class.)[21]

An example of this is the propaganda in connection with the opening of a home for convalescent workers at Vincennes, near Paris, in 1857. From the day that the administration revealed its project for the convalescent home, the press, placards, and government orators outdid each other in praising the generosity of Napoleon III who had allegedly inspired the institution. A large placard described in detail the ceremony at the laying of the corner stone and praised the ruler and the government for its aid to the working class.[22] At the dedication of the new institution, the Minister of the Interior devoted most of his talk to reminding workers in the audience of their debt to Napoleon III and his government. (The Minister's enumeration of the services of the Empire to the working class filled more than two columns of *Le Moniteur*.)[23] And he closed his remarks with an appeal for the loyalty of workers to the regime: "May this completely new institution henceforth be justly appreciated by the workers for whom it is founded! May they repay in affection and gratitude all the benefits which the paternal solicitude of the Emperor does not cease to plan and to realize for them."

The "cradle to the grave" assistance that the government claimed it provided for the needy, including the very words, was another common subject of Imperial propaganda. An article in a government newspaper describing the aid provided for the

[21]See p. 43.

[22]B.N. Lb⁵⁶ 256, "Pose de la première pierre de l'Asile Impérial de Vincennes pour les ouvriers convalescents." (1855). At the top in large print we read:

"Depuis son avènement, Sa Majesté Napoléon III a cherché toutes les occasions de venir au secours des classes laborieuses. Combien de cités ouvrières, d'établissements modèles de bains et lavoirs publics, gratuit ou à prix réduits, d'asiles pour l'enfance, de sociétés de secours mutuels, ont été autorisés et crés, soit à Paris, soit dans les départements!"

[23]*Le Moniteur*, September 1, 1857. Other government newspapers also gave generously of their space to describe the dedication.

needy in Paris stated: "The organization of public assistance in Paris is worthy of serving as a model for states which take pride in their charitable institutions. . . . The nation takes the needy person at birth and comes to his aid at each epoch of his life until old age."[24] A leaflet whose vocabulary, style, and frequent anecdotes indicate that it was aimed at workers stated, "The Imperial effort extends throughout the life of the worker; it does not cease to protect him from the cradle to the grave."[25] Examples of the assistance provided by the state and society for the worker and the needy were: for the new born child, a doctor and layette; for the working mother, public nurseries; for orphans, care in families subsidized by the government; for craftsmen requiring money for tools or materials, the *Société du prince Impérial* provided credit without security. The Empress, with her tender concern for the suffering, sponsored schools for poor girls, assisted a school for deaf-mutes, and had founded a hospital for workers' children. In 1867, Napoleon III ordered that soup kitchens be established in the poorer sections of Paris. The name given to these institutions, the *Fourneaux du prince impérial*, was in itself propaganda.

The Second Empire sought to stimulate the construction of low-priced workers' apartments, usually through the granting of subsidies to private builders. A workers' *Cité Napoléon* was built in Paris, and similar cities, at Marseille, Lyons, Lille, Amiens, and Mulhouse. Government spokesmen did not, of course, overlook the propaganda value of such housing projects. A published report to the Emperor on workers' housing by the Minister of the Interior Persigny praised the success of the *Cité Napoléon*, with its five hundred inhabitants.[26] When, in 1853, the govern-

24*Le Constitutionnel*, April 25, 1857.
25B.N. RP 12170 Norbert Brillat, *Le groupe de l'Empereur à l'Exposition universelle* (Paris, n.d.), probably 1867.
26*Le Moniteur* (April 6, 1854). The report occupied four columns on the first page.

ment concluded an agreement with a builder for the construction of workers' housing, placards describing the project were posted about Paris.[27] The *Moniteur* (April 27, 1854) described a similar agreement at Lille as a *"véritable bienfait."* During the 1857 electoral campaign for the *Corps législatif*, the administrator of the *Cité Napoléon* posted a placard on the premises to remind the residents of their debt to the Emperor.[28] The inhabitants of the *Cité Napoléon*, he pointed out, owed their low-priced apartments, as well as baths, laundries and a nursery to the "solicitude of His Majesty the Emperor for the working classes and particularly for you." The administrator concluded with an appeal to his *"chers locataires"* to show their gratitude by voting for the official candidate.

The public works of the Second Empire, particularly the rapid transformation of Paris and other large cities, provided government spokesmen with both an opportunity and a challenge.[29] They attempted to convince the working class that it gained more from the program of public works than did other classes. In order "to enlighten public opinion," the Prefect of the Bouches-du-Rhône publicized the contribution of the government's public works program, including the fact that they provided "employment for workers."[30] An additional advantage of public works, he pointed out to the Minister of the Interior, was that they were evidence of "the concern of the government with

[27]Pierre-Léon Fournier, *Le Second Empire et la législation ouvrière* (Paris, 1911), 120-121.

[28]"Circulaire de M. Aublet, l'Administrateur de la Cité Napoléon" (1857).

[29]Several recent works have discussed the motives, the financing, and the achievements of the Second Empire's public works program. Louis Girard, *La Politique des travaux publics du Second Empire* (Paris, 1952); David H. Pinckney, *Napoleon III and the Rebuilding of Paris* (Princeton, 1958); Charlene M. Leonard, *Lyon transformed. Public Works of the Second Empire 1853-1864* (Berkeley and Los Angeles, 1961).

[30]*Archives nationales* (hereafter A.N.) F1c III, Bouches-du-Rhône 7, prefect to the Minister of the Interior, May 4, 1858.

the laboring classes." The announcement of plans for public works was always immediately turned into propaganda. A placard praised Louis Napoleon for authorizing the construction of a new boulevard, a project which would both improve a densely populated neighborhood and provide employment for many workers.[31] A lengthy article in a government newspaper cited the opening of the Boulevard de Sébastopol as "a splendid specimen of the great works of public utility whose benefits will perpetuate in future generations the memory of the reign of Napoleon III."[32] Napoleon III himself inaugurated the boulevard of Prince Eugène in 1862; his speech emphasized what the regime had done for workers.[33]

There was, however, another side to the public works program of the Second Empire that government spokesmen could not ignore. The demolition of apartment houses in Paris to clear space for the new boulevards and streets was responsible for a rise in rents that placed government spokesmen on the defensive. Thus, several long articles in Le Moniteur insisted that the rise in rents was only temporary and that they would decline as new apartment buildings took the place of those that were torn down.[34]

The 1850's and 1860's, despite periods of economic crises, were generally years of prosperity, not only in France but also throughout Europe and the United States. Whatever the reasons for this prosperity, the government of Louis Napoleon claimed credit for it, and, at the same time, warned workers that unrest, by weakening confidence, threatened their well-being more than that of

[31]B.N. Le⁷⁷ 155, "Aux Habitants et électeurs du 5ème arrondissement de Paris" (1852).

[32]La France, April 10, 1858.

[33]La Revue de l'Empire, December 14, 1862.

[34]An article in Le Moniteur of April 21, 1853 took two columns on the first page to present the government's argument.

any other class. On September 4, 1852, *Le Moniteur* wrote that the "act of public safety" of December 2 (a common euphemism for the *coup d'état*) had already exerted a favorable influence upon business; the economy was expanding, the workshops were busy, "assuring workers of high wages." In fact, workers were so satisfied with conditions at Paris that no one of them had accepted a very favorable offer of employment in the Department of the Oise. "This is an important fact," editorialized the article; "it proves more than anything one can say that industry has regained its impetus, that the workers have jobs, that they are satisfied and confident." During the campaign of 1863, a placard posted by a mayor in the industrial Department of the Nord gave the Emperor credit for the unprecedented prosperity of the country, "prosperity which resulted in increased wages for the worker."[35] In the electoral campaign of 1869, the government press attributed the prosperity of the country ("seventeen years of prosperity," wrote the *Courrier de Marseille*)[36] to the regime. On the other hand, political opposition and disturbances threatened this prosperity and the well-being of the working class. "You are tired of revolutions which increase unemployment among workers," announced the official candidate Devinck in 1862.[37] And two days later he added, "Tranquility stimulates employment."[38]

Imperial publicists utilized a device that contemporary students of propaganda have labelled the "band-wagon" technique. They tried to convince workers that since everyone, including the working class, except for a handful of incorrigible victims of the *idées démagogiques*, had rallied to the Empire, resistance could only be isolated and futile. Government propagandists

[35] B.N. Le77 1049, "Le maire d'Hazebrouck à ses administrés" (Hazebrouck, 1863).
[36] *Les élections de 1869*. Bibliothèque de la révolution de 1848, Tome XXI (Paris, 1960), 77-78.
[37] *Le Pays*, February 27, 1862.
[38] *Le Pays*, February 29, 1862.

seized upon, exaggerated, and even invented incidents to prove that the working class was behind the regime. The government tried particularly to show that workers in cities and areas with revolutionary histories and traditions had abandoned their old ways and were rallying around Napoleon III.

During the uncertain period that followed the *coup d'état*, the government cited evidence to show that workers throughout France approved of Louis Napoleon's seizure of power. Day after day during the month of December 1851, *Le Moniteur* published reports from all parts of France seeking to prove that workers favored the new regime. On December 6, for example, the official newspaper made a kind of *tour d'horizon* of the French working class: at Paris, workers had demolished several barricades raised by resistants to the *coup d'état*; at Roubaix, they greeted the proclamations of December 2 with shouts of *"Vive Napoléon"*; in the Ardennes, workers remained calmly at their jobs; at Le Creusot, a similar response ("not a man was missing in the workshops; . . . not the slightest trace of agitation"); at Metz, iron-workers paraded a bust of Louis Napoleon about the city. Other issues of *Le Moniteur* reprinted articles and news items from provincial newspapers describing the enthusiasm of workers for the *coup d'état*; a letter to the *Salut public* of Lyons from inhabitants of the revolutionary Croix-Rousse section repudiating "the fomenters of disorder" (December 21, 1850); a report from *Le Concorde* of Reims which attributed the large "yes" vote in the plebiscite on the *coup d'état* "particularly to the working population" (December 24, 1851); from the *Union bourguignonne* a report that workers at Dijon had placed a crown on a bust of Louis Napoleon (January 7, 1852). The *Constitutionnel* (January 8, 1852) even reprinted an item from the *Nouvelle gazette de Munich*: "The mass of workers did not resist the [*coup d'état*] and aided its execution by a calm and dignified attitude, and, in large part, by their approval of it." A statement by the Prince-President praising the conduct of French workers was frequently reproduced: "In those popular quarters where in the past insurrection quickly found recruits among the workers . . . this time anarchy met only a profound repugnance."[39] A similar statement by Morny also received wide publicity: "The plan of the anarchists had been disrupted in the capital by the courage of the army and by the contempt of the fine workers who so often had been their dupes."[40]

Such efforts to convince workers that opposition was against the current and senseless continued throughout the reign of Louis Napoleon. On June 11, 1852, *Le Moniteur* described the enthusiasm of workers for the Prince-President in the traditionally revolutionary Faubourg Saint-Antoine; as he traversed the neighborhood a young girl tossed a large bouquet of flowers into his carriage. Similar incidents were described frequently in government newspapers, placards, and pamphlets. When Louis Napoleon returned to Paris, in October 1852, after a tour of the provinces, workers in the city greeted him warmly, some holding up a poem printed in large letters praising the ruler.[41] Returning from a ride in the Bois de Vincennes by way of a workers' neighborhood, the Emperor and Empress were constantly surrounded by its cheering inhabitants.[42] A heavy rain did not deter workers employed at the nearby iron founderies from cheering the Emperor when he visited Plombières.[43] At Epernay, railroad

[39]*Le Moniteur*, December 8, 1851.

[40]*Le Moniteur*, December 14, 1851.

[41]*Le Moniteur*, October 17, 1852. The third stanza of the poem reads:
> "Ami des travailleurs et leur ami sincère,
> Non content de leur rendre un labeur quotidien,
> Pour eux, dans l'avenir, combattant la misère,
> Il veut de leurs vieux jours être encore le soutien."

[42]*Le Moniteur*, March 9, 1862.

[43]*Le Moniteur*, July 25, 1856.

workers welcomed Napoleon III enthusiastically.[44] At Arras, stated a pamphlet describing a royal tour, the "working population . . . never tired of acclaiming and gazing at the sovereigns whom they had freely chosen."[45] The loyalty and affection of workers for the ruler also embraced the heir to the throne. When the Prince Imperial visited a factory, enthusiastic workers gathered about him and offered him flowers.[46]

The city of Lyons with its centuries long history of worker unrest was, we have seen, a particular object of Imperialist propaganda. In 1865, the government made a dramatic gesture towards workers in the silk center; it announced plans to raze the wall separating the worker Croix-Rousse section from the remainder of the city. The government pointed to this action as further evidence of its confidence in the loyalty of the working class. And in a frequently reprinted letter to the Minister of the Interior, Napoleon III explained why it was now safe to level the barrier:[47]

We are no longer in the period when we thought it necessary to erect formidable defenses against disturbances. The working population of

[44]*Le Moniteur*, August 30, 1857.

[45]B.N. Lb56 1809, *Voyage de Leurs Majestés l'Empereur et l'Impératrice dans les Départements du Nord (Août 1867)* (Paris, 1867), 3.

[46]*Le Pays*, July 4, 1867.

[47]The letter appeared, for example, in a propaganda pamphlet published in Lyons, B.N. Lb56 1517, *S.M. Napoléon III à Lyon* (Lyons, 1865). The pamphlet includes, in addition to the Emperor's letter, a song written by two local *café-concert* artists praising the ruler's action, "Les vieux murs de la Croix-Rousse." The final stanza of the song reads:

> "Chantons en choeur en ce jour d'allégresse
> Vive la France et vive l'Empereur!
> Gais ouvriers, honorons tous sans cesse
> Le souverain soutien du travailleur;
> Pour le travail, que chacun se trémousse:
> Mes chers amis, nous sommes affranchis;
> Réjouis-toi, bonne et vieille Croix-Rousse,
> Car tes vieux murs vont être anéantis."

Lyons is too intelligent, it knows too well how much I have their interests at heart to wish to compromise them by creating trouble.

I wish, therefore, to replace the customs barrier, product of the distrust of another epoch, by a vast planted boulevard, enduring evidence of my confidence in the good sense and in the patriotism of the population of Lyons.

The main subject of government propaganda during the Second Empire was Napoleon III. This was, in part, because the administration realized that the Emperor was more popular than his government, that the electoral victories of the Second Empire owed more to the ruler's personal prestige than to any other cause. In part, also, because Napoleon III, whether as a result of vanity or an insight into popular psychology, insisted upon the personification of the regime in himself.

Government propaganda pictured Napoleon III as a kindly, clement ruler whose great desire was to pardon imprisoned or exiled foes of the regime, if only they would come to their senses and abandon their opposition. Although the government crushed opposition ruthlessly and even employed terror as an instrument of rule when it felt threatened, as soon as the emergency was over, well-advertised Imperial clemency made itself felt.

Even before his arrival in power, Louis Napoleon attempted to establish a reputation for generosity towards the working class. After the "June Days" he told the socialist Proudhon that "he disapproved unreservedly of the policies of General Cavaignac, the suppression of newspapers, the state of siege, and all those repression measures borrowed from the monarchy for the defense of the Republic."[48] (In view of the record of Napoleon III's government there is good reason to suspect the sincerity of his concern for political and personal liberty.) After his election, the

[48]Alfred Darimon, *A travers une révolution (1847-1855)* (Paris, 1894), 68 ff. This is Darimon's account of a meeting between the two men.

Prince-President continued to proclaim his kindly disposition towards misguided opponents, a category that included many workers. The government, he declared before the *Corps législatif* in November, 1850, had been indulgent towards political prisoners on every occasion that it could do so without danger.[49] Thus, since June, 1849, it had freed 2,400 persons, and holding forth hopes for still more pardons, he added, "Unfortunately, there are still 348 political prisoners in France, without counting the transportees [of June 1848]." A circular from the Minister of the Interior that was printed in government newspapers informed the prefect that Louis Napoleon wished to liberate all political prisoners who had only been misled and whose freedom would not endanger society.[50] The majority of the prisoners, said the circular, were "unfortunate workers or country people who were involved in the revolt [probably the resistance to the *coup d'état*] only because of weakness or ignorance." A government newspaper praised the generosity of the chief of state who "after having vanquished like Caesar pardons like Augustus."[51] When the participants at a ball in Montpellier greeted the touring Louis Napoleon with shouts of *"Vive l'Empereur"* and *"Vive l'amnestie,"* the ruler replied: "I hear the shouts of *Vive l'amnestie*. Amnesty is in my heart more than it is in your mouths."[52] A cursory examination of *Le Moniteur* for January, 1853, revealed decrees or articles on amnesties on January 1, 5, 6, 7, 13, and 22. Throughout the early years of the Second Empire, government newspapers, pamphlets, and placards continued to print decrees, articles, and editorials on amnesties and to praise Napoleon III's generosity towards political foes. When, during the Crimean War, the political prisoner Barbès, a revolutionary leader in 1848, ex-

[49]*Oeuvres*, III, 161-162.
[50]*Le Constitutionnel*, January 30, 1852.
[51]*La Patrie*, January 31, 1852.
[52]*Le Moniteur*, October 5, 1852.

pressed hopes for a French victory, Napoleon III immediately ordered his liberation, declaring, "A prisoner who retains such patriotic feelings, despite his long suffering, cannot rot in prison during my reign."[53] This example of Napoleon III's clemency was, of course, given adequate publicity. And when, in 1859, a general amnesty pardoned all but a few of the political exiles, government spokesmen found no praise too high for their merciful sovereign.

The "public relations men" of the Second Empire valued the appeal of "human interest stories" and repeated and embroidered upon incidents in the lives of the rulers, real or apocryphal, revealing the virtues of the Emperor and the royal family. A propaganda pamphlet of 1859 lists several examples of the Emperor's inherent kindness—examples which I have also seen a number of times in other government literature:[54] When Louis Napoleon was only three or four years old, he gave the entire contents of his purse to a poor lad. On another occasion, the young Louis Napoleon returned home without shoes and almost naked after giving his clothes to a needy family. Nor had power altered the ruler's kindly nature. The Emperor listened sympathetically to the request of a young girl that her father, a deportee, be permitted to return to France. Royal visits to hospitals, particularly if the sovereigns visited patients with contagious diseases, were a favorite subject of Imperial propaganda. Napoleon III's first visit after the proclamation of the Empire, went a frequently repeated story, was to the *Hôtel Dieu* (a charity hospital) and to a military hospital; the sovereign was said to have explained his choice with the statement, "I want my first visit as Emperor to be to those who suffer."[55] In 1864, the Emperor insisted in a letter, which soon be-

---

[53]*Oeuvres*, III, 398-399.

[54]B.N. Lb56 402, *Histoire et Bienfaits de 8a Majesté Napoléon III* (1859), 3, 6.

[55]Charles Robert recounts the incident in a pamphlet based upon a course offered at the Vincennes home for convalescent workers, *Les améliorations sociales du Second Empire* (Paris, 1868), II, 19-20.

came familiar to the entire country, that construction of a new *Hôtel Dieu* start immediately and that work on the Opera, already under way, be delayed so that both structures could be completed together.[56] "It is very important to me," wrote the Emperor, "that the monument dedicated to pleasure does not rise before the shelter for suffering." A report by the Minister of the Interior to the Empress, which found its way into the government press, stated that Eugenie had decided to distribute sewing machines to needy workers.[57] Another common theme of government propaganda was royal assistance to individual workers or families who had suffered misfortunes: five hundred francs to the family of a worker killed in an industrial accident;[58] four hundred francs to several workers injured on the Rue des Mauvaises-Paroles;[59] two thousand francs for workers at Metz whose factory had been destroyed by fire;[60] aid for a worker injured in an accident in the twelfth arrondissement of Paris and for the widow of a worker killed in another accident.[61]

Government publicists tirelessly repeated incidents intended to reveal the humanity and the simplicity of the royal couple. On a visit to Lyons, in 1856, the Emperor ordered his escort to permit a woman who had been following his carriage and shouting *"Vive l'Empereur"* to approach and gave her a handful of coins with the remark, "Take it poor woman; this is to purchase bread."[62] A variation of this incident occurred in the Department of the Aisne, where Napoleon III called to his carriage a worker, ques-

[56]*Le Moniteur universel du soir*, August 1, 1864.

[57]*Le Moniteur universel du soir*, February 6, 1867.

[58]*Le Moniteur*, May 5, 1852.

[59]*Le Moniteur*, August 7, 1852.

[60]*L'Etincelle*, June 23, 1866.

[61]B.N. Lb56 37. "Clémence et bienfaits de S.M. Napoléon III" (1853). This placard consists of items from *Le Moniteur*, December 2, 1852-January 8, 1853.

[62]B.N. Lb56 346, "Arrivée de S.M. l'Empereur à Lyon" (Lyons, 1856), a four-page leaflet.

tioned him paternally about his family, and left a gift of twenty francs.[63] When a delegation of girls at a workers' ball at Poitiers presented the touring Louis Napoleon with a crown and "His Highness deigned to dance with them," there was no containing the enthusiasm of the crowd.[64] The reaction was the same at Bordeaux where Louis Napoleon danced with the daughter of a foreman.[65]

Even before twentieth century totalitarian regimes, Napoleon III sensed the value of the "cult of the hero" for increasing the affection of the masses for the leader. A myth-surrounded ruler, who was also the source of all beneficence, could be an appreciable asset to the regime. Napoleon III, therefore, insisted that all of the accomplishments of the regime be attributed to him. As Karl Marx said in his own sarcastic way, "He [Napoleon III] would like to steal the whole of France in order to be able to make a present of her to France."[66] The Catholic social reformer, Armand de Melun, who worked with Napoleon III, observed that the Emperor insisted that all his activities in behalf of the needy be of advantage to him, that they increase his "power and popularity."[67] Emile Ollivier wrote that the Emperor claimed the credit for all the generous acts of the government and cited a letter by the Emperor complaining that his name had not been mentioned in connection with a gift to the victims of an earthquake.[68] Ollivier also wrote that the minister Baroche and the Bonapartist deputy Jerôme David objected that he had not given

[63]*La France*, November 14, 1857.

[64]*Le Moniteur*, October 16, 1852.

[65]Georges-Eugène Haussmann, *Mémoires du baron Haussmann* (Paris, 1890-1893), I, 573.

[66]Karl Marx, *The Eighteenth Brumaire of Louis Bonaparte* (New York, n.d.), 119.

[67]Armand de Melun, *Mémoires du Vicomte de Melun* (Paris, 1891), II, 42.

[68]Emile Ollivier, *L'Empire libéral* (Paris, 1895-1915), III, 73-74.

[111]

proper credit to the Emperor for his role in preparing legislation legalizing strikes.[69]

Imperial officials, acting on instructions or sensing what was expected of them, attributed everything accomplished by the government to the Emperor. It was the constant preoccupation of Napoleon III's entourage, wrote Alfred Darimon, to praise the Emperor for everything done for the masses.[70] In 1856, a report by the Prefect of Police stated that assistance to Parisian workers displaced by public works was always given in the name of the Emperor and the Empress.[71] Another police report in the same year said that the royal couple received credit for the bread, meat, and firewood distributed to unemployed workers.[72] During the crisis of 1866-1867 in the Lyons area, the prefect announced that all aid distributed to the needy was due to and by order of the Emperor.[73]

It was only partly out of the natural desire to escape criticism that Napoleon III, who claimed credit for the achievements of the regime, refused to accept responsibility for its shortcomings and failures. He realized that for the security and the prestige of the state the ruler must be above attack. As a result, the failures of the regime were attributed to others, to obstruction or to circumstances beyond the control of the ruler. Thus in June, 1851, in a speech delivered at the opening of a new railroad line, the Prince-President charged that the factions in the Assembly were to blame for the government's failure to realize all the reforms

[69]Ollivier, *L'Empire libéral*, VI, 528; 533. Baroche complained that "le nom de l'Empereur ne fût jamais prononcé et que la loi parut être d'initiative parlementaire." David criticized Ollivier's report because it lacked "le bon goût et la justice de parler de l'initiative généreuse de Sa Majesté l'Empereur."

[70]Alfred Darimon, *Histoire d'un parti. Les Cinq sous l'Empire (1857-1860)* (Paris, 1885), 86-87.

[71]A.N. BB[30] 366, "Affaires politiques diverses," October 10, 1856.

[72]A.N. BB[30] 366, November 1, 1856.

[73]Sreten Maritch, *Histoire du mouvement social sous le Second Empire à Lyon* (Paris, 1930), 107.

that it desired; although they were always ready to second him when he requested repressive measures, the factions of the Assembly opposed their inertia when he attempted to "take measures to improve the condition of the population."[74] A government newspaper commenting on the opposition of the legislature to Louis Napoleon's projects for public baths and laundries, exclaimed, "What difficulties the government had to surmount to obtain these laws."[75] In his address to the opening session of the legislature in 1854, Napoleon III denied responsibility for the economic crisis and attributed it to "circumstances alone."[76] And on a similar occasion in 1862, he asserted that he knew the people did not blame him for the existing unemployment and high prices.[77] In an anonymous newspaper article, Napoleon III wrote that despite the continuing popularity of the Emperor, the prestige of the government was declining.[78] This was because the agents of the government failed to imitate the "extreme kindness" of the chief of state; impressed by the power delegated to them such servants of the state were neglecting the interests of the people.

The Electoral Campaigns

The government's propaganda machine did not exist only for electoral campaigns and plebiscites. Spokesmen for the regime also had day to day responsibilities; they were not idle between elections and plebiscites.[79] However, the machine was used to its maximum power and efficiency during electoral campaigns. This

[74]*Oeuvres*, III, 210-211.

[75]*Le Constitutionnel*, January 9, 1852.

[76]*Le Pays*, March 3, 1854.

[77]*Le Moniteur*, January 27, 1862.

[78]*Papiers et correspondance de la famille impériale* (Paris, 1870-1872), I, 387-388.

[79]However, as we shall see, some officials and friends of the regime believed that a weakness of government propagandists was their tendency to relax between electoral campaigns, pp. 202-203.

became necessary because of the new institution of universal manhood suffrage, the only major reform of the Second Republic maintained by Napoleon III. It was, in fact, the Second Empire that accustomed France to the new institution. Louis Napoleon called upon the entire electorate to approve his acts or policies on three different occasions: the *coup d'état*, the establishment of the Second Empire, and the Empire after the liberal reforms of the 1860's. There were also four nation-wide elections for the *Corps législatif*: 1852, 1857, 1863, and 1869, as well as frequent elections for departmental and *arrondissement* councils. These many elections and plebiscites created both an opportunity and a need for propaganda.

Elections during the Second Empire differed from elections in twentieth century democratic states in two significant ways. In the United States and western Europe most political parties accept the institutions and the constitutions of their countries and electoral campaigns are a contest to determine who will guide the state. During the Second Empire, on the contrary, most opposition parties did not accept the basic institutions of the state, and, in theory at least, hoped to overthrow them. For the followers of the fallen dynasties and for republicans, the regime was illegal and Napoleon III a usurper. This meant that at every plebiscite and election the voters were asked to pronounce on the very existence of the regime. As the government candidate, Granier de Cassagnac, said during the 1863 campaign for the *Corps législatif*, "It is not my person or the person of my rival that the electors have before them. The question is more important and more serious: they must pronounce between a friend and an enemy of the Empire."[80]

The second way in which elections during the Second Empire differed from contemporary elections in democratic states was

<hr>

[80]B.N. Le⁷⁷ 840, "A Messieurs les électeurs de la 3ème circonscription du Gers."

the practice of "official candidates," who were named and supported by the government. The Second Empire was not the first government to support candidates that favored it, but as Ollivier pointed out, it differed from preceding regimes by making "the designation of its candidates an official action."[81] In a circular to the prefects, the Minister of the Interior Persigny defended the practice of official candidates on the grounds that "the people must be able to discern who are the friends and who are the enemies of the government."[82] There was, therefore, no pretence of governmental neutrality in elections.[83] All newspapers, for example, including the opposition press, had to publish the names of official candidates.

Before elections the government distributed a kind of propaganda line for the guidance of its officials, who were, of course, expected to work actively for the approved candidates. In 1857, a circular from the Minister of the Interior to the prefects on the approaching elections to the *Corps législatif* suggested the line that government propaganda should take.[84] The Minister urged the prefects to remind property owners of the security that they enjoyed under the Empire, workers of their improved conditions, those who suffered, of the Emperor's constant concern for them, and, all voters of the glorious and respected international position of France. Again, for the 1863 elections, the Minister of the Interior offered his ideas on propaganda to the prefects, this time

[81]Ollivier, *L'Empire libéral,* III, 15.

[82]De la Gorce, *Histoire du Second Empire,* I, 54-55.

[83]At times, however, the government did seem embarrassed about its intervention in elections, and tried to keep some of its activities from reaching the public. Thus, a circular to the *procureurs impériaux* on the elections of 1863 was marked "*très confidentielle.*" A.N. BB[30] 427, *procureur général* at Aix to the Minister of Justice, May 18, 1863. The Prefect of the Department of the Rhône urged the *maires* in his jurisdiction to encourage a favorable vote in the plebiscite of 1852, but "*sous un prétexte convenable*," A.N. F[1c] III, Rhône 4, November 2, 1852.

[84]J. Albiot, *Annales du Second Empire. Les campagnes électorales (1851-1869)* (Paris, 1869), 219.

[115]

emphasizing the popular origins of the Empire and the government's activities in behalf of the needy.[85] The Minister of Justice also regularly distributed a circular on elections to the *procureurs généraux*, which the latter sent to the justices of the peace in their jurisdictions, often adding a word of encouragement and additional suggestions for the campaign.

On the regional level, the prefects and the *procureurs généraux* directed the government's electoral campaigns. The prefects worked mainly through the *maires* of the communes, the *procureurs généraux*, through the justices of the peace. The *procureurs général* at Angers wrote that the success of an election depended upon the justices of the peace, public officials who were in very close contact with the people.[86]

The means of communication with the electorate were those that I have already discussed. The government press had, of course, a role to play during electoral campaigns. Contacts between the government and sympathetic newspapers were even more frequent than usual. And towards the end of the Empire the government attempted to found new newspapers during electoral campaigns and to suborn opposition journals. Electoral placards were a common form of propaganda. Their form and contents have changed little since the Second Empire (bright colors, varied type, endorsement of candidates); only the photographs of candidates were lacking. On the other hand, public meetings to support candidates were illegal until late in the Empire; only in the 1869 campaign did they become common.

The success of an official candidate, the government realized, depended to some extent upon his person and record. It sought, therefore, to present candidates who were popular in their electoral districts. In industrial areas this meant, of course, candi-

[85] Jules Ferry, *La lutte électorale en 1863* (Paris, 1863), 113-114.

[86] A.N. BB[30] 403, no. 625, circular of the *procureur général* at Angers to the justices of the peace, February 21, 1852.

[116]

dates agreeable to workers. Thus, the *procureur général* at Rennes urged the government to accept as an official candidate an industrialist who had an "influence upon the workers" because of his charitable activities.[87]

The official candidate based his campaign on his own record, as well as on the achievements of the government. In industrial areas, he sought, therefore, to convince constituents of his devotion to working-class interests. Perret, a government candidate in 1852, boasted that he had always lived among workers, and promised that he would support energetically "all measures proposed in the interest of the working class."[88] In 1852, an article urging the election of Fouché-Lepelletier to the *Corps législatif*, reminded the working class that "during the crisis which followed February, 1848, M. Fouché-Lepelletier, thanks to considerable sacrifices, did not close a single one of his workshops and kept on all of his workers.[89] Eleven years later Fouché-Lepelletier, again a candidate, once more recalled to the working class his sacrifice of 1848, and pointed out that since then he had served as vice-president of the *Conseil de prudhommes* and as a member of the *Comité de surveillance de l'administration générale de l'Assistance publique*.[90] A campaign placard of 1863 supporting the official candidate, Frédéric Lévy, mayor of the twelth arrondissement, informed his worker constituents that he had lived among them for twenty-five years.[91] His services to the working class included the founding of many mutual aid societies, the reorganization of public assistance, the opening of several branches of the *Mont-de Piété* (public pawnshops); he was responsible also

[87]A.N. BB[30] 426, "Elections diverses (1857-1871)," November 3, 1859.

[88]B.N. Le[77] 118, *Candidature au corps législatif de M. J. Perret*; in *Elections du Corps législatif*. This is a bound collection of campaign placards and platforms.

[89]*Le Constitutionnel*, February 22, 1852.

[90]*Le Constitutionnel*, May 27, 1863.

[91]B.N. Le 1241 A, *Aux électeurs de la 5ème circonscription électorale*.

for many new schools and charitable institutions in his *arrondissement*. The industrialist Constant Say, a government candidate in 1863, boasted of the practical reforms he had introduced in his factories.[92] In 1869, a pro-government newspaper praised the official candidate, Savart, a simple workman in 1850, who now employed 4,000 persons.[93] M. Savart did not, however, work solely in his own interests. "He has always loved to aid and to elevate those who shared his daily labors," and it was rare that one who had worked with him for a number of years did not have some savings. M. Savart had also founded a mutual aid society, a savings bank for his employees paying ten percent interest per year, a society to help sick workers, a burial society, an orphanage, and each year he distributed several thousand pairs of shoes to the needy in his neighborhood.

Appeals for the election of official candidates signed by workers, whether voluntarily or under duress, were common during the Second Empire. In 1852, a statement, *Aux ouvriers de la 3ème Circonscription* (of Paris) signed by a number of workers and soldiers urged the election of the government candidate, Germain Thibaut.[94] The following year a proclamation, *Aux ouvriers électeurs dans la 4ème circonscription* (of Paris), signed by a journeyman butcher, a shoemaker, two printers, a cabinetmaker, and a tanner, urged workers to vote for the official candidate, Moreau: "The resumption of work requires that we remain united and that we vote together for a friend of order, for without order we and our families will suffer."[95] An electoral statement (undated) signed by a large number of workers sup-

---

[92]"Pour l'ouvrier, le nom de M. Say exprime quelque chose de supérieur à tout; il veut dire Philanthropie, Bienfaisance, Humanité, Dévouement. B.N. Le⁷⁷ 1270, *Aux électeurs de la 7ème circonscription.*

[93]*La Patrie*, May 22, 1869.

[94]B.N. Le⁷⁷ 166.

[95]B.N. Le⁷⁷ 155.

ported the candidacy to the *Corps législatif* of Monnin-Japy, "indefatigable defender of the worker because he knows all his needs, being placed at the head of important factories employing more than 6,000 workers."[96] On May 25-26, 1863, *Le Pays* published the text of a statement signed by a large number of workers ("the original of this address," said the statement, "is covered by more than a thousand signatures") urging the election of Constant Say, who instead of elaborating fine-sounding theories for improving the condition of the working class, had established in his factory a pension system and a fund to care for injured workers.

Such electoral propaganda for the working class was, of course, most abundant in towns with large worker populations. But even in predominantly agricultural regions, official candidates often included a few generalities in their campaign literature for the benefit of whatever small agglomerations of workers lived in their districts.

The propaganda message that I have described appealed particularly to unsophisticated workers who still looked to the benevolence of the upper orders for help in their moments of need. However, by the mid-nineteenth century a new kind of worker also existed—a worker who was not satisfied by charity and who questioned the values of a society that seemed to condemn him to perpetual poverty. Did government propaganda during the Second Empire have anything to say to such a worker?

[96]B.N. Le[77] 322.

Government Propaganda New Style
Workers Organizations—Bonapartist Agents

In the 1860's, the Bonapartist message to workers grew more subtle and sophisticated than it had been during the first decade of Louis Napoleon's rule. As we have seen, the earlier message was simple and direct. It proclaimed the devotion of the Emperor and his government to the working class and cited as evidence the achievements of the regime. The new propaganda, on the contrary, was more reserved; it did not praise the Second Empire blindly and without reservation, and insisted more upon the hope for social reform under existing institutions than upon the actual achievements thus far, which it often admitted were quite meager. The old propaganda was, moreover, obviously government inspired; few informed persons, for example, did not know of the relationship between such newspapers as *Le Constitutionnel* and *Le Pays* and the government. The new propaganda, on the other hand, encouraged the activities of sympathetic workers' organizations and employed the services of secret agents.

The new message was the product of a deeper understanding of propaganda and of working class attitudes. From about 1859, a number of friends of the Empire, often recent converts from republicanism, began to question the value of the existing propaganda, particularly among the better educated and more class-conscious workers. These friendly critics of government propaganda doubted whether assurances that the Emperor was charitable and merciful satisfied workers who read about and discussed the problems of their class. Such workers were interested in questions like the right to strike, to form trade unions, the organization of cooperatives, the repeal of the obligatory *livret*, and of Article 1781 of the Civil Code (an article providing that in disputes over wages between a worker and his employer the court must, in the absence of evidence, accept the word of the latter). One of the reasons for the success of republican propaganda among these workers, said the advocates of a new propaganda, was that it told workers what they wanted to hear about issues of this kind.

Furthermore, they urged, there was reason to hope that some of the more thoughtful workers might be convinced of the virtues of the Empire. Many such workers, disillusioned with political parties, would support any government that seemed genuinely interested in improving the condition of the working class. Workers in general were also impressed by the endurance of the Second Empire; it was the existing regime and gave every evidence of surviving, at least for the foreseeable future. Moreover, as government officials confirmed, the most politically alert workers approved of the Emperor's nationalities' policy, particularly his intervention in Italy. The *procureur général* at Lyons reported that because of their enthusiasm for the Italian cause workers were becoming more favorable towards the government; "the Emperor was becoming its hero."[1] Another potential advantage of the Empire, it was claimed, was the fear of class-conscious workers that a republic dominated by the bourgeoisie might be even more indifferent to the needs of the working class than the existing regime.

[1]A.N. BB30 379, *procureur général* at Lyons to the Minister of Justice, July 10, 1859.

A report by the *procureur général* at Lyons summed up the hopes of those who believed that the working class was not irretrievably lost to the Empire, and that some workers might be won over if the government made a wiser effort to attract them.[2] Even though the majority of urban workers voted for opposition candidates in the 1863 elections to the *Corps législatif*, the *procureur général* did not despair. Divisions already existed within the working class, he reported: "A new democracy has taken shape along side the old democracy; it is Imperialist and moderate, enamored of progress but better inspired than its elder." And the government "by its initiative, its advice, by frequent communication" should seek to exploit this division within the working class; "circumstances have never seemed more favorable."

The government, faced by the opposition of Catholics to its Italian policy and of many industrialists to lower tariffs, as well as by increasing evidence (election results and official reports) that many workers still believed in the republic, permitted the advocates of a new propaganda message to try their experiment. There was not, it should be said, a complete change from one propaganda message to another. The simple message of the 1850's was not abandoned; quite the contrary, as opposition to the Empire grew, the old slogans appeared even more frequently. Only side by side with it existed another propaganda message intended for the politically alert and class-conscious workers, particularly the craftsmen and the artisans of such cities as Paris and Lyons.

The legislation and social policy of the Second Empire in the 1860's was also, in large part, dominated by propaganda considerations. These were the years when the government conceded more political and personal liberties and sought to placate the working class by such measures as the legalization of strikes and the encouragement of cooperatives of all kinds. There is little

[2] A.N. BB[30] 379, *procureur général* at Lyons to the Minister of Justice, December 28, 1864.

doubt that one of the purposes of the new policy was to gain worker support. The government consented to amendment of the law banning strikes with hesitation and reluctance. According to Emile Ollivier, Rouher, who was charged with defending the bill before the *Corps législatif*, did so "without enthusiasm" and warned that "workers deceive themselves in believing that strikes will increase their wages; wages do not obey their caprices and fantasies; they are determined by the law of supply and demand."[3] The legislative and financial aid that the government and the Emperor extended to cooperatives, particularly producers' cooperatives, was also primarily for propaganda purposes. Producers' cooperatives, wrote Michel Chevalier, the Emperor's favorite economist, were impractical, because workers lacked the capital and the *"esprit des affaires"* so necessary for the success of a business enterprise.[4] And well into the 1860's the government discouraged attempts by workers to found producers' cooperatives. However, in the late 1860's, the policy of the government changed. In 1866, the Emperor contributed 500,000 francs to a *Caisse d'escompte des societés coopératives*, established to aid producers' cooperatives, and later in the same year he gave 300,000 francs to a producers' cooperative founded by silk workers at Lyons.[5] The government's new policy towards producers' cooperatives was not the result of a change of opinion but of a desire to satisfy workers. The reports of government officials frequently described the interest of workers in cooperatives. "The cooperative movement," declared the *procureur général* at Rouen, "is becoming a popular enthusiasm."[6] And although he

[3]Emile Ollivier, *L'Empire libéral* (Paris, 1895-1915), VI, 553.

[4]Michel Chevalier, *Cours d'économie politique fait au Collège de France*, 2nd ed. (Paris, 1855), I, 138-139.

[5]For the Second Empire and cooperatives, see Jean Gaumont, *Histoire générale de la coopération en France* (Paris, 1924), v. I, passim.

[6]A.N. BB[30] 387, report of the *procureur général* at Rouen to the Minister of Justice, January 12, 1867.

doubted that they would succeed, he urged the government to permit workers to found producers' cooperatives. This was also the opinion of the *procureur général* at Lyons; although producers' cooperatives had rarely succeeded in the past, he saw no danger in allowing workers to try again.[7] Additional pressure was applied on the government when the opposition seized upon the issue of cooperatives. In 1864, the republican Darimon urged the government to legalize cooperatives of all kinds.[8] The republican Jules Simon and the Orleanist Count of Paris both studied and wrote on the cooperative movement in England.[9]

The new propaganda and the legislation in behalf of workers were both facilitated by the existence within the Bonapartist movement of a liberal or "leftist" tendency. In 1832, Louis Blanc distinguished between those Bonapartists who were "blind admirers of the Napoleonic monarchy" and those who were "friends of equality."[10] More than twenty years later a prefect of the Second Empire wrote that the same divisions still existed in the Bonapartist party.[11] Another prefect also pointed to this split among the Bonapartists, adding that one "nuance" of Bonapartism had "sympathies for the party of the reds."[12]

The acknowledged leader of the Bonapartism of the left during the Second Empire was Napoleon III's cousin, the Prince Napoleon. From the very beginning of Louis Napoleon's rule, the Prince was the symbol of liberal Bonapartism. Elected to the

[7]A.N. BB[30] 379, *procureur général* at Lyons to the Minister of Justice, January 8, 1866.

[8]*Le Moniteur universel*, January 20, 1864.

[9]Sreten Maritch, *Histoire du mouvement social sous le Second Empire à Lyon* (Paris, 1930), 119.

[10]Louis Blanc, *Histoire de dix ans (1830-1840)* (Paris, 1846), III, 270-271.

[11]A.N. F[1c] III Bouches-du-Rhône 7, Prefect of the Bouches-du-Rhône to the Minister of the Interior, November 18, 1853.

[12]André Armengaud, *Les populations de l'Est-Aquitain au début de l'époque contemporaine* (Paris, 1961), 399. Prefect of the Haute Garonne, April 24, 1853.

National Assembly in 1848, he sat with the Mountain, usually voted with the republicans, supported the cause of Polish and Italian nationalism, and urged clemency for workers arrested after the June Days. In the spring of 1849 he called upon the voters to cast their ballots for republican candidates so that the Prince-President could free himself from the yoke of the "chiefs of the reactionary movement."[13] Apparently surprised by the *coup d'état*, the Prince Napoleon openly opposed his cousin's illegal act, and retired from public life for about a year. He later became reconciled with the Emperor and, despite his frequent outspoken criticism of government policy, held a number of high positions during the Second Empire, as senator, member of the Council of State, Minister of Algeria and the Colonies. At the same time, the Prince Napoleon continued to maintain cordial relations with opposition leaders such as Darimon and Havin, and even with the socialist Proudhon who made discreet visits to his home. He constantly urged the Emperor to liberalize the institutions of the regime and to permit more political and personal freedom. Thus, in 1865, the Prince Napoleon reminded Napoleon III that he had formerly favored liberal ideas; "that was the theme of the Bonapartist and the liberal party from 1815 to 1848."[14] The Prince Napoleon also had a leading role in the attempts to create a Bonapartist workers' movement during the 1860's. He was, for example, one of the most active persons in the organization and direction of workers delegations to the London Exposition of 1862; he maintained regular contact with and gave instructions to a leader among the worker delegates, the Bonapartist tin worker Chabaud.[15]

[13]Ernest d'Hauterive, *Napoléon III et le prince Napoléon, correspondance inédite* (Paris, 1925), 53-55.

[14]Hauterive, *Napoléon III*, 376.

[15]*Bibliothèque de l'Institut, Archives Le Play*, letter of Prince Napoleon to Le Play, August 2, 1867.

The Palais Royal Group

The Prince Napoleon also helped to organize the most active Bonapartist workers' movement of the Second Empire. About 1860, he offered his protection and encouragement to a group of Parisian craftsmen who had been meeting informally to discuss the problems of the working class.[16] These workers came to be known, in fact, as the Palais Royal group, after the Prince Napoleon's residence. It is not known how the Prince established contact with the group, but there is reason to believe that the intermediary was Armand Lévy, a revolutionary of 1848 who later rallied to the Empire.[17]

Many workers in the Palais Royal group remained fervent partisans of the Empire until the very end and some even after its fall. Their motives varied. There were paid agents, but other Palais Royal workers believed that the Empire offered more to the working class than other regimes, a belief reinforced by the legislation and policies of the 1860's. Such workers had not forgotten what they regarded as the betrayal of the Revolution of 1848 by the republicans, and they believed that the liberal opposition to the Empire was more interested in political reform than improvement of the condition of the working class. One Palais Royal worker denounced the "democratic liberal bourgeoisie" who substituted the word "liberty" for a "serious" program of aid for the people.[18] Another complained that the opposition to the Empire was interested only in political liberties, and while these liberties were "undoubtedly precious things," they were not as vital as the material needs of man; those who possessed the physical necessities for life might well believe that "intellectual liberty" was the greatest of all values, but for the masses ameliora-

16Henry Fougère, *Les délégations ouvrières aux expositions universelles sous le Second Empire* (Montluçon, 1905), 46.

17See pp. 137 ff.

18B.N. Lb36 2288, A. Coutant, *Les candidatures ouvrières* (Paris, 1869), 5-6.

tion of their condition, "social progress," was more important.[19] Other Palais Royal workers, who remained republican at heart, cooperated with the regime because it existed and seemed likely to exist for the foreseeable future.

It is, perhaps, not entirely just to label the Palais Royal workers Bonapartist propagandists. As I have just pointed out, many of them supported the regime because they believed that workers could make greater progress under Napoleon III than under a republic ruled by the bourgeoisie. Frequently these pro-Bonapartist workers accompanied their praise of the regime with demands for social reform. Many Palais Royal workers came from the printing trades, and were traditionally considered the most alert and informed group of workers, or, as one printer proudly observed, the corporation that led the working class.[20] It remains a fact, however, that the Palais Royal group did disseminate pro-government propaganda among workers and that some Imperial officials helped them in their task.

Little is known about the Palais Royal group besides the names and a few other details concerning some of the leaders. In fact, both contemporaries and historians have been unable to decide whether particular workers belonged to the Palais Royal group. A printer, J.-J. Blanc, who was himself charged with Bonapartist sympathies during the Second Empire, attacked the spirit of suspicion prevalent among French workers on the subject of membership in the Palais Royal group.[21] And at the beginning of the present century, the socialist historian, Albert Thomas, discussed the question whether Tolain, one of the founders of the French

[19]B.N. Lb56 1512, A. Bazin, *L'Opposition, le gouvernement et les classes ouvrières* (Paris, 1865), 5-6.

[20]*Les délégations ouvrières à l'Exposition universelle de Londres en 1862* (Paris, 1862), 4.

[21]J. J. Blanc, "Les hommes et les souris," *Almanach de la coopération* (1870), 96-97: "Celui-ci dépend de la préfecture de police, celui-là de tel ministre; cet autre appartient au Palais Royal."

Section of the First International, had been associated with the Palais Royal group, a charge that was frequently made during the Second Empire (Thomas concluded that he had not).[22] Some Palais Royal workers do, however, emerge out of the anonymity into which history usually pushes obscure leaders.

One of the most active of the Palais Royal group was the tin worker Chabaud. He served as president of the workers' commission established to organize the delegations from the different crafts to the London Exposition of 1862. We have already seen that he received instructions on the workers delegations from the Prince Napoleon. Chabaud wrote articles and pamphlets to the *Brochures ouvrières* published by the Palais Group, and was one of the most prolific contributors to the *Chroniques ouvrières*, a column in the pro-government *Le Pays* reserved for workers' letters.[23] Although Chabaud wrote pamphlets and articles on a variety of subjects, he usually managed to include in them some praise of the government and particularly the Emperor. He also constantly urged moderation upon the workers. Thus, in 1864, he warned the working class against heeding revolutionaries who called for radical reforms and who tried to stir up class hatred: "In opposition to those who desire a prompt and radical change of our social organization, I want these changes to occur gradually and without shock, for it is only in this way that they will be established upon unshakable foundations."[24] At a workers' meeting in 1867, to discuss vocational training, Chabaud recommended calling the problem to the attention of the Emperor, who would undoubtedly establish more trade schools when he realized the need for them.[25] Again, in 1868, at a public meeting

[22]Albert Thomas, *Le Second Empire* (Paris, 1907), 200.

[23]See pp. 152-154.

[24]*L'Opinion nationale*, March 13, 1864.

[25]Georges Duveau, *La Pensée ouvrière sur l'éducation pendant la Seconde République et le Second Empire* (Paris, 1947), 106.

of workers protesting against the law banning trade unions, Chabaud urged the assembly to petition the Emperor to remove the ban and stated that this method had been successful in obtaining the right to strike.[26] Other Palais Royal workers also frequently recommended appeals to the government and especially to the Emperor.

The typographical worker, Coutant, was another leading member of the Palais Royal group. Coutant always insisted that he was a socialist, even after he rallied to the Empire. Before the Second Empire he was associated with the worker newspaper, *La Ruche populaire*, and later became editor-in-chief.[27] One of Coutant's articles for the newspaper contrasted the luxury of the wealthy with the poverty of the "martyrs of industry."[28] *La Ruche populaire* greeted the February Revolution joyfully. Coutant became a candidate for the Constituent Assembly with a platform that called for a more equitable organization of society "to assure the individual of work and the fruits of his labor."[29] Twenty years later Coutant's language, if a bit more restrained, was essentially the same, and he still called himself a socialist.[30] Moreover, he found no contradiction between his socialism and his support of the Empire. In 1869, he attacked the republican and democratic policy of "systematic" opposition to the regime.[31] During the 1860's, Coutant served as secretary of the workers' commission for the London Exposition and contributed articles

[26]A.N. 45 AP⁶ (dossier 4), "Papiers de Rouher," November 28, 1868. Although this police report refers to a "Chabot," it is undoubtedly Chabaud.

[27]Georges Weill, "Les journaux ouvriers à Paris (1830-1870)," *Revue d'histoire moderne et contemporaine*, IX (1907-1908), 94; 99.

[28]B.N. Lb⁵¹ 3938, "Organisation du travail. Discussion entre le journal, *le Globe* et un ouvrier typographe," Extrait de la *Ruche populaire*, by Coutant "ouvrier typographe."

[29]B.N. Le⁶⁴ 1305 "A M.M. les électeurs du département de la Somme" (Péronne, 1848).

[30]B.N. Rp 13538, Coutant, *Propriété et travail association* (Paris, 1868), 1.

[31]Coutant, *Les candidatures ouvrières*, 2.

and letters to the *Brochures ouvrières,* the *Chroniques ouvrières,* and to the pro-government newspaper, *L'Opinion nationale.*

Other workers, who may or may not have been associated with the Palais Royal group, also urged support or acceptance of the Second Empire for the same reasons. The typographical worker, A. Bazin, protested against the view that "a good citizen must, above all, be an opponent of the regime."[32] Such an attitude was all the more regrettable, he wrote, in view of the fact that the government was "profoundly changing its policy" and had already "accomplished significant reforms." Like many other workers, Bazin attacked the opposition's exclusive preoccupation with political reform rather than with the improvement of the condition of workers. The Second Empire, on the contrary, based as it was upon universal manhood suffrage and dependent upon public opinion, must seek to satisfy the needs of the people. Bazin, therefore, called upon the working class to end its opposition to the regime and, instead, to tell the government what it wished. This was a policy, he said, that had already gained for workers the right to strike. The shoe leather cutter Jacques Durand, a violent anti-clerical and future Communard, praised Napoleon III's social views and urged workers to petition him for the right to organize trade unions.[33]

Even after the fall of the Second Empire in 1870, some workers, still convinced that a Bonapartist Empire offered the best hope for the working class, carried on propaganda for the restoration of Napoleon III. Albert Richard, leader of the First International at Lyons from 1866 to 1871 and an exile after the Commune, continued to agitate for a return of Napoleon III, claim-

---

[32]Bazin, *L'Opposition, le gouvernement et les classes ouvrières,* 4 ff.

[33]B.N. Vp 22523 Jacques Durand, *Mémoires adressés à la réunion générale des coupeurs et brochures en chaussure de la ville de Paris,* (Paris, n.d., but after 1864), 6; Georges Duveau, *La vie ouvrière en France sous le Second Empire* (Paris, 1946), 390.

ing that the working class had more to gain from a Bonapartist Empire than from any other regime, including a republic.[34]

The most ambitious propaganda effort of the Palais Royal group was the publication of a series of pamphlets for workers, the *Brochures ouvrières*. The pamphlets printed by Dentu, who was frequently referred to as the "Emperor's printer" during the Second Empire, appeared in a similar format and sold for the low price of thirty centimes. I have been unable to find statistics on the number of *Brochures ouvrières* printed or sold, but frequent references to them by contemporaries and their relative abundance in French libraries indicate that they had a wide circulation. The pamphlets were not only Imperialist propaganda. In almost all of them praise for the regime was accompanied by pleas for further reforms to aid the working class, and in many of them the praise was very perfunctory. Some of the pamphlets called for broad reforms that interested the working class as a whole.[35] Others discussed specific reforms[36] or the grievances of particular crafts.[37]

But even the pamphlets written to urge a specific reform or to defend the interests of a particular craft rarely failed to say something good about the regime or Napoleon III. (This was, of course, frequently good "public relations" as much as propa-

[34]Albert Richard and Gaspard Blanc, *L'Empire et la France nouvelle, appel du peuple et de la jeunesse à la conscience française* (Brussels, 1872). Richard soon rejected Bonapartism and returned to socialism. Another example of the survival of Bonapartist feeling after 1870 occurred at Anzin, in 1878, when striking miners raised the cry "*Vive Napoléon IV*"; other striking miners, it is true, replied with "*Vive la République*." Daniel Halévy, *La République des ducs* (Paris, 1937), 335.

[35]B.N. Lb56 1175, *Le peuple, l'Empereur et les anciens partis*; Paris, 1861. B.N. Vp 9023; Vp 9024, *A l'Empereur, Les cahiers populaires I & II* (Paris, 1861).

[36]B.N. Vp 9027, *L'Organisation des travailleurs par les corporations nouvelles* (Paris, 1861); *A l'Empereur Napoléon III, manifeste des ouvriers*.

[37]B.N. Vp 9029, *Voeux et besoins des ouvriers corroyeurs* (Paris, 1862); B.N. Vp 9025, Coutant, *Du salaire des ouvriers compositeurs* (1861); *Des intérêts typographiques devant la conférence mixte. Des maitres imprimeurs et des ouvriers compositeurs* (Paris, 1861).

ganda.) One *Brochure ouvrière* referred to the Emperor as the author of that "excellent book, the *Extinction du paupérisme*," and "the liberator of Italy."[38] Another pamphlet that urged the government to aid needy and unemployed workers cited the reforms already granted by the Emperor as evidence of the "liberalism of his government," and of the fact that "privilege had had its day"; it expressed the hope that France would soon see "the realization [of the wish] so dear to the heart and mind of the Prince Louis-Napoleon Bonaparte: *L'EXTINCTION DU PAUPERISME* [in capitals in text]."[39] A *Brochure ouvrière* called the attention of the royal couple to the deplorable conditions that prevailed in homes for the aged, a subject, said the pamphlet, sure to interest rulers who were so concerned with the well-being of the people.[40] The pamphlet also praised the Emperor for maintaining the gains made by the working class in 1848.[41]

The most theoretical of the Palais Royal works was, *Le Peuple, l'Empereur et les anciens partis*, written in response to an open letter by the Orleanist Duc d'Aumale, *Lettre sur l'histoire de France*, which, said the pamphlet, was circulating in the factories.[42] This pamphlet provides the fullest statement of the ideas of the Palais Royal workers. It included an introduction, five articles, and closed with an appeal for confidence in the Emperor. The Duc d'Aumale's letter, said the introduction, attacked the

---

[38] *Voeux et besoins des ouvriers corroyeurs*, 21; 23.

[39] *A l'Empereur Napoléon III*.

[40] *A l'Empereur. Les cahiers populaires*, I, 8.

[41] *A l'Empereur. Les cahiers populaires*, I, 21; "Aujourd'hui, en politique, le peuple est l'égal de la bourgeoisie, puisque, grâce aux conquêtes de février, maintenues par l'Empereur, il nomme les députés au corps législatif, les membres des conseils municipaux et des conseils généraux.

[42] Aumale's pamphlet may be found in Henri d'Aumale, *Ecrits politiques (1861-1868)* (Brussels, 1868). The letter, addressed to the Prince Napoléon, contrasted Louis Philippe's generous treatment of the Bonapartes with Napoléon III's harsh treatment of the Orleanist family, and also attacked the foreign policy of the Empire.

principles of the February Revolution at the very time that the government of the Emperor seemed to be active "more and more in the national and popular interests, internally as well as abroad."

The first article by B. V. Viguier, a proof-reader, denounced the political economy of the July Monarchy—a policy "summed up in the formula, laissez-faire, laissez-passer!" The working class, said Viguier, judged governments by their economic policy: "We have had enough of speeches; we must also know how to obtain bread." Napoleon III had, on the contrary, demonstrated his sympathy with the needs of the working class, and if progress was slow and the good intentions of the Emperor not yet realized, the fault lay with the many adherents of former regimes who still held high offices.

An article by Chabaud, *"Ne soyons plus dupes,"* attacked the Orleanist monarchy for ignoring the cries of the oppressed nationalities of Europe, and praised the Second Empire for favoring social progress. It urged workers to petition the Emperor for practical and useful reforms:

We do not believe that Napoleon III, better advised than those who have preceded him, will wait until the Legitimists, Orleanists, and clericals have sown discouragement in all the minds and fomented a senseless disorder, but will rather spontaneously accord the practical reform desired by the workers.

A third contributor, the printer Berthelemy, also accused the July Monarchy of having done nothing for the nations under foreign rule. Nor had he found in Aumale's letter a single word on the people or "ameliorations in favor of the laboring classes attempted or proposed by the Orleanist family." True, he lamented, the condition of French workers were still miserable, "but we hope that the elected of the nation [Napoleon III] . . . will at last listen to our demands."

In an article that interpreted the history of France since 1789,

the bookbinder Coquard condemned the selfishness of the bourgeoisie and lauded the Bonapartes, as a dynasty which had always
been concerned with the welfare of the entire nation. After ending the prerogatives of the nobility at the time of the French Revolution, the bourgeoisie, by making strikes illegal, revealed that
it did not intend to share its newly acquired liberty with the
working class. At first the bourgeoisie supported Napoleon I as
a bulwark against a return to the Old Regime, but when the
Emperor refused to govern in the interest of the bourgeoisie
alone, the disappointed middle class abandoned him for the
Bourbons. When, however, the Bourbons conferred excessive
power upon the nobles and priests, the bourgeoisie incited the
people to overthrow the old dynasty and then crowned itself in
the person of Louis Philippe. The government of Louis Philippe
proved, however, to be too personal for the bourgeoisie, which,
seeking reform, once again called the working class to its aid. But
the bourgeoisie in 1848 had not anticipated universal suffrage
and turned against the Republic which proclaimed it. To the
bourgeoisie, Napoleon III then seemed to be a guaranty against
revolution, but now that it felt secure and realized, moreover,
that the Emperor would never rule in the interests of a single
class, the bourgeoisie yearned for a return of the dynasty of its
choice, the Orleanists. For this reason it was now trying to create
distrust between people and the government:

If the bourgeois oligarchy incites the people to distrust the one whom
it has elected, this is because it seeks to persuade the people to throw
itself once again into the arms of the bourgeoisie, who are the most
implacable enemy of the people and of the Emperor. For the people,
like the Emperor, desire that the government be the government of all
and not of a party.

The final article, by the printing worker Leroy, also drew
upon the lessons of French history to prove to the working class

that it was wise to cooperate with the government. Leroy drew an analogy between the struggle of the working class for the satisfaction of its demands and the struggles of the communes in the twelfth century to gain their freedom. Faced by a powerful feudal nobility, the communes sought the support of the monarchy, which, in turn, welcomed the aid of the towns against the seigneurs and Rome. "Without this union, these two forces would have been absorbed one after the other by feudalism." From this analysis Leroy concluded that the working class should follow the example of the medieval townsmen and cooperate with the government.

The pamphlet closed with an avowal that despite the good intentions of the government, the condition of the working class had deteriorated during the Second Empire. However, the working class itself bore the responsibility for this; first, because of the mistrust with which it received the reforms *"granted"* (underlined in the text) by the government; and second, because workers did not make their needs known. The pamphlet urged workers to inform the Emperor of their needs in a "firm and respectful voice," and assured them that the people and the Emperor, working together, would in a short time realize the reforms that had been needed for so long a time.

It is not clear whether Palais Royal workers or workers independent of the regime first suggested sending delegates from the various crafts to the London Exposition of 1862.[43] However, the Palais Royal group had a major role in the delegations, and the government encouraged and aided them financially. The enthusiasm of government newspapers for the project suggests strongly

43Fougère says that the government and Palais Royal workers initiated the movement to send workers' delegations, *Les délégations ouvrières,* 46 ff. Léon Fournier, *Le Second Empire et la législation ouvrière* (Paris, 1911), 159 ff. emphasizes the efforts of workers without ties to the Palais Royal.

that they had received instructions from the Press Bureau to support the delegations. The government also relaxed the ban upon public meetings so that workers could meet to elect delegates. The Palais Royal workers dominated the *Commission ouvrière* established to organize the delegations to the Exposition; all four officers of the *Commission ouvrière* were associated with the Palais Royal group (Chabaud, president, Wanschooten, Coutant, Coquard).[44]

The government encouraged the workers' delegations primarily for economic reasons. The tariff treaty of 1860 with England made it vital for French industry to increase its efficiency in order to compete successfully, and the government hoped that the worker delegates and through them other French workers would profit from their observation of English industry and their contact with English workers.[45] The government also recognized, however, the propaganda value of the delegations and pointed to official encouragement of them as another example of its concern with and confidence in the working class. Coutant wrote enthusiastically of the delegations:[46]

Everything in this project is original, down to the slightest circumstances, to the smallest detail. It is, moreover, an act worthy of an epoch of progress and in perfect accord with the fundamental principle of popular sovereignty which is today the indestructible basis of French law and society.

Napoleon III contributed the much publicized gesture of naming three workers delegates *chevaliers* of the Legion of Honor.[47]

---

[44]B.N. Vp 9028, *Les délégations ouvrières à l'Exposition universelle de Londres en 1862* (Paris, 1862), 10. This is a *Brochure ouvrière*.

[45]Fournier, *Le Second Empire*, 165-167.

[46]Fougère, *Les délégations ouvrières*, 43.

[47]Fougère, *Les délégations ouvrières*, 173.

Bonapartist Propagandists Among the Working Class

The Palais Royal was a workers group. In addition, the Second Empire cooperated with and used persons from other classes, particularly writers and intellectuals, whom it believed could influence worker opinion. Often such persons had been revolutionaries and frequently violently anti-Bonapartist. Much is obscure about the relationship between these former revolutionaries and the government; it was naturally not a well-documented relationship. In addition to problems created by the secrecy that surrounded the ties between Imperial officials and these missionaries to the working class, another handicap to the scholar is the lack of understanding within the government. Ministers and officials often attacked and hampered the work of persons, who, unknown to them, were in the service of or had been encouraged by others in the administration, while the latter hesitated to defend or to acknowledge their agents or associates. The motives of government propagandists varied: some were sincere and enthusiastic converts to Bonapartism; others accepted it half-heartedly, since the possibility of a republic seemed remote; some were hired agents, interested only in gain.

The journalist, Armand Lévy, was the most prominent of the former revolutionaries who during the 1860's attempted to convince workers of the advantages of cooperation with the Empire. At the outbreak of the February Revolution, Lévy, then a law student, threw himself into revolutionary activity.[48] He founded a club where his violent speeches led to his being fined twice. He

[48]A.N. F18 281. This is a *dossier personnel* on Lévy in the Bureau of the Press. The biographical data on Lévy during the Second Republic in the dossier is from a police report on him requested by the Minister of the Interior, July 1, 1861. A brief and at times apologetic biography of Lévy exists: B.N. 40 Ln 27 81718 Jean Gaumont, *Un républicain révolutionnaire romantique Armand Lévy (1827-1891)* (Paris, 1932).

was arrested following the *journée* of May 15, 1848, but was found not guilty of participating in this effort to overthrow the governmen of the Republic. After the suppression of the *journée* of June 13, 1849, he fled to Belgium but soon returned to France, and in 1850 Lévy was once more distributing "socialist works." He also wrote pamphlets in favor of the "Social Republic" and denouncing Louis Napoleon.[49] And in the presidential campaign of 1848 he supported the socialist Raspail.

After about 1850 Lévy's revolutionary ardor seems to have cooled, although he frequently ran as an opposition candidate in the elections of the decade. Thus, in 1857, he became a candidate for election to the *Corps législatif* with the aid of a "committee of the republican opposition."[50] The following year he again posed his candidacy in a by-election, claiming that he did so at the insistence of workers: "'The workers have imposed upon me the duty of maintaining my candidacy!'"[51] Lévy's claim of worker support was not without basis; the Prefect of the Côte d'Or reported that in the 1858 election "all the factory regions voted for him."[52] On the other hand, moderate republicans had little respect for him. Darimon, who had known Lévy for some time, referred to him as "a revolutionary imbecile" whom no one took seriously.[53] Emile Ollivier regarded him as an unprincipled schemer.[54]

It is not clear just when Lévy began to draw closer to the Empire. By 1858, however, he was sufficiently sympathetic to the

[49]B.N. Lb55 206, Armand Lévy and Henri Valleton, *Les Emeutiers!* (Paris, 1849); B.N. Lb55 126, Armand Lévy and Henri Valleton, *Démocratie Sociale* (Paris, 1849).

[50]A.N. BB18 1567, "Elections législatives de 1857," *Procureur général* at Dijon to the Minister of Justice, June 19, 1857.

[51]B.N. Le77 390, "Aux électeurs de la 6ème circonscription."

[52]Gaumont, *Un républicain révolutionnaire*, 32.

[53]Alfred Darimon, *Histoire d'un parti. Les cinq sous l'Empire* (Paris, 1885), 155.

[54]Emile Ollivier, *Journal* (Paris, 1961), I, 328-329.

regime to write a pamphlet, at the Prince Napoleon's request, praising Napoleon III's nationalities policy (*l'Empereur Napoléon III et les principautés roumaines*).[55] The Emperor spoke highly of the pamphlet to the Prince Napoleon; it was, he said, the work of a "master's hand."[56]

Although this was not the last service that he performed for the Prince Napoleon and despite the fact that he undoubtedly used his prestige among some workers to gain their support for the regime, Lévy can hardly be called a government agent. I have not seen anything to indicate that his motives were venal, and Lévy was even more of a propagandist for social reform than for the regime.

There were several reasons for Lévy's support for the Empire, some of them shared by other republican converts to Bonapartism in the 1860's. Lévy was tied by family tradition to Bonapartism. His father had been a secretary to the great Napoleon. Lévy's biographer refers to his "sentimental inclination" to a Jacobin and liberal Bonapartism during his student days,[57] and Lévy himself wrote that since childhood he had been imbued with "the tradition of the *Grande Nation*."[58] More weighty, however, than Lévy's "sentimental inclination" towards Bonapartism was his approval of the Second Empire's nationalities policy and his conviction that Napoleon III sincerely wished to ameliorate the condition of the working class. Since his schooldays, when he had been greatly influenced by a Polish exile, Jacques Malinowski, Lévy had been a passionate defender of the cause of the oppressed European nationalities, and when he came to believe

[55]Darimon, *Histoire d'un parti. Les Cinq*, 195-196. Darimon writes that the Prince Napoleon first requested him to prepare the pamphlet, a statement which also tells us something about Darimon who was at the time a republican deputy in the *Corps législatif*.

[56]Hauterive, *Napoléon III*, 112.

[57]Gaumont, *Un républicain révolutionnaire*, 109.

[58]A.N. F18 549, File on *L'Espérance*; letter to Persigny, March 27, 1861.

that Napoleon III felt as he did on the nationalities problem, he could no longer withhold his support. In addition to the pamphlet already mentioned, Lévy wrote several others praising Napoleon III's foreign policy. (I have been unable to learn whether these were also at the request of the Prince Napoleon or some other member of the government.)⁵⁹ Lévy's other great concern was social reform and the condition of the working class; by 1860 he had become convinced that the Second Empire, dependent as it was upon popular support, must attempt to aid the working class. A letter to Persigny written by Lévy and signed by some 330 workers expresses Lévy's basic views on the subject.⁶⁰ The letter stated that workers were no longer interested in "sterile discussions about forms of government," but rather in the improvement of their condition, and that this was also an objective of Napoleon III's regime. Lévy did not become an Imperialist; he believed, however, that under the circumstances the working class would do best to accept the regime and seek to obtain help and favorable legislation from it. There was, therefore, nothing inconsistent in his behavior in September 1870. After the defeat at Sedan, Lévy was among those who invaded the *Corps législatif* to call for the establishment of a republic. He also participated in the Paris Commune.⁶¹ After the defeat of the Commune, he fled France not to return until an amnesty was granted to the *communards* in 1879.

Lévy's message to the working class during the 1860's was, then, to forget political questions and to press the government for social reforms. And Lévy, himself, set an example. He wrote several pamphlets calling upon the government to give workers the right

⁵⁹*L'Empereur, Rome et le Roi d'Italie* (Paris, 1861); B.N. Lb⁵⁶ 1206, *L'Empereur Napoléon et le roi Guillaume* (Paris, 1861).

⁶⁰A.N. F¹⁸ 549, March 1861. There were many copies of this letter in the dossier; the original was, however, in Lévy's handwriting.

⁶¹Gaumont, *Un républicain révolutionnaire*, 43; 50.

to strike,[62] and in 1862, he helped to defend a group of printers charged with violating the ban on coalitions. Lévy always insisted, however, that the working class could obtain satisfaction of its demands from the government and urged confidence in Napoleon III. Thus, one of his pamphlets reprinted a letter to the Emperor from several workers asking him to repeal legislation banning the right to strike. Lévy's comment on the letter was that, confident in the good will of the Emperor, the workers had placed their fate in the hands of a ruler "whose concern for everything affecting the well-being of the people they know very well."[63]

An example of Lévy's propaganda both for reform and for the Empire, as well as of his relations with the government, may be seen in a newspaper that he founded at Geneva in October 1859, *L'Espérance*.[64] It is very likely that the Prince Napoleon helped Lévy found the newspaper; a report on *L'Espérance* in the press section of the Ministry of the Interior stated, "His Royal Highness, the Prince Napoleon, is interested in M. Armand Lévy."[65] The newspaper frequently printed notices on the Prince's activities and movements and during an illness it published a number of bulletins on his conditions. Thus, on January 25, 1860, *L'Espérance* declared: "The Prince Napoleon is radiant over the present policy [of the French government]," a policy which "he has so often and so ably demanded for the nationalities." Less than two weeks after the appearance of *L'Espérance*, Lévy requested approval to circulate his newspaper in France, and, on March 26,

62B.N. FM. 25064, *Mémoire pour les ouvriers typographes* (Paris, 1862); B.N. Lb56 1429, *La loi contre les coalitions et la liberté des travailleurs* (Paris, 1864).

63Lévy, *Mémoire pour les ouvriers typographes*, 62.

64A.N. F18 549. This file on *L'Espérance* included a few issues of the newspaper, apparently the only ones to be found in France.

65A.N. F18 549, January 1860.

1860, his request was approved.[66] He did not, however, succeed in obtaining authorization to move *L'Espérance* to Paris.[67]

The first issue of *L'Espérance* (October 25, 1859) announced the policy of the newspaper: "to take up the defense of the nationalities, to support the cause of liberty and practical progress." It called upon France to assist nations seeking their independence: "It would be denying the French tradition to have a policy of everyone for himself." Lévy also urged practical reforms to help the lower classes: "In our time many progressive ideas have been proposed, most of them generous, but too often impractical. At present it is especially necessary to explore those ideas which can most rapidly improve the condition of the many." Lévy's policy statement concluded with the assurance that Napoleon III shared this view. Had not the Emperor declared that the purpose of government should be to end poverty?

Although not a newspaper for workers alone, *L'Espérance* devoted much space to the problems of the working class. The Sunday issue included a regular section, *"Tribune des travailleurs,"* with articles by workers; one of the most prolific contributors was Coutant. His worker readers were one of Lévy's selling points in negotiations with the government over transfer of his newspaper to Paris. In a letter to Persigny, he wrote that he sent *L'Espérance* to "men respected in the workshops and to whom I am known."[68] A short time later Lévy assured Persigny of his devotion to the dynasty and of the need for a newspaper like his:[69]

My democratic ideas are known to Your Excellency. But he can count upon my eagerness to combat the present enemies of the government who are also ours. For I am convinced that only the loyal and firm union of the Napoleons and democracy can save our country from new

[66]A.N. F18 549.
[67]See p. 200.
[68]A.N. F18 549, March 27, 1861.
[69]A.N. F18 549, April 22, 1861.

misfortunes. Believe me that no existing newspaper is in a situation to exercise the necessary influence upon the masses.

In a letter to the Emperor, Lévy wrote that a newspaper like his was "one of the most effective ways of ending the unfortunate influence of the old parties upon the masses, of calming a certain restlessness of the people, and of assuring prudently liberal and truly patriotic progress."[70]

In addition to Lévy's own statement that *L'Espérance* had been able "to influence the workers towards a new attitude,"[71] there is other evidence that the newspaper did have a following among the workers and artisans of Paris. On several occasions the *Brochures ouvrières* commented favorably upon *L'Espérance*.[72] And as part of his long drawn out and unsuccessful campaign to obtain authorization for the transfer of *L'Espérance* to Paris, Lévy presented Persigny with a petition signed by some 330 workers.[73] Most of the signers were artisans and skilled workers: tin workers, cabinetmakers, printing workers, bookbinders, carpenters, bronze workers. The petition cited the need for a newspaper where workers could express their wishes and needs and declared that *L'Espérance* was such a newspaper; "it has gained . . . the sympathy of many in the workshops."

Gabriel Hugelmann was another revolutionary of 1848 who in the 1860's emerged as an apostle of the Empire to the working class.[74] His relations with Napoleon III and the government are,

70A.N. F18 281, "Dossier personnel," June 30, 1861.

71A.N. F18 549, March 27, 1861, letter to Persigny.

72B.N. Vp 9025, *Des intérêts typographiques*, 33; B.N. Vp 9027, *L'Organisation des travailleurs par les corporations nouvelles*, 10: "un journal dévoué aux intérêts nationaux et populaires qui eut l'inspiration vraiment libérale d'ouvrir ses colonnes aux ouvriers."

73A.N. F18 549, March 1861.

74Police reports and the article in *La Grande Encyclopédie* are the main sources for the career of Hugelmann.

however, even more obscure than those of Lévy. During the Second Republic, Hugelmann's revolutionary activities earned him exile to Algiers. From there he escaped to Spain where, changing his political color, he founded a newspaper so friendly to the Second Empire that he obtained a pardon. After his return to France Hugelmann became involved in a number of financial adventures which twice ended in bankruptcy, wrote pro-government pamphlets and books, and became a candidate for the *Corps législatif*. His name appears on a list of government press subsidies for the year 1863,[75] and, in 1869, then editor of the Bonapartist journal, *Le Nain jaune,* he closed a letter to the Minister of the Interior with an appeal for financial aid, citing the needs "of a family as numerous as mine."[76] After the fall of the Empire, Hugelmann edited several Bonapartist journals, and, at the same time, served Thiers as a secret agent. In 1874, he was condemned to five years imprisonment for bankruptcy, swindling, and extortion. Although both served the Second Empire, the motives of the opportunist Hugelmann offer a contrast to those of Lévy, who was something of a zealot.

In 1863, Hugelmann published a two-volume dithyramb to the Bonapartist dynasty.[77] The entire history of France, he wrote, was only a prelude to the accession of the "fourth race," the Bonapartes. The task of the "fourth race," proclaimed Hugelmann, was to introduce the age of equality.[78] All social reformers, for example, Saint-Simon, Enfantin, Fourier, were the instruments "voluntary or involuntary of the Napoleonic idea," since "every profession of social faith is an expression of Napoleonic faith."[79] In the tradition of the Bonapartes, who had always been sympa-

[75]A.N. F18 306, Press subventions (1862-1863).
[76]A.N. F18 277, "Dossiers personnels, Bureau de la presse," October 28, 1869.
[77]*La IVème Race* (Paris, 1863).
[78]*La IVème Race*, I, 259.
[79]*La IVème Race*, I, 255-256.

thetic with the needs of the working class, Napoleon III, too, had studied and reflected long upon the problem of poverty at the prison of Ham.[80] And it was the working class, always faithful to the Bonapartes, that had paved the way for the "Imperial resurrection" and remained "the most solid column of the Empire."[81]

Hugelmann also wrote a number of pamphlets praising the Empire. In 1866, he announced a series of biographies of government leaders with the title, *Le Panthéon du travail*. However, he apparently wrote but one, a eulogy of the minister Rouher.[82] Another brochure, probably written during the war with Prussia, was entitled *Le Salut c'est la dynastie*.[83]

In 1869, Hugelmann announced his candidacy for the *Corps législatif*, and, although not an official candidate, proclaimed his confidence in the Empire. His campaign brochure, *Pourquoi vous devez élire Gabriel Hugelmann candidat socialiste dans votre intérêt et dans celui de vos familles*, demanded amelioration of the condition of the working class, but insisted that "only our voluntary but vigorous union around a strong government can enable us to realize social reforms."[84] He also urged the election of deputies who would encourage Napoleon III in his work of social reform, the real task of the Empire: "The People have elected the prisoner of Ham even more than the nephew of Napoleon I. They expect well-being even more than glory."

Hugelmann's most ambitious enterprise was, however, to found, in the 1860's, the *Société nationale pour l'extinction du paupérisme*. This strange society seems to have been a pressure group for social reform and an old age retirement plan, as well

[80] *La IVème Race*, II, 55.

[81] *La IVème Race*, II, 373.

[82] B.N. Ln[12] 14, *Le Panthéon du travail. M. Rouher* (Paris, 1866). I have been unable to discover any other biographies in the series and none is listed in the catalogues of the *Bibliothèque nationale*.

[83] B.N. Lb[56] 3215.

[84] B.N. Le[77] 2415 A.

as a center for Bonapartist propaganda. A note in the Ministry of the Interior describing the founding and the organization of the society states that it had about 30,000 or 40,000 members.[85] According to the statutes of 1867, the organization had a "triple mission": education of children, organization of labor, and the establishment of the *Invalides civils*.[86] Article 25 founded the *Invalides civils*, an old-age retirement plan offering its members the choice of drawing a pension or entering a home for the aged at the age of sixty.

Our interest is, of course, in the propaganda carried on by the society, an important part of its activities not mentioned in the statutes. At meetings of the society and in its pamphlets, Hugelmann and other officers praised extravagantly the Emperor's concern with the workers and the needy. The very name of the society recalled, of course, the social consciousness of the author of *L'Extinction du paupérisme*. "What Prince," demanded the president of the society, the Marquis du Planty, "has done more for the people than Napoleon III?"[87] Before a meeting of the society Hugelmann cited *L'Extinction du paupérisme* as evidence of the Emperor's abiding concern for the working class and called upon the audience to "thank the man who desires the same thing we desire by raising . . . the cry of *Vive l'Empereur!*"[87a]

The government distrusted Hugelmann,[88] and his personal contacts were probably with the Emperor or perhaps Persigny,

[85]A.N. 45^AP (dossier 5), "Papiers de Rouher." These figures seem, however, to be based upon the claims of the society.

[86]*Société nationale pour l'extinction du paupérisme. Assemblée générale du 3 Février 1867* (Paris, 1867). I found this propaganda pamphlet in A.N. 45^AP (dossier 5), "Papiers de Rouher."

[87]*Société nationale pour l'extinction du paupérisme* (Paris, 1866). Despite the similar title this is not the same pamphlet as the one cited above. It was also in A.N. 45^AP (dossier 5).

[87a]*Société nationale pour l'extinction du paupérisme* (Paris, 1866).

[88]See p. 200.

whose patronage he also claimed. Although I have been unable to discover evidence that Hugelmann had an understanding with the Emperor, it is likely that some kind of relationship existed. Article II of the statutes announced that the society had been "constituted under the protection of the Emperor Napoleon III from whom the founders have obtained protection and thanks to whom their initiative has been able to triumph over all obstacles."[89] The organization's letterhead carried the words, *"Protectorat de l'Empire."* When Hugelmann's claim to Imperial favor was challenged, he replied that the society had openly proclaimed the Emperor's protection for two years without a disavowal.[90] Whatever the true situation, in the spring of 1867 the government became alarmed at Hugelmann's activities among the working class and forced him to abandon the claim of Imperial patronage.

Alfred Darimon, formerly secretary to Proudhon, a contributor to socialist journals, and from 1857 a republican deputy to the *Corps législatif* also performed various services for the Empire among the working class. Darimon, who always called himself a democratic socialist, maintained close relations with the Prince Napoleon during the entire Second Empire. In 1857, when he ran as an anti-government candidate for the *Corps législatif*, the Prince Napoleon seemed to approve of his campaign, and a short time after his election invited the successful candidate to a reception.[91] Darimon's former associate, Proudhon, believed that the republican deputy took his orders from the Palais Royal.[92] By 1865, Darimon had all but rallied to the Empire. In June 1865, at Rouher's request, he prepared a note for the work-

[89]*Société nationale* (1866).
[90]*Société nationale* (1866).
[91]Darimon, *Histoire d'un parti. Les Cinq,* 28, 76-77.
[92]Darimon, *Histoire d'un parti. Les Cinq,* 205.

ing class to explain the government's delay in preparing a bill to facilitate the organization of cooperative societies.[93] Darimon made a virtue out of the delay. The proposed legislation was of such importance to the working class that the government did not want to act hastily; it even planned to consult those most affected, the workers who belonged to cooperatives:

The author of the present note has been concerned with workers' questions for fifteen years. He has lived with workers for a long time, and he knows from experience how much they will be moved to see that on a question which is so close to their interests a decision is taken to consult them directly.

A curious report in the police archives at Lyons refers to a certain de Wollfers, who seems to have been a Bonapartist agent among the workers, perhaps an informer even more than a propagandist.[94] After editing a pro-government newspaper at Strasbourg, de Wollfers became editor of *Le Progrès* of Lyons, a newspaper popular among workers. (This is the newspaper described in a government report as "radical for the public but amenable to arrangements with the government.")[95] De Wollfers, said the report, claimed the protection of the Minister Billaut and spent far more than his salary permitted, "unless he received from an unknown, but suspected source, a supplement to his salary." De Wollfers and his co-editor Vermorel also held workers' meetings in their home.

The government also tried unsuccessfully to gain the support or, at least, the benevolent neutrality of the French section of the

[93]Alfred Darimon, *Histoire d'un parti. Le Tiers Parti sous l'Empire (1863-1866)* (Paris, 1887), 303-305.

[94]B.N. Lb56 471, *Pièces saisies aux archives de la police politique de Lyon* (Lyons, 1870), 6-8. The report is, however, not very clear and permits only the most tentative conclusions.

[95]See p. 58.

International Workingman's Association, the First International. For the first few years after the founding of the First International in 1864, the Second Empire looked upon the organization with some favor, even authorizing the French section to open its office on the Rue de Gravilliers without submitting to all the legal formalities.[96] Many French workers believed that the members of the International, and particularly its leader Tolain, were followers of the Palais Royal.[97] When workers who belonged to the First International appeared at work dressed better than usually, their fellows would demand ironically whether the police had paid for the clothes.[98] Tolain stated that radical socialists suspected the International of "an Imperialist tendency" and of seeking to organize "a kind of Imperialist Socialism."[99]

Fribourg, one of the founders of the French section of the First International, relates how an aid of Hugelmann sought to form an alliance between the *Société nationale* and the International.[100] The French members of the International refused, however, to work with an organization under the protection of a political power (Fribourg had no doubts that Hugelmann's organization was an instrument of the Empire). Fribourg also described an effort by the Minister Rouher to persuade the French section of the International to issue a few complimentary remarks about

[96]Paul Leroy-Beaulieu, *La question ouvrière au XIXème siècle.* 3rd ed. (Paris, 1871), 142-143, deplored the Empire's policy of tolerance towards the International: "Pendant les premières années de son existence, l'Association internationale était vue avec faveur dans les régions officielles; on la regardait presque comme une alliée. Elle fut l'objet d'une tolérance mal dissimulée; elle prit ainsi racines à l'ombre du pouvoir."

[97]E. E. Fribourg, *L'Association internationale des travailleurs* (Paris, 1871), 22; 31-32.

[98]Pierre de la Gorce, *Histoire du Second Empire*, 7th ed. (Paris, 1905), V, 430.

[99]Maurice Dommanget, *Blanqui et l'opposition révolutionnaire à la fin du Second Empire* (Paris, 1960), 192.

[100]Fribourg, *L'Association internationale*, 37-38.

the Emperor.[101] When Rouher refused to authorize publication of a memorandum presented at the Geneva Congress of the International in 1867, the French delegation requested and was granted an interview with the Minister. At the meeting, Rouher suggested a compromise: in return for a few words of thanks to the "Emperor who had done so much for the working classes," the French section could publish its memorandum. The delegate of the International replied that his organization did not engage in politics.

[101]Fribourg, *L'Association internationale*, 162-163.

VI

The Government Press and the New Propaganda: The Crises of the 1860's

The new propaganda and the more complex problems of the regime in the last decade of the Empire also influenced the message of the government press. This was, in part, due to the sensitivity of editors to changes in the government's "line," and, in part, to suggestions from the administration. In the 1860's, some government newspapers, without abandoning the simple message of the 1850's, also discussed the demands of the working class more seriously and praised the social legislation enacted and proposed by the government. Conservative government newspapers lauded the reforms of the 1860's—reforms which they had often opposed in the first decade of Napoleon III's rule. The *Revue de l'Empire* (January 23, 1864) applauded the government's bill to amend the coalitions law, pointing out that the future and aspirations of the working class was "without contradiction the leading problem of our epoch." The *Pays* (February 24, 1864) also approved of changes in the coalitions law, but hoped that the number of strikes would not increase; workers knew, it wrote, that strikes could lead to disasters which threatened them more than any other class. On the day following the favorable vote on amending the coalition law, *Le Constitutionnel* (May 4, 1864) wrote that it was confident that the working class would appreciate the advantages offered them by the new law.

Government newspapers also made much of the Emperor's proposal to repeal legislation requiring workers to carry the *livret*. The existence of the *livret*, said *Le Constitutionnel* (January 5, 1869), contradicted the tendencies "of our administrative and economic legislation." The journalist, Charles Gaumont, termed it a remnant of the Old Regime and a practice which violated the dignity of the workers.[1] But thanks to the initiative of the government, he wrote, working conditions had improved greatly in the past few years as the result of such actions as amendment of the coalitions law, tolerance of trade unions, repeal of article 1781; and now it was time for the *livret* to go.

In 1865, one of the leading pro-government newspapers, *Le Pays*, opened a regular column for workers' letters. On May 30, the newspaper announced that henceforth it would publish letters from workers on their problems and grievances in two issues per week (actually, the letters appeared once a week), and assured correspondents that they could write freely and without censorship by the editor. The announcement called upon workers to express their desires to the government openly and without fear. "We are profoundly convinced," it affirmed, "that in the situation in which the working class is today, it cannot improve its status without the support and the aid of the state." As a result, from June to November 1865, the Tuesday issue of *Le Pays* published letters from workers under the rubric, *"Chroniques ouvrières."*

Many of the contributors to the *"Chroniques ouvrières"* were members of the Palais Royal group or delegates to the London Exposition of 1862. On June 13, Chabaud offered his cooperation: "I shall make it a duty to produce my quota of observations." The following month (July 18), Coutant also pledged his support to *Le Pays*: "I am sending you an article which will not be the last." These two men and the typographical worker Bazin, a

---

[1] *Le peuple*, February 6, 1869.

delegate to the London Exposition, became the most prolific contributors and on several occasions almost monopolized the "*Chroniques*." It was, in fact, a pamphlet by Bazin, *L'Opposition, le Gouvernement et les classes ouvrières* (1865), urging the working class to abandon its faith in political parties and to concentrate on social reform, which inspired the "*Chroniques ouvrières*."[2]

Although the letters often included a good word for the government and more frequently for the Emperor, the purpose of the column was to show workers that the government had not forgotten them, that it realized the need for change, and that it wanted to hear their views on reform and social legislation. The relationship between *Le Pays* and the government was no secret, and the mere fact that the newspaper printed proposals for reform seemed a hopeful sign.

The "*Chroniques ouvrières*" published communications on a wide range of workers' problems. The issue of June 27 included a letter from leather workers describing conditions in their craft after an unsuccessful strike, an article by Chabaud ("*De la necessité des chambres syndicales ouvrières*"), and resumés of reports by delegates to the London Exposition. On July 18, Coutant wrote on the importance of education to the working class. On September 5, Bazin lauded the *Société du Prince Impérial*, an institution that provided low-interest loans for workers, and J. Henry, a foreman, urged the organization of workers' cooperatives. The September 12 issue included a letter from bakery workers on the unfortunate effects of night work, two articles by Bazin, one calling for a shorter work week in the interest of full employment, health, morality, and education; the other, urging

[2]*Le Pays*, May 30, 1865: "Que veut M. Bazin, après tout? Que la lumière se fasse? Nul plus que nous ne la désire. Que mettant enfin la politique au second rang, les ouvriers commencent par le véritable commencement, par ce qui leur importe avant tout. . ."

the government to establish employment offices. Another article described a cabinet makers' strike.

Adolphe Guéroult and L'Opinion nationale

As I have already said, a number of new pro-government newspapers appeared in the late 1850's, and in the 1860's. One of these journals, *L'Opinion nationale*, although intended also for the liberal bourgeoisie, was as close as the Second Empire came to a workers' newspaper. It devoted more space than any other pro-government newspaper to social problems and frequently published letters and articles by workers. For example, the famous "Manifesto of the Sixty," a landmark in the history of the French working class, appeared first in *L'Opinion nationale*. The newspaper was read by some of the more militant and class-conscious workers, including the Parisian members of the First International.[3]

The founder of *L'Opinion nationale*, Adolphe Guéroult, was a former Saint-Simonian, who never lost his respect for the school and for its leader during the Second Empire, Prosper Enfantin.[4] His admiration for both Saint-Simon and Napoleon III emerged in the epithet that he coined to describe the latter, "Saint-Simon on horseback."[5] Guéroult had a varied career. He started in journalism during the July Monarchy, but also served briefly as a consul in Mexico. After the February Revolution, he became a republican and an editor of the newspaper, *La République*.

[3]Georges Duveau, *La pensée ouvrière sur l'éducation pendant la Seconde République et le Second Empire* (Paris, 1947), 312.

[4]On March 24, 1863, *L'Opinion nationale* devoted almost four columns to Enfantin's letter outlining a plan for the extension of credit to students (*"le crédit intellectuel"*). At Enfantin's funeral, in September 1864, Guéroult lauded the services of the Saint-Simonians to society, and *L'Opinion nationale* gave about three and a half columns to the *"Obsèques de M. Enfantin."*

[5]Sébastien Charlety, *Histoire du Saint-Simonisme (1825-1864)*, 2nd ed. (Paris, 1931), 343-344.

Guéroult's republican activities resulted in his arrest at the time of the *coup d'état*, but after ten days imprisonment he was released after the intervention on his behalf of the Saint-Simonian bankers, the Péreire brothers. And until 1857 he was associated with the *Crédit mobilier*, the great new bank founded by the Péreires. In 1858, Guéroult returned to journalism as editor of *La Presse*. His first article, says Darimon, was "a series of genuflections before the Imperial government," and under his direction the newspaper established close relationships with the regime.[6] The following year he left *La Presse* because of policy differences, and shortly thereafter he founded *L'Opinion nationale*. In 1863, Guéroult was elected to the *Corps législatif* from the Department of the Seine as an opposition candidate, although, again quoting Darimon, he "was almost a government candidate."[7] During the campaign Guéroult and *L'Opinion nationale* made a great effort to gain the workers' vote, but despite a liberal platform his ties to the government proved to be too great a disadvantage. By 1869, Guéroult's political allegiance was clear to all, and the republicans successfully ran their candidate, Jules Ferry, against him. After the fall of the Empire, Guéroult rallied to the Third Republic. The bare recital of the facts of Guéroult's career suggests that he was an opportunist, without principles of any kind. This was, however, far from being the case. Guèroult had a Saint-Simonian indifference to forms of government which made it easy for him to shift his allegiance to any regime that he he believed was on the right path. During the electoral campaign

[6]Alfred Darimon, *Histoire d'un parti. Les Cinq sous l'Empire (1857-1860)* (Paris, 1885), 114; Maurice Reclus, *Emile de Girardin le créateur de la presse moderne* (Paris, 1934), 205.

[7]Alfred Darimon, *L'Opposition libérale sous l'Empire (1861-1863)* (Paris, 1886), 414-415. Ollivier objected to republican opposition to Guéroult: "On n'avait à reprocher à cet homme de talent, écrivain excellent et orateur suffisant que son amitié avec le prince Napoléon." Emile Ollivier, *L'Empire libéral* (Paris, 1895-1910), XI, 492.

of 1863 he declared: "I am not one of those who see salvation for society only in a particular form of government, and for whom a revolution is the necessary condition for all progress, the preface for all reforms."[8] And his fellow journalist, the republican Taxile Delord, said of Guéroult that "like all Saint-Simonians he believed more in the importance of interests than in ideas [and was] indifferent to forms of government and party programs."[9] Therefore, when the Empire adopted what seemed to be a policy of aid for the oppressed nationalities Guéroult believed that it merited his support. Guéroult's motives, it is clear, were similar to those of Armand Lévy, with whom, moreover, he often collaborated.

The *Opinion nationale* was the first newspaper authorized under the press laws of the Second Empire to discuss political and social issues. Here, again, we see the influence of the Prince Napoleon who lent Guéroult funds to found his newspaper and also intervened with the government to obtain authorization for it.[10] In return, *L'Opinion nationale* often praised the Prince and proclaimed the role he should play in the government, "the interpreter of the desires of Liberal France" (July 8, 1860). The Emperor also wished Guéroult success with his newspaper. On May 8, 1859, when Guéroult requested Napoleon III's help to obtain authorization for his newspaper, he reminded the ruler that he had urged him to return to journalism, and assured him that the newspaper would support the policies of the Empire.[11]

8B.N. Le77 1222, *Elections de 1863, 6ème circonscription. Candidat Ad. Guéroult aux Electeurs.*

9Taxile Delord, *Histoire illustrée du Second Empire*, nouvelle ed. (Paris, 1880-1883), V, 381.

10When Guéroult rallied to the Republic after the fall of the Empire, the Prince Napoleon angrily demanded repayment of the loan. Article on Guéroult in Larousse, *Grand dictionnaire universel du XIXème siècle.*

11A.N. F18 396, file on *L'Opinion nationale*; letter of May 8, 1859: "Votre Majesté a bien voulu m'engager à rentrer dans le journalisme."

The propaganda in *L'Opinion nationale* differed markedly from that in other pro-government newspapers. Unlike the latter, it did not praise the Empire uncritically, and at times its attacks upon the government even equalled those of the opposition press in violence.[12] Guéroult differed fundamentally, however, from the opposition press in that he always insisted that social progress was possible under the Empire. On August 29, 1860, for example, *L'Opinion nationale* agreed that although the Constitution of 1852 had flaws, "in our eyes, it has a great quality: it is perfectible. It can be changed, modified. The Emperor, in agreement with the Senate, can introduce all the changes which moral progress and experience will have shown to be indispensable." In an announcement for former subscribers, Guéroult declared that *L'Opinion nationale* was neither a systematic adversary nor a *"partisan quand même"* of the Empire.[13] It was unjust, he said elsewhere, to condemn the government because it had not immediately enacted all the reforms desired by its critics,[14] and later he chided the uncompromising foes of the Empire who boasted of their independence: "real independence consists not only of criticizing the bad but also of approving and encouraging the good and of being satisfied with the possible."[15] Moreover, despite the constant hopes of the opposition that every crisis, such as the Crimean and Italian wars, would topple the government, it had managed to survive: "good or bad the Empire exists," and, therefore, anyone who wished to influence events or to change the policies of the government must accept it and work through its institutions.[16]

[12]This, perhaps, explains the fact that in his bibliography for *The Cambridge Modern History* (N.Y. 1909), XI, 928, Albert Thomas lists *L'Opinion nationale* under the rubric, "Independent (democratic or liberal)." Other historians have referred to *L'Opinion nationale* as an opposition newspaper.

[13]Adolphe Guéroult, *A mes anciens abonnés* (Paris, 1861).

[14]*L'Opinion nationale*, October 2, 1859.

[15]*L'Opinion nationale*, March 16, 1861.

[16]*L'Opinion nationale*, April 10, 1863.

Despite Guéroult's cautious and critical appreciation of the Empire, *L'Opinion nationale,* like other government newspapers, also frequently printed articles and editorials praising the concern of the government with the working class and the charity of the royal couple. On October 1, 1859, it joined the chorus of government newspapers to describe in detail the inauguration of the convalescent home for workers at Vésinet, including the prefect's speech with the usual praise of the Emperor and Empress and enumeration of government institutions for workers and the needy. On August 27, 1860, *L'Opinion nationale* reprinted from *Le Moniteur* a lengthy description of a royal visit to Lyons, and two days later another account, this time adding, "Various letters which we have received from our friends residing at Lyons agree in recognizing that the welcome accorded the Emperor had been very friendly, and that the working part of the population had made itself particularly noticed by the dash and warmth of its manifestations." An article applauding the recently concluded tariff treaty of 1860 quoted from Louis Napoleon at Ham ("the reign of castes is over"), and affirmed that the former prisoner, now invested with the supreme authority, had used his power "to ameliorate the condition of the laboring masses" by concluding a treaty which provided work, reduced the price of articles of primary necessity, and assured the prosperity of the country (June 22, 1860). A collection of several of Guéroult's articles declared that the Empire had not been founded by a few millionaires but by universal suffrage; "the worker, the peasant, these have been up to now its most devoted and surest partisans."[17] "Its natural policy," continued Guéroult, "is to improve the moral, intellectual, and material condition of the many; it is only by that policy that it can endure and grow."

The contribution of *L'Opinion nationale* to Bonpartist prop-

[17]Adolphe Guéroult, *La liberté et les affaires. La cherté des loyers et les travaux de Paris* (Paris, 1861), 29-30.

aganda among the working class was, however, not limited to re-
prints from *Le Moniteur* or kind words about the prisoner of
Ham. Other newspapers could do this more convincingly, and
Guéroult's praise of the Empire was at least balanced by his criticism.[18] The propaganda role of *L'Opinion nationale* was to convince workers that, even if conditions remained unsatisfactory
and the reforms of the government failed to meet their expecta-
tions, the Empire still merited confidence, and that revolution
would only lead to disaster. It was significant that a newspaper
which made no secret of its admiration for the Emperor dared
describe the condition of the working class objectively and to
demand reforms; it seemed to be a sign that the government also
sought solutions for the social problem.

The real value of *L'Opinion nationale* to the government consisted, then, not primarily in its praise of the Empire, but simply
in its exposition and discussion of workers' problems and activities. As in the case of Lévy and the Palais Royal workers, who
were, moreover, among the contributors to *L'Opinion nationale,*
pressure for reforms and pro-government propaganda were combined. One of these problems, the result of Haussmann's gigantic
construction efforts in Paris and the growing population, was rising rents. The *Opinion nationale* frequently published articles,
editorials, and letters on the plight of the poor in the face of rising rents. "In order to inhabit the new Paris which they are building for us," complained Guéroult, "there is one necessary condition to fulfill, one must be rich."[19] On January 14, 1862, an article,
"Les ouvriers dans la rue," called attention to another problem,
that of the worker who, hired by the task, day, or week, had to

[18]Guéroult apparently was sometimes concerned about the attitude of the government towards his critical articles. He once told Ollivier that he had asked the
Minister of the Interior whether he was dissatisfied with articles Guéroult had written on the reconstruction of Paris. Emile Ollivier, *Journal* (Paris, 1961), II, 9, Jan.
22, 1861.

[19]Guéroult, *La liberté et les affaires,* 29.

remain out-of-doors in all kinds of weather, resisting the temptation of the tavern, while waiting for employment. "Would it not be possible," asked the article, "to open simple buildings where workers could await the offer of employment under a shelter?" The *Opinion nationale* published frequent articles calling attention to the condition of unemployed textile workers in the crisis-ridden cotton industry during the American Civil War. On January 11, 1863, the newspaper called upon the 6,000,000 French workers to aid their needy comrades, even if only by working an additional five minutes per day. Another article (January 20, 1863), *"Aux ouvriers,"* signed by a number of workers, opened a drive for working class contributions to aid the unemployed in the Department of the Seine-Inférieure, and subsequent issues published the names of contributors.

Workers' activities and meetings also received attention from *L'Opinion nationale*. It never overlooked the annual award of prizes to workers who had taken the adult education courses offered by *L'Association polytechnique* and *L'Association philotechnique*.[20] On February 10, 1863, an article of almost four and a half columns, *"Une fête populaire,"* described the ceremony accompanying the awards. The *Opinion nationale* often published articles and editorials praising mutual aid societies; "is not mutual aid the application of the great principle of fraternity and the surest means of eliminating poverty?" (June 29, 1860). In 1862, *L'Opinion nationale* enthusiastically supported the project for workers' delegations to London. It published numerous communications from the workers' commission, the results of elections in the various crafts, and the names of delegates; it also opened a subscription to permit additional workers to attend the Exposition and reported in detail on the work of the delegations at London. After the London Exposition had brought them into

[20]See pp. 182 ff.

contact with English workers and working conditions, the elite of the French working class became more and more interested in foreign workers and in international labor solidarity. Guéroult, who recognized and shared this new interest, often published accounts of the activities of foreign workers: *"Congrès des associations ouvrières de l'Allemagne"* (June 18, 1863); *"Congrés d'Edinbourg Grand meeting d'ouvriers"* (October 30, 1863).

Always a consistent foe of legislation forbidding strikes, Guéroult, from the beginning of 1862, began a campaign of articles and letters calling for amendment or repeal of the ban. During a famous strike of printers in 1862, *L'Opinion nationale* published the views of both sides to the dispute, and used the trial and conviction of the striking workers as a springboard for attacks upon the law. After amendment of the coalitions law, the newspaper frequently printed letters from strikers and described labor conflicts objectively and sometimes sympathetically. On July 3, 1864, it printed a letter from striking porcelain workers at Limoges after the local newspaper had refused to do so. Later in the same year (October 16), *L'Opinion nationale* published a letter from striking furniture workers, adding the comment, "Without constituting ourselves judges in the issue, we hasten to open our columns to this letter, desiring to prove once again to the workers that they will never make a fruitless appeal to our publicity." On March 7, 1867, a communication from the International Workingman's Association on a strike of bronze workers appeared in *L'Opinion nationale*. A police statistic and analysis of strikes complained that Guéroult's newspaper often encouraged strikers.[21] The *Opinion nationale* (November 12, 1868) printed a letter of protest signed by nine workers who had been condemned to prison terms for belonging to the International Workingman's Association, and in April of 1869 published a

---

[21]A.N. 45 AP⁶ (dossier 3), no date but probably in late 1860's.

manifesto by followers of the perpetual revolutionary Blanqui.[22] From about 1862, the Palais Royal worker Coutant became a frequent contributor to *L'Opinion nationale*. On December 27, 1862, he wrote an article, *"Rapports des délégués lyonnais à l'Exposition de Londres*; on March 4 and 12, 1863, articles urging repeal of the coalitions law and article 1781; and on September 12, 1864, in praise of a pension system established at Lyons and Rouen for injured workers.

Imperial Propaganda and the Resurgence of the Working Class

Government propaganda, in the 1860's, had, moreover, to reach workers whose attitudes and demands were no longer the same as they had been in the previous decade. Despite some signs of dissatisfaction with the regime, workers during the 1850's had generally been quiescent.[23] However, with the emergence of the Liberal Empire in the 1860's and the enactment of more tolerant press and assembly laws, French workers, unable since the *coup d'état* to express their views freely or to engage in concerted action to improve working conditions, began to agitate for social reform and to organize trade unions. As worker unrest increased and socialism, thought moribund since 1848, showed signs of vigorous life, fear of revolution increased among the upper classes.

Among the signs of working class discontent was the appearance of workers' candidates to the *Corps législatif*, as self-conscious and declared representatives of their class.[24] Another sign was the publication of "The Manifesto of the Sixty" (1864), one

[22]Maurice Dommanget, *Blanqui et l'opposition révolutionnaire à la fin du Second Empire* (Paris, 1960), 178-179.

[23]David I. Kulstein, "The Attitude of French Workers Towards the Second Empire," *French Historical Studies*, v. II, no. 3 (Spring, 1962), 360 ff.

[24]For workers' candidates during the Second Empire, see I. Tchernoff, "Les candidatures ouvrières sous le Second Empire," *La Revue socialiste*, XLIII (Jan.-June 1906), 161-167.

of the most significant statements in the history of the French working class. Although the Manifesto rejected the concept of class conflict, it revealed unmistakably that the signers believed that they had class interests that were not satisfied by the existing economic and social order. The press law of May 11, 1868, facilitating the founding of political newspapers, and the law of June 6, 1868 on public assemblies enabled socialists and radicals to come out into the open. As a result, a great variety of projects for social reform and schools of socialism were expounded in the public meetings which flourished in Paris in the last years of the Empire. In addition, the years 1869-1870 were also marked by numerous strikes, often accompanied by violence. On June 16, 1869, thirteen miners were killed and nine wounded in the Loire region during a battle between strikers and troops; at the mines of Aubin, on October 8, 1869, fourteen miners were killed and some twenty wounded in a skirmish with the military; in 1870, a lengthy and historic strike occurred at the Le Creusot works. The goverment faced, therefore, the problem of combatting such movements and ideas without alienating the working class.

One answer to the growth of class consciousness revealed by the appearance of workers' candidates and the "Manifesto of the Sixty" was to insist that France was a democratic, classless society. In reply to the announcement of workers' candidates to the *Corps législatif* in 1863, a government newspaper raised the question, what was the bourgeoisie and the working class?[25] The bourgeoisie, it responded, was the worker who had risen to a comfortable position, while the worker was "the pedestrian advancing upon the path of the bourgeoisie, always ready to welcome him." Many workers moreover, already sat in the *Corps législatif*: Schneider (a wealthy industrialist) was an iron worker; Dolfuss (a leading Alsatian textile manufacturer), a weaver. In *L'Opinion*

[25]*La Revue de l'Empire*, March 28, 1863.

nationale, Guéroult criticized the class concept that provided the basis and justification for workers' candidates.[26] In a society which accepted the concept of the equality of all citizens, voters should not choose deputies to the legislature because they represented the working class or the bourgeoisie, as in the past the clergy, the nobility, and the third estate had sent their own delegates to the Estates General.

The "Manifesto of the Sixty," with its class-consciousness and demands for basic social reform, aroused a similar response by government spokesmen, plus an effort to convince workers that its program was visionary and would lead to class strife. Several government newspapers published the statement, which appeared first in *L'Opinion nationale,* and then proceeded to criticize it. On February 27, *La Revue de l'Empire* published the text of the "Manifesto," and a week later (March 5) sought to convince the signers of their errors. The "Manifesto," said the newspaper, called for the abolition of the wage system, something which "social science and experience" say is not reasonable. No real difference, it continued, existed between the capitalist and the worker: "Capital and labor are two identical terms just as interest and wages; capital is accumulated labor; interest is the wage of previous labor." In *Le Constitutionnel* (February 20, 1864), Paulin Limayrac approved of some of the ideas of the "Manifesto" and had kind words for the moderation of the authors, but attacked the document as "an anachronism, a false idea, an unjust protestation. At first people think that they are reading a selection from the literature popular in 1848." The "Manifesto," he complained, rejected the social order and "the whole wage system."

The government's answer to the radical schemes proposed by the orators at the public meetings of 1868-1870 was to insist upon the benefits of moderation and gradualism. It contrasted its own

[26]*L'Opinion nationale,* June 8, 1863.

practical and moderate reforms with what it termed the wild ideas of the public meetings, and praised those workers who spurned agitation. A government publicist, Claveau, in a newspaper intended for the lower classes, contrasted the accomplishments of the worker delegates to the Universal Exposition of 1867 with those of the public meetings.[27] Where the delegates to the Exposition had served the working class faithfully by their clear and precise reports and recommendations on such questions as the *livret* and article 1781, the orators at the public meetings proclaimed only absurdities and generalities. "Nothing clear, nothing precise, no program, no formula. There are not even questions. There are general terms of a grotesque banality upon which the first comer improvises all the variations which pass through his brain to the great amazement of his auditors." Another article in the same newspaper (May 17-18, 1869), contrasted the public meetings with a meeting of 1500 workers of the paternalistic employer Leclaire on the occasion of the thirtieth general assembly of the firm's *Société de prévoyance*:

There, [at the public meetings] antagonism, hate, over-excited passions . . . Here, [at Leclaire's meeting] harmony, contentment, moral and material well-being, and in the workers' mouths, eloquent and enthusiastic words to honor social peace and to express the most ardent gratitude and the most sincere respect to their employer.

"Good workers," declared another newspaper, refused to accept "the strange and subversive theories" proclaimed in their name at the public meetings.[28]

At the same time, the government engaged in a little "red scare." Government newspapers condemned the attacks upon the social order at public meetings and hinted at repression and even at a return to the Authoritarian Empire. They published fre-

[27]*Le Peuple*, February 12, 1869.
[28]*Le Pays*, January 2-3, 1869.

quent accounts that emphasized the disorder of the meetings, the extravagant doctrines of the orators, the appeals to violence, and the attacks upon the Church. Public meetings, said *Le Constitutionnel* (January 27, 1869), have had "for some time a violent character which disturbs peaceful citizens." During the month of February 1869, *Le Pays* published almost daily accounts of the meetings in order to expose the dangerous doctrines proclaimed by the speakers. Charles Gaumont wrote frequent patronizing articles on the public meetings for *Le Peuple*. He jeered at the disorder and confusion of the meetings and attacked the orators who spoke in platitudes, ignoring both the laws of economics and "acquired rights" (February 3, 1869). Even Guéroult, usually sympathetic to demands for social reform, joined in the attack upon the public meetings. Although it was clear, he said, that the people of Paris did not wish a riot or a *journée*, it was equally clear that some 10,000 or 12,000 men obeyed the word of order given by two or three ultra-red newspapers and were disposed towards revolt.[29] During the campaign preceding the plebiscite of 1870, Guéroult frequently attacked the agitators; their activities, he warned, might lead to a revival of the dictatorship. More than 100,000 copies of a government-inspired pamphlet were distributed, mainly in rural areas, attacking the public meetings.[30]

Unlike the years 1862-1864, when government newspapers sometimes sympathized with strikers, there was, in 1869-1870, almost universal condemnation. Even *L'Opinion nationale* tried to convince workers that they harmed everyone. An article, *"Une conséquence des grèves"* (April 21, 1870), insinuated that aid proffered by English hat workers to striking French hat workers

[29]*L'Opinion nationale*, April 9, 1870.

[30]Auguste Vitu, *Les réunions publiques à Paris 1868-1869.* (Paris, 1869). The Prefect of the Department of the Nord reported to the Minister of the Interior: "La brochure sur les réunions répandues dans le département y a produit un excellent effet." F1c III Nord 8, report for March, 1869.

was not disinterested; during the strike English manufactured hats had entered the French market. The following day the newspaper charged that strikes hampered French competition in foreign markets. Guéroult also condemned the great strike at Le Creusot in 1870.[31] Workers at Le Creusot earned better than average wages, and, even if they were not entirely adequate, the company could not increase wages and compete successfully in domestic and foreign markets. Only a prosperous industry could increase wages; therefore, any thing which rendered industry unprofitable harmed the working class.

One of the dangers that the Second Empire feared and sought to prevent was cooperation between the liberal bourgeois foes of the government and the working class. As liberal opposition to the regime increased in the late 1850's and the 1860's, the government attempted to drive a wedge between the working class and the partisans of political reform. The problems of the working class, said Imperial publicists, were social and economic, not political; the reforms and liberties demanded by the liberals served the interests of the bourgeoisie, not the workers.

Duvernois, one of the Emperor's favorite journalists, criticized the opponents of the government for their exclusive concern with political liberty and with obtaining more power for the *Corps législatif,* and attacked the liberal bourgeoisie for its indifference to social questions:[32]

What difference does it make [to the bourgeoisie] whether or not the law on workers' *livrets* is abrogated? What difference does it make whether article 1781 is repealed or maintained? What difference does it make whether workers can defend themselves by striking or that they have no means of defense . . .What is important is that authority be transferred and that the Assembly be sovereign.

[31]*L'Opinion nationale,* April 9, 1870.
[32]*Le Peuple,* February 5, 1869.

Those persons, he continued, whose social position and education rendered them capable of ruling the country fought over the division of power between the assembly and the crown, but "for the mass of the governed, the important thing is not that the power be divided in one way or another, it is that power be exercised in the interests of all."

To separate workers from the liberal opposition, the government frequently denounced the bourgeois selfishness and indifference to the needs of the working class in a manner reminiscent of Bonapartist propaganda in 1848. It is surprising to discover statements attacking the bourgeoisie even in the conservative Bonapartist press. As early as the 1857 elections to the *Corps législatif*, the Prefect of the Department of the Meurthe published a statement in the *Moniteur de la Meurthe* denouncing the candidacy of General Cavaignac; the statement recalled the General's role in the "June Days" and pointed out that he was being supported by the very groups whom he shot down in 1848.[33] During the electoral campaign of 1863, Auguste Vitu denounced the opposition candidate Thiers as a reactionary who had always opposed measures to aid the working class.[34] Thiers, he charged, had an "horror of every amelioration, of every new concept." A few days later (May 27) an article in the conservative *Le Constitutionnel* declared that under the government of Napoleon III as many workers were admitted to the charitable institutions of Vincennes and Vésinet as "there were wounded workers in former times at the cloister of Saint-Merri and on the Rue Transnonian [scenes of street fighting during the July Monarchy]."

Between the avarice and the self-interest of the bourgeoisie and the needs of the people, said Imperial propagandists, stood the Emperor, the representative of the entire nation. The people

[33] A.N. BB[18] 1567, *Procureur général* at Nancy to Minister of Justice, June 19, 1857.

[34] *Le Constitutionnel*, May 22, 1863.

knew very well, said Duvernois, that so long as it lacked the education to sit in the legislature, government by an assembly assured the omnipotence of the bourgeoisie.[35] A pamphlet urging a "yes" vote in the plebiscite of 1870 declared that while the *Corps législatif* represented the bourgeoisie, the Emperor represented the people.[36] The working class, said the author, was not interested in constitutional changes which altered the form of government, but in a profound and radical transformation of the social order. The *Corps législatif* could not carry through such changes, since it was "with a few exceptions the representative of the employers." The Emperor's past, on the other hand, guaranteed his sympathy for workers. A "no" vote, he concluded, would mean that workers had abdicated in favor of the employers.

Since it was common for liberals to praise English institutions and liberties, the government pointed to the condition of workers across the Channel and insisted that, despite English freedom, French workers were better off. The press frequently printed accounts of strikes and violence in England. On February 6, 1857, *Le Constitutionnel* described the sufferings and unrest of unemployed English workers and contrasted it with conditions in France where, even during difficult times, workers did not suffer as much as in England. Another article in *Le Constitutionnel* (March 3, 1857) declared, "Considered as a whole the working classes are materially better off or, if you prefer, less miserable in France than in England." In an article on the *"Oligarchie anglaise,"* *L'Opinion nationale* (November 4, 1859) maintained that if liberty contributed to the happiness of a people, it alone could not create prosperity and social progress. Nor was liberty a substitute for the principle of equality, a principle applied only in France.

[35]*Le Peuple*, February 2, 1869.
[36]Jean Martin, *Les travailleurs et le plébiscite* (Bordeaux, 1870).

VII

Economics Instruction for Workers

During the Second Empire numerous private individuals and organizations, municipalities and the central government encouraged and founded institutions to instruct French workers in economic principles, or, as Napoleon III said a number of times, in the "sane doctrines of political economy."[1] Economics instruction is not, of course, necessarily propaganda, but the objectives of economics courses for workers during the Second Empire justify, this writer believes, the use of the term. And although foes, as well as friends of the regime, participated in the movement, its popularity owes much to the favorable attitude of the public authorities. In the early 1850's, economics instruction was usually informal and unorganized. Government spokesmen and members of the upper classes who spoke before workers sought to impress upon them the salutary lessons of economics. Towards the end of the decade, however, and throughout the 1860's formal courses and lectures for workers, as well as simple texts or pamphlets on economics subjects, appeared in great number. It is interesting that this occurred in a country which, despite the presence of a distinguished group of economists, showed relatively little concern for the "dismal science."[2]

[1] This frequently quoted phrase became a euphemism for liberal economics.

[2] In 1864, the Minister of Education, Victor Duruy, complained to Napoleon III that only two chairs in economics existed in Paris and none in the Departments. *Le Moniteur universel*, September 18, 1864.

Proponents of economics education for workers advanced a number of reasons for it; in fact, they regarded such instruction as a basic need of society. Without question the weightiest motive was fear for the stability of the social order believed to be threatened by the increasing influence of radical and socialist ideas on the working class. Knowledge of the economic laws governing such phenomena as production and distribution, profits and wages, would, it was hoped, prove to workers that attacks upon existing economic institutions and practices were both unjustified and futile. Would the events of 1848 have occurred, asked the Minister of Public Instruction Victor Duruy, and would we have "the insane dreams which still agitate some minds, the fatal errors which the masses still accept, if a widespread program of instruction in economics had been in effect during the past eighty years?"[3] Social progress and public order, declared a speaker before the *Société d'économie politique*, the economists' professional association, depended upon whether the lower classes learned the meaning of such terms as wages, capital, property, and freedom of labor.[4] Henri Dameth, who in the 1860's taught public economics courses at Lyons, pointed out the menace in the downward diffusion of socialist ideas.[5] Although, he said, radical ideas no longer appealed to the upper classes as in the past, they were now penetrating the working class, particularly in the great industrial centers. Enflamed by socialist schemes for reform, the working class threatened the stability of society. Economics, he concluded, should expose these false solutions to the social problem. Not until economic precepts had entered the

[3]M. G. Molinari, *Le mouvement socialiste et les réunions politiques avant la révolution du 4 Septembre 1870* (Paris, 1872), 45-46.

[4]*Annales de la société d'économie politique*, VI, 504-505, meeting of September 5, 1866.

[5]H. Dameth, *Le mouvement socialiste et l'économie politique* (Paris, 1869), 20-21; 16-17.

home of every peasant and worker, said the economist Paul Leroy-Beaulieu, would the social order be secure.[6]

Gazing enviously across the Channel, French economists attributed the apparent imperviousness of the English laboring class to socialist and revolutionary ideas to the instruction in economics which they believed the latter received in the Mechanics' Institutes and similar institutions.[7] Despite the violence which sometimes accompanied strikes in England, said a high official in the Ministry of Education, English workers, with their superior knowledge of economic principles, had fewer illusions than French workers.[8] He also quoted a statement on communism in England in 1848 by the Primate of Ireland, Monseigneur Whateley: "That plague will never reach us; the economic catechism protects our workshops from it." And, he continued, twenty years later another Englishman confirmed his judgment: "Our workers will never riot or revolt; they understand political economy too well."

Economics also improved morality. True all education, claimed the advocates of popular enlightenment, had such an effect. In fact, only two ways existed, suggested one writer, to maintain order and respect for the law, the prison and the gallows or the school.[9] But if education in general improved morality, instruction in the "sane doctrines of political economy" did so in par-

[6]Paul Leroy-Beaulieu, *De l'état moral et intellectuel des populations ouvrières et de son influence sur le taux des salaires* (Paris, 1868), 289-290. This work won first prize in a competition opened by the *Académie des sciences morales et politiques*.

[7]The most recent account of the English Mechanics' Institutes is in Richard Altick, *The English Common Reader. A Social History of the Mass Reading Public 1800-1900* (Chicago, 1957), 188 ff. Actually these institutions for popular education did not teach as much economics as their French admirers believed. In fact, says Altick, "in many places there was an absolute ban on 'controversial topics,'" 194.

[8]Charles Robert, *La Suppression des grèves par l'association aux bénéfices* (Paris, 1870), 126.

[9]Emile de Laveleye, "De l'instruction du peuple au dix-neuvième siècle," *Revue des deux mondes*, January 1, 1866, 215-216.

ticular. Moreover, if workers observed these doctrines, they would also ameliorate their material condition and increase their industrial efficiency. Immorality and not the much maligned factory system, said many economists, was responsible for the poverty of the worker. "If ever the workshop is full and the cabaret empty, poverty will be conquered," predicted Jules Simon.[10] Economists hoped that economics instruction would combat the improvidence of the worker, his addiction to the cabaret, the custom of taking Mondays off, and shirking on the job, which one of them regarded as a more serious offense than absenteeism, since the worker received no wage when he was not at his bench.[11]

Economics instruction would assist religion in inculcating morality in the lower classes. In fact, avowed the young economist Leroy-Beaulieu, despite the deep respect he felt for religion, it must be admitted that during the centuries that it had been trying to do so, religion had not succeeded in raising the moral standards of the working class to the slightest extent. It was time, he concluded, after centuries of unprofitable preaching about man's duties, to speak of man's interests.[12]

The titles of books written for workers reveal the close connection believed to exist between morality and economics instruction: J. J. Rapet, *Manuel de morale et d'économie politique à l'usage des classes ouvrières* (Paris, 1858); Antonin Rondelet, *Les Mémoires d'Antoine ou notions populaires de morale et d'économie politique* (Paris, 1860). In 1866, the *Académie des sciences morales et politiques* announced a competition for an essay on "The influence of the moral and intellectual condition of the working population on the rate of wages."[13]

[10]Frédéric Passy, *Les machines et leur influence sur le développement de l'humanité* (Paris, 1881), 152 ff. This is a new edition of two lectures given by the author in 1864.

[11]Leroy-Beaulieu, *De l'état moral*, 18-20.

[12]Leroy-Beaulieu, *De l'état moral*, 136.

[13]Leroy-Beaulieu, *De l'état moral*, preface.

It was also claimed that a clear understanding of economic principles would dispel false ideas and prejudices which often stood in the path of industrial progress: the fear of new machines and processes, resistance of some interested groups to railroads, efforts by workers and peasants in periods of shortage to impede the free movement of foodstuffs, objections to female labor and apprentices. Among the common and uninformed demands of striking workers, pointed out Leroy-Beaulieu, was a reduction in the number of apprentices.[14] Greater knowledge of economic laws and the needs of industry might also overcome the reluctance of the worker to relocate, to learn a new trade, to leave a declining industry, and to desert the attractions of the city for more remunerative work in smaller towns.

New legislation in the 1860's provided additional motives for instructing workers in economics. First, the Cobden-Chevalier Treaty of 1860 between France and England establishing lower tariffs on certain exports of both countries. French economists, who generally favored the Treaty, believed that they had to convince workers of the advantages to them of lower tariffs. And also to incite them to a greater effort in order to meet foreign competition since idling on the job, negligence of equipment, the wasteful use of materials, and failure to deliver orders on time would handicap French industry on the international market. A second new reason was the recognition, in 1864, of the right to strike. Now that workers could strike legally, they had to be warned against abuse of the new weapon.

The motives for instructing workers in economic principles determined the contents of the lessons. These lessons did not discuss the technical aspects of economic institutions and theory, and whenever a lecturer or printed matter discussed finance, banking, foreign trade, it was always with the broader aim of re-

14Leroy-Beaulieu, *De l'état moral*, 285.

futing socialist doctrines and exposing popular "misconceptions." As a speaker said at a meeting of the *Société d'économie politique,* it was not the purpose of a certain economics course for workers to initiate them into the complexities of the science, but to define principles useful for "our conduct in the social order."[15] When an entire course on a technical subject was offered, such as Dameth's on banking (*Résumé d'un cours . . . sur les banques publiques*), it was probably not intended for workers.

A second characteristic of economics courses for workers was their uncompromising economic liberalism. Even though by the 1860's many economists already questioned some of the principles of classical economics, they reserved whatever doubts they had for their more scholarly works. In their popular works and courses, economic science was presumed to be based on principles beyond question. Courses and texts assured workers that just as the natural world followed laws so did economic activity. "Human societies," wrote an economist, "are subject to economic laws, [and] these laws are not arbitrary, but derived from the physical and moral constitution of man."[16] Another economist gave an example of such a natural law: "although every individual works for his own well-being, "the nature of things is such that each of us in thinking only of himself, of the satisfaction of his own needs, in working from morning to evening in his own interests, is also forced to work in the interests of others."[17] A lecturer at Lyons insisted that the laws of the market, not the desires of workers or of employers determined the wage rate.[18]

[15]*Annales de la société d'économie politique,* VII, 602-603, meeting of September 5, 1868.

[16]J.-B. Lescarret, *Conférences sur l'économie politique faites en 1867-1868 à Bordeaux et à Bayonne* (Paris, 1869), 23.

[17]*Cours d'économie industrielle, recueilli et publié par Evariste Thévenin,* 1ère série (Paris, 1866). Introductory lecture by Joseph Garnier.

[18]H. Dameth, *Introduction à l'étude de l'économie politique,* 2nd ed. (Paris, 1878), 345-346.

Economists defended the social role of capital and the justice of interest upon it. Capital, complained one, "that instrument of production, has been the object of the most vehement, of the most passionate attacks" by individuals who mistakenly believed that it is an enemy of labor. We are all capitalists, he declared, even the worker with only a few savings and the tools of his trade. Interest is the merited reward of the capitalists' restraint and abstinence. Therefore, he admonished his audience to respect the security and freedom of capital.[19] Labor and capital, said Frédéric Passy, have the same interests; what hurts one, hurts the other, and he ended his lecture with the exhortation: "Love each other, help each other, for, employers and workers, you are all brothers."[20]

Another common theme of popular economics was the defense of competition, the whipping-boy of the socialists; competition, replied the economists, provided an incentive to better methods and, therefore, lower prices. Economists also agreed that, however unfortunate the condition of many members of society, the lot of the worker was incomparably superior to that of the slaves of antiquity and the serfs of the Middle Ages. Human misery, declared an economist, is nothing new, and only by closing one's eyes to the lesson of history can we blame modern society for it.[21]

Before the founding of the Second Empire, the Revolution of 1848, which, for a few months, seemed to place the destiny of France in the hands of the turbulent Parisian working class, inspired an educational counter-offensive by the defenders of the social order. Between the years 1848 and 1851, wrote a contem-

[19]Henri Beaudrillart, "Le Capital" in *Cours d'économie industrielle*, lère série, 87; passim.

[20]Passy, *Les machines et leur influence*, 161; 218-219.

[21]Lescarret, *Conférences sur l'économie politique*, 243.

porary economist, more was done to popularize economic doctrines than in the previous fifty years.[22]

The *Académie des sciences morales et politiques* published a series of popular pamphlets on economic questions, and the Committee of the Rue de Poitiers, the conservative high command, distributed hundreds of thousands of pamphlets to refute socialist propaganda.[23] Adolphe Thiers wrote a 388 page work, *De la propriété*, whose cheap edition, with the aid of an *Association pour la défense du travail national*, sold for one franc.[24] Frédéric Bastiat, a distinguished French economist, wrote many pamphlets in defense of existing institutions.[25] So respected was Bastiat as a popularizer that several of his pamphlets were translated into English for distribution to workers across the Channel. Michel Chevalier, former Saint-Simonian and during the Second Empire Napoleon III's favorite economic adviser, wrote a widely distributed attack upon socialist doctrines, particularly Louis Blanc's plan for social workshops; a system so contrary to human nature, he said, would only increase the poverty of the working class.[26] Chevalier denied that he was opposed to reform and pointed to his Saint-Simonian past and to his reputation as a reformer as evidence of his sympathy for the working class.

However, in the years immediately following Louis Napoleon's *coup d'état* such efforts at popular instruction in economics became rare. Although some officials and members of the upper classes continued to fear revolution, most persons believed that socialism was dead. Not until the 1860's did interest in economics

22Molinari, *Le mouvement socialiste*, XVI-XVIII.

23Molinari, *Le mouvement socialiste*, 68.

24Adolphe Thiers, *De la propriété* (Paris, 1848), I-IV.

25Frédéric Bastiat, *Essays on Political Economy* (London, n.d.). I consulted the "Fifth (Peoples) Edition." For Bastiat's pamphlets use, *Oeuvres complètes de Frédéric Bastiat*, 5th ed. (Paris, 1884), vol. 4-5.

26Michel Chevalier, *Question des travailleurs* (Paris, 1848). The pamphlet first appeared in a less developed form in the *Revue des deux mondes* (March 15, 1848).

instruction for workers revive. I have already suggested two new factors that help explain this renewed concern, the Tariff Treaty of 1860 and the legalization of strikes. But even more important was increasing worker agitation and unrest.[27]

The multiplication of popular courses and literature on economics in the 1860's also owes a great deal to the benevolent attitude of the government. Throughout his reign Napoleon III insisted upon the need for teaching economics to workers, and the advocates of such instruction never tired of quoting the Emperor on the subject. Before a meeting of French industrialists on August 4, 1849, the Prince-President declared: "Do not forget to disseminate the sane doctrines of political economy among your workers."[28] And in his message to the opening of the legislative session in 1857, he repeated the admonition: it was "the duty of good citizens to disseminate everywhere the same doctrines of political economy."[29]

Ministers and high officials of the Empire shared Napoleon III's views on the subject. In a prophetic article that appeared a short time before the Revolution of 1848, the future minister of the Second Empire, Morny warned: "Communism is secretly undermining the basis of society and government."[30] Since it was natural, he went on, for the poorer members of society to accept egalitarian doctrines, the government and upper classes must "prove to the unfortunate by the use of logic and common sense that the rich are not responsible for their condition, and enable them to understand the secret of the social mechanism." Victor Duruy, Napoleon III's liberal Minister of Public Instruction in the 1860's, urged more instruction in economics, not only for

27See pp. 162-163.

28*Oeuvres de Napoléon III* (Paris, 1856-1869) (hereafter *Oeuvres*), III, 104-105.

29*Le Moniteur*, February 17, 1857. On a similar occasion, in 1867, the Emperor repeated his counsel in almost identical words, *Oeuvres*, V, 258-259.

30A. de Morny, "Quelques réflexions sur la politique actuelle," *Revue des deux mondes*, XXI, New Series (January 1, 1848), 152; 161-162.

workers, but for all classes of French society. He complained that there existed in France so few courses in economics, "that science which is taught in all countries about us and which recently enabled a neighboring state to traverse without peril a crisis which had been extremely hard on the working class."[31] And, in 1868, he urged the government to open a competition for text-books on various subjects, including economics, suitable for workers and peasants.[32] Michel Chevalier approved of a proposal to establish a chair of "political and industrial economy" in every department of France.[33] A few years later he declared that the unsound ideas prevalent among workers were the product of their profound ignorance of social and political economy, a condition that must be corrected by proper instruction.[34] Such sympathetic attitudes by the ruler and highly placed persons facilitated the task of the partisans of popular economics. For example, it made it easier for them to obtain authorization for courses.

The initiative came, however, not from the government, but from private organizations and towns. Municipal chambers of commerce, institutions for adult education, and other local organizations frequently invited economists to offer public courses for workers and other interested citizens. Although such municipally or locally sponsored courses were not always for workers alone, the sponsors showed pleasure when workers attended and made special efforts to attract them. At Perigueux, for example, the town reserved one third of the available seats for railroad workers in the vicinity.[35]

[31]*Le Moniteur*, September 18, 1864.

[32]Victor Duruy, *Notes et souvenirs (1811-1894)* (Paris, 1901), I, 237-238.

[33]*Le Moniteur*, February 13, 1864. For some reason, Michel Chevalier, despite his concern for popular education and his work in 1848, did not participate actively in the movement to carry economics instruction to workers.

[34]Michel Chevalier, *Exposition universelle de 1867. Rapports du jury interrnational. Introduction* (Paris, 1868), 444-445.

[35]*Annales de la société d'économie politique*, VIII, 324, meeting of March 5, 1870.

The first such public course was offered in 1860 at Pau by Frédéric Passy, publicist and economist, whose enthusiasm and devotion to popular economics earned for him the title of the "apostle of political economy."[36] The same year the town of Montpellier invited Passy to offer a similar course. He accepted and during the winter of 1860-1861 gave twenty-nine lectures, which were later published in two volumes under the title, *Leçons d'économie politique faites à Montpellier*. Other towns also called on Passy to offer economics courses. In 1861-1862 and again in 1862-1863, he taught economics at Bordeaux under the auspices of the *Société Philomatique*, an organization interested in popular education. In 1863-1864 and 1864-1865, he lectured at Nîmes. At the same time, after overcoming the objections of local authorities who feared that economics instruction might incite rather than pacify workers,[37] Passy gave two lectures at Paris on the use of machines in production, which were subsequently published under the title, *Les machines et leur influence sur le développement de l'humanité*.

Other economists began to offer similar courses as more and more municipalities became convinced of their social utility. At Castres, M. Rozy, a professor of political economy, taught a public course that was "followed with the greatest interest by an appreciative audience of workers and bourgeois."[38] The *Société Philomatique* at Bordeaux, pleased with their first venture, sponsored another series of lectures by J. B. Lescarret.[39] At Marseille, the municipality founded a course in 1867, which was taught un-

[36]Emile Levasseur, "Résumé historique de l'enseignement de l'économie politique et de la statistique," *Journal des économistes* (November 1882), 315. Levasseur offered this report at a meeting of the *Société d'économie politique*, November 6, 1882.

[37]See pp. 183-184.

[38]*Annales de la société d'économie politique*, VI, 413-414, meeting of May 5, 1866.

[39]Lescarret, *Conférences sur l'économie politique*. This is a published version of Lescarret's lectures.

til 1891 by a M. Jourdan, dean of the faculty at Aix.[40] Among the other towns that offered public economics courses were Nantes, Reims, Grenoble, Nancy, Toulouse, Bayonne, and Perigueux.

The Chamber of Commerce at Lyons organized the most successful of the locally-sponsored courses.[41] The Chamber had already discussed the founding of an economics course as early as 1842, but the fears of the Orleanist government and then the Revolution of 1848 put a halt to the project. From about 1860 interest in the plan revived. Two Lyonnese newspapers, the *Gazette de Lyon* and *Le Progrès*, began to urge the founding of economics courses for workers "in order to arm them against the absurd theories which are unfortunately current among us."[42] When the workers at Lyons cast a large republican vote in the 1863 elections to the *Corps législatif*, the Chamber of Commerce became even more alarmed, and several times requested the government to found a public chair of political economy at Lyons, even offering to pay half the salary of the instructor and all other expenses. Impatient after a year of government delays, the Chamber, in 1864, established its own course. At the first lecture the President of the Chamber of Commerce insisted on the need for the course: "How many false ideas must be corrected concerning the accumulation of capital and what the socialists call its tyranny, concerning the laws determining wages, variations in prices, credit, etc., etc.! How much prejudice there is to dissipate!"[43]

Classes started in November 1864, and continued regularly until the end of the Empire. The instructor, Henri Dameth, despite a Fourierist past, taught the purest liberal economics before

[40]Emile Levasseur, *Résumé historique de l'enseignement de l'économie politique et de la statistique en France de 1882 à 1892* (Paris, 1893), 44.

[41]For the background and organization of the course at Lyons, see Sretin Maritch, *Histoire du mouvement social sous le Second Empire à Lyon* (Paris, 1930), 180-181, and Dameth, *Introduction à l'étude de l'économie politique*, "Avantpropos des éditeurs," IX-XIV.

[42]Maritch, *Histoire du mouvement social*, 180.

large-sized audiences. If the President of the Chamber of Commerce is to be trusted, hundreds had to be turned away at the first lesson, even though Dameth lectured in a large hall.[44] With the aid of a subsidy from the Chamber of Commerce, Dameth published separately each of the twenty lectures he gave during the first year, and at the completion of the course he published the entire series of lectures.

At Paris the *Association Polytechnique* and the *Association Philotechnique,* institutions concerned with worker education, took the lead in offering economics courses.[45] The former and older organization took its name from its founders, graduates of the *Ecole Polytechnique,* the great engineering school established during the First Empire. Shortly after the Revolution of 1830, which most of them favored, a group of *polytechniciens* founded an association for popular education as a means of expressing their gratitude to the workers and artisans of Paris who had made the Revolution. With its center at Paris, the *Association Polytechnique* organized "sections" both in the capital and the provinces. (A "section" consisted of a series of courses offered in the same locality.) From the beginning the *Association* had the cooperation of the city of Paris and the central government. The authorities at Paris lent it classroom space in public buildings, and in the 1830's the Minister of Public Instruction began a policy of government subsidies which continued during the Second Empire.[46] During the first years of the *Association Polytechnique*

[43]Dameth, *Introduction à l'étude d'économie politique*, XIII-XIV.
[44]Dameth, *Introduction à l'étude d'économie politique*, XV.
[45]Georges Duveau has dealt ably with some aspects of worker education and reading habits: *La vie ouvrière en France sous le Second Empire* (Paris, 1946), Ch. 4, and *La pensée ouvrière sur l'éducation pendant la Seconde République et le Second Empire* (Paris, 1947). However, there is still need for a history of the education, formal and informal, of the French working class in the nineteenth century.
[46]Both it and the *Association Philotechnique* received an annual subsidy of 5,000 francs from the municipality of Paris, and 1500 francs from the Minister of Public Instruction. Auguste Perdonnet, *Notice sur les associations polytechnique et philotechnique* (Paris, 1865), 10.

all instructors were *polytechniciens*, but as the institution grew others began to teach, and the *polytechniciens* became a minority. They continued, however, to dominate the organization with the result that the new instructors left the parent organization to found a new one, the *Association Philotechnique*. The objectives, methods, and organization of the new institution resembled the older one, and, although efforts to unite them failed, they did, from time to time, cooperate.

The beginnings were very modest; in 1830, the *Association Polytechnique* listed only eight courses. However, with increasing literacy and a greater appreciation of the usefulness of education, both institutions expanded rapidly during the Second Empire. By 1867, the *Association Polytechnique*, "the workers' Sorbonne" as someone called it during the Second Empire, offered more than 200 courses and the *Association Philotechnique* more than 100.[47] The courses offered by the *Association Polytechnique* included: French grammar and composition, arithmetic, geometry, descriptive geometry, trigonometry, algebra, accounting, drafting, artistic designing, hygiene, physics, chemistry, mechanics, astronomy, legislation (law), geography, natural history, technology, political economy, foreign languages, and singing.[48]

Political economy was, however, a recent addition to the curriculum. From the beginning, the *Association Polytechnique* had a policy of excluding from its offerings subjects likely to arouse controversy. As late as 1865, its director, Perdonnet, declared that the *Association Polytechnique*, "enlightened by experience," refused to offer courses that might incite political or religious controversy, "for example, courses in history, political economy,

---

[47]Auguste Perdonnet, *De l'utilité de l'instruction pour le peuple* (Paris, 1867), 13-14.

[48]Perdonnet, *De l'utilité*, 27-28. This strange order is the way Perdonnet lists the subjects.

morality, etc."[49] And when Frédéric Passy urged Perdonnet to offer a course on political economy at the *Association Polytechnique*, the latter replied that it was dangerous merely to pronounce such words as "capital" and "labor" before a worker audience.[50]

If the *Association Polytechnique* thought it imprudent to offer courses in economics, its students did occasionally hear economic "truths," and sometimes from the Ministers of the Interior and of Public Instruction themselves. The *Association*'s annual award of distinctions was an important event which high Imperial officials honored with their presence. Ministers and other speakers at these ceremonies never forgot to impress upon their large audiences that they lived in a free society where each individual could go as far as his abilities permitted, nor failed to warn them of the dangers of class strife. In 1858, the Minister of the Interior told the assembled students and their friends that although God had condemned men to inequality by granting them different capacities, the laws no longer set artificial limitations upon the able. And he warned them against accepting such sterile slogans as "the right to work."[51] The following year the Minister of Public Instruction denied that the rich and powerful were unconcerned about the condition of the poor, and cautioned his audience against the fomenters of class hatred.[52] In 1862, the Minister of Public Instruction denounced the chimeras which led only to hatred and ruin. France, he declared, seemed to be saying to all her citizens: The field is open to those who want to employ their capacities. There is a place in the sun for those who work and persevere.[53]

[49]Perdonnet, *Notice*, 6.
[50]Levasseur, "Résumé historique" (1882), 315-318.
[51]*Le Moniteur*, February 1, 1858.
[52]*Le Moniteur*, January 24, 1859.
[53]*Distribution des prix aux élèves réunis des deux associations polytechniques* (Paris, 1862), 14.

Such intermittent morsels of wisdom did not, however, satisfy the ardent advocates of economics instruction who believed that only the dissemination of sound doctrines could save society from disaster. And, in 1864, the "apostle of political economy," Frédéric Passy, overcame the fears of Perdonnet that economics was too controversial a subject and gave two lectures on the use of machines in industry, under the auspices of the *Association Polytechnique*. The success of Passy's lectures, their failure to stir up a revolution, as well as the fact that the Minister of Public Instruction had himself sponsored a series of public lectures, including several on economic and social problems,[54] convinced the *Association Polytechnique* that it could thereafter safely offer instruction in economics.

In 1866, after obtaining authorization from the Prefect of the Seine, Perdonnet called upon the *Société d'économie politique,* which had long been urging economics courses for workers, to supply ten instructors for a series of public lectures. And, on February 4, 1866, Joseph Garnier, a member of the *Société*, gave the first lecture in the auditorium of the *Ecole Turgot*. Garnier's opening lecture, entitled "Industrial Economy," outlined the project and its purpose. (The term "industrial economy" was used to describe the entire series of lectures, because, for some reason, it seemed more innocuous to the *Association Polytechnique* than "political economy.") Other lectures followed on such subjects as: "Capital," "Labor and Wages," "Interest and Usury," "Co-operative Societies," "Money and Exchange," and "Credit."

Perdonnet was so pleased with the lectures that he not only organized a new course the following year, but also envisaged a nation-wide system of economics courses. On May 5, 1866, he told a delighted meeting of the *Société d'économie politique* that the *Association Polytechnique* hoped to found economics courses

[54]See p. 187-188.

wherever it had sections and friends; no better insurance against class warfare existed.[55] After Perdonnet's death in 1867, the *Association Polytechnique* seemed to lose its enthusiasm for such ambitious ventures as he had outlined, but it continued to offer instruction in economics and even opened new courses. In 1868, it organized courses in two working class neighborhoods, La Villette and the turbulent Faubourg Saint-Antoine.[56] The following year it founded two more courses "intended primarily for workers."[57]

A few months after the opening of the *Association Polytechnique's* course a somewhat similar series of lectures was inaugurated at the new home for convalescent workers at Vincennes. Since an average of 10,000 workers spent some time at Vincennes each year, this seemed to offer an ideal opportunity to implant economic "truth" among the idle convalescents. The government took a direct interest in the lectures at Vincennes, whose official title was "*Conférences populaires faites à l'asile impériale de Vincennes sous le patronnage de S.M. l'Impératrice.*" The Minister of the Interior named a civil-servant to organize the lectures, and the director of the convalescent home always included a section on them in his semi-annual reports. On May 30, 1866, Monseigneur Darboy, Archbishop of Paris, opened the series and thereafter three lectures were given each week.[58] Usually each lecture was complete in itself; it did not form part of a course. The founders of the "*Conférences populaires*" hoped, however, that the lectures would stimulate the auditors so that they would maintain an interest after completing their convalescence.

Although lecturers discussed a variety of subjects—hygiene, the sciences, history and biography, literature—it is clear that politi-

---

[55]*Annales de la société d'économie politique*, VI, 416 ff.

[56]*Annales de la société d'économie politique*, VII, 629.

[57]*Annales de la société d'économie politique*, VIII, 211.

[58]According to *Le Moniteur* (May 2, 1868), "S. M. l'Impératrice a décidé que les conférences seraient faites trois fois par semaine."

cal economy was the main interest at Vincennes. A report to the Minister of the Interior stated that the Empress herself had insisted that the speakers emphasize social and economic questions.[59] The distribution of lectures shows this interest. By the end of 1866, there had been ninety-two lectures plus the inaugural lecture by the Archbishop of Paris; of these, forty-eight had discussed political economy; eighteen, hygiene; ten, history and biography; eight, the sciences.[60] Even this does not tell the full story. The "sane doctrines of political economy" found their way into lectures on subjects apparently quite remote from economics. The economist Baudrillart, for example, turned his three lectures on the life of the inventor Jacquard into a demonstration that an ambitious and abstemious member of the lower classes could overcome all the obstacles in his way.[61]

Even before the *Association Polytechnique's* courses and the Vincennes lectures, the Minister of Public Instruction, in cooperation with a committee of private persons, had sponsored a series of public lectures at the Sorbonne, *"Soirées littéraires et scientifiques."* From March 1864, apparently to the end of the Empire, two distinguished scholars or public officials spoke at the Sorbonne each week, one on a scientific subject, the other on a "literary" subject.[62] Although not intended primarily for the lower classes, workers did attend the lectures according to newspaper accounts of the *"soirées."* Political economy also had a place on the program. On April 25, 1864, Henri Baudrillart lectured on the social utility of political economy, pointing out how the science refuted the attacks on the existing order by reformers and

[59]*Conférences populaires sous le patronage de S. M. l'Impératrice* (Paris, 1867), 12.
[60]*Conférences populaires*, 13-18.
[61]*Le Moniteur*, July 21-23, 1866.
[62]*Le Moniteur*, March 4, 1864. Among the subjects discussed at the *"soirées littéraires et scientifiques"* were: "Sur les divers états de la nature," "Poussin," "La Jeunesse de Marc Aurèle d'après les lettres de Fronton," "Génération dite spontanée" (by Pasteur).

socialists.[63] In December of the same year, A. P. Batbie, Professor of Political Economy at the law faculty of the University of Paris, traced the origins of the science of economics.[64] Among the lecturers in 1865 was the devoted Frédéric Passy who spoke on the *"Histoire du travail."*[65]

During the last two years of the Second Empire economists had the chance to carry their message to meetings organized by the workers themselves. The law of June 6, 1868, easing the restrictions on public meetings hitherto in effect, permitted a more open discussion of social and economic questions. To the dismay and the horror of the government and the upper classes, spokesmen at the public meetings which flourished at Paris in a way reminiscent of 1848 not only revived the socialist ideas of the Second Republic, but also proclaimed new and even more radical schemes to transform society.

French economists, accepting the challenge, mounted the barricades of the public meetings and sought to answer the attacks of socialists on the economic order.[66] Many of them, it is true, questioned whether the popular meetings provided the right environment for the exposition of their science. At the February 5, 1869 meeting of the *Société d'économie politique*, the members discussed the utility of debating with the socialists in the public meetings.[67] Joseph Garnier, a veteran of the meetings, described the physical conditions at the public assemblies. Overcrowded

[63]*Le Moniteur*, April 29, 1864.

[64]*Le Moniteur*, December 24, 1864.

[65]*Le Moniteur*, December 5, 1865.

[66]For the public meetings of the last years of the Empire and the activities of orthodox economists in them, see Molinari, *Le mouvement socialiste*, and Auguste Vitu, *Les réunions publiques à Paris, 1868-1869* (Paris, 1869). A police report of 1868 on the public meetings tells of several such encounters between socialist orators and economists: June 6, 1868, October 10, 1868, November 7, 1868, November 14, 1868. *Archives Nationales* 45 AP6 (Dossier 4).

[67]*Annales de la Société d'économie politique*, VIII, 42-45.

halls made it necessary for the speaker to shout, an undignified procedure not conducive to calm discussion. Late arrivers not only disturbed the others, but forced to stand in the rear of the hall and unable to hear the speaker, became impatient. More serious, however, than the unfavorable physical environment, complained Garnier, was the ignorance of the auditors, their addiction to "systems," their refusal to listen to views contrary to their prejudices. The economist Molinari wondered how worthwhile it was to teach economics before an audience which listened patiently while an orator attacked the Bank of France in Alexandrine verse![68]

In addition to lectures and courses, many pamphlets and books on economics for workers were published in the 1860's. Increasing literacy and government encouragement led to the founding during the Second Empire of a number of collections offering the lower classes instruction in a wide variety of subjects: the *Bibliothèque utile,* the *Bibliothèque des connaissances utiles, L'Ecole mutuelle, cours complet d'éducation populaire.*[69] A sign of the popularity of these collections is that editions of some self-education manuals ran as high as 5,000 copies. Printed materials on economics for workers were generally of two kinds: published versions of single lectures or entire courses, or original instructional manuals. The former kind, particularly the single lecture or several lectures combined in a single pamphlet, had the largest circulation.

Soon after the founding of the *Association Polytechnique's* course on economics, the lectures began to appear in a series of small, low-priced pamphlets with the title, *Cours d'économie industrielle.* During the first year of the course, the *Association*

[68]Molinari, *Le mouvement socialiste,* 43.

[69] Duveau, *La vie ouvrière,* 456-458.

Polytechnique published six pamphlets, each containing three lectures. Statistics on the number printed are not available, but they probably had a considerable circulation.

An even greater effort was made to distribute printed versions of the Vincennes lectures among workers. Printing the lectures, said the director of the convalescent home, would allow other workers to profit from the "solid and brilliant" lessons given at Vincennes.[70] These printed lectures, which sold for twenty-five or thirty-five centimes, had a wide circulation, although Charles Robert, who lectured at Vincennes, probably exaggerated when he spoke of millions of copies.[71] In 1867, a report to the Minister of the Interior on the Vincennes lectures stated that the publishing house L. Hachette et Cie selected for publication the lectures it thought would be of most service to the working class, and printed them in editions of 5,000.[72] Not all of the printed lectures discussed economic or social questions, but of about 35 published at the time of the report, some 27 seem to have been in these areas.[73]

Some of the more formal and ambitious courses offered under the sponsorship of local organizations also appeared in print. At Lyons, Henri Dameth published several courses, including the first he offered in 1864-1865—a book of more than 500 pages subsidized by the Chamber of Commerce.[74] A. Rondelet, professor of

[70]Reboul-Daneyrol, *Aperçu historique sur l'asile et les conférences* (Paris, 1867), 67.

[71]Charles Robert, *Les améliorations sociales du Second Empire* (Paris, 1868), I, 29.

[72]*Conférences populaires*, 28 ff.

[73]Following are some of the titles: *Luxe et travail, L'Argent et ses critiques* (both by Baudrillart); *La Prévoyance et l'Epargne*; *L'Ouvrier autrefois et aujourd'hui*; *Des Erreurs et des préjugés populaires* (many of the prejudices are on economic questions); *La Vraie et la fausse égalité*; *Les Améliorations sociales du Second Empire*.

[74]Dameth, *Introduction à l'étude d'économie politique*. The second edition simply polished up the first edition which was a stenographic record of his course. Another of Dameth's published courses was entitled, *Le mouvement socialiste et l'économie politique* (Paris, 1869), 142 pp.

philosophy at the University of Clermont-Ferrand, and J.-B. Lescarret, Passy's successor at Bordeaux, also published their courses.[75]

In addition, a number of original textbooks or introductions to economics for workers appeared during the Second Empire. A text by J. J. Rapet, *Manuel de morale et d'économie politique à l'usage des classes ouvrières* (Paris, 1858), went through two editions. Its history, moreover, attests to the contemporary concern with economics for workers. Rapet's *Manuel* won the first prize of 10,000 francs in a competition opened by the *Académie des sciences morales et politiques* for a work on morality and economics accessible "to the laboring classes, to men who rarely and with difficulty dispose of a few moments of leisure."[76] The *Académie*'s report announcing the results of the competition stated that there were twenty-four entries, and that Rapet's work received the award because the best entry was at too high a level for workers.[77]

Authors of texts, lecturers, administrators of economics courses all admitted the need for making the "dismal science" interesting to worker students. A report on the lectures at Vincennes insisted that the *convalescent* workers at the institution did not lack intelligence and enthusiasm, but nevertheless urged lecturers to be clear and precise and cautioned that sometimes the attention

[75]Antonin Rondelet, *Petit manuel de l'économie politique* (Paris, Lyons, 1867), 282 pp. J.-B. Lescarret, *Conférences sur l'économie politique faites en 1867-68 à Bordeaux et à Bayonne* (Paris, 1869), 352 pp.

[76]A.-L. Duc de Broglie, "Rapport sur le concours Félix de Beaujour relatif au manuel de morale et d'économie politique," *Séances et travaux de l'Académie des Sciences morales et politiques*, v. 40 (1867), 161-162.

[77]Among the other texts for workers were: Antonin Rondelet, *Les Mémoires d'Antoine ou notions populaires de morale et d'économie politique* (Paris, 1860), a lengthy work of 342 pages; Henri Baudrillart, *La liberté du travail, l'association de la démocratie* (Paris, 1865); Otto Hubner, *Petit Manuel populaire d'économie politique* (Paris, 1861), translated from the German by a French economist, Charles Le Hardy de Beaulieu.

of the students drifted.[78] We have already seen that in a competition for an economics text for workers the best entry was disqualified because it was written on too high a level. Rapet, who won first prize in the contest, himself observed that most books for the lower classes seem to have been written for the well-to-do bourgeoisie; "they are . . . too grave, too abstract, too difficult to read."[79]

Lectures and printed material for workers were, therefore, usually simple, filled with anecdotes and analogies from daily life —and condescending. (More than one lecturer and writer interrupted his exposition to insist upon his lifelong devotion to the working class, to the *braves ouvriers*.) The popularizers borrowed freely from each other so that the same anecdotes, the same examples occurred again and again. It is interesting that many of the illustrative anecdotes came from farming or rural life, indicating how close workers during the Second Empire were to the soil.

Economics instructors sought to drive home the point of their lessons by dramatic analogies and by citing outstanding examples of "sane" economic behavior. A text compared the suffering of the poor during an economic crisis to the crew of a ship or the members of a desert caravan delayed by unanticipated conditions; in such a situation the captain or the leader of the caravan must reduce the rations of his men in order to keep them alive.[80] An analogy that one often encounters is that of the blind man and the paralyzed man, who alone are both helpless, but when the blind man lifts the paralyzed man onto his shoulders as a guide, the two get along very well. Spelling out the moral, one author adds: "Labor, capital, property, powerful and fecund motors, are unable to accomplish anything alone, but united

[78]*Conférences populaires*, 34.
[79]De Broglie, "Rapport sur le concours Félix de Beaujour," 172-173.
[80]Rondelet, *Petit Manuel*, 214.

nothing is beyond their capacity."[81] Another economist, Lescarret, called upon his readers to consider the case of a savage who has built and furnished a hut and procured weapons for himself. Doesn't the savage, demanded the author, have the right to use and dispose of his hut, furnishings, and weapons as he pleases? Forget the false doctrines that you may have heard, he wrote, and simply ask yourself if the individual who uses his labor and intelligence to transform an object to make it useful, does not have the right to it.[82] Lescarret, as well as others, cited approvingly a group of typographical workers, "men of their century," who had it in them to "salute progress" in the form of a new composing machine, even though it threatened their jobs.[83]

Some of the more ambitious economic texts sought to hold their readers' interest by means of a plot or narrative. There are, for example, few formal lessons in a work by A. Rondelet, *Les mémoires d'Antoine ou notions populaires de morale et d'économie* (Paris, 1860). The principles of morality and political economy emerge from the experiences and observations of Antoine, a carpenter and the fortunate possessor of all the virtues, who eventually becomes a successful entrepreneur. Entire chapters in Rondelet's work are intended only to hold the reader's interest. Antoine has last minute escapes, such as one from a disgruntled revolutionary who expounds upon the injustice of the wage system. The author exercised his ingenuity to discover new situations by which his point might be made evident in a dramatic way. Often conflicting views were presented in dialogue form with the "sane" view always impressing itself upon the auditors. Frequently a kind and sage employer set Antoine

---

[81]L. Wolowski, *Notions générales d'économie politique* (Paris, 1868), 36-37. This is a published lecture from Vincennes. On the title page we read of the author: "Membre de l'Institut, Professeur au Conservatoire des Arts et Métiers et à l'Association Polytechnique."

[82]Lescarret, *Conférences sur l'économie politique*, 68 ff.

[83]Lescarret, *Conférences sur l'économie politique*, 276-277.

straight as he was about to succumb to temptation or to a "demagogic" idea. Antoine concluded his memoirs with the assurance that every *"honnête homme"* could look forward to "the reign of justice and the triumph of labor."[84]

The *Manuel de moralité* by Rapet introduced a progressive and humanitarian physician who transformed his town from a poverty stricken to a prosperous community by observing the laws of economics. (The resemblance to Balzac's *Le médecin de campagne* is obvious.) When the good Doctor Dupré overheard some of the townspeople attacking the wealthy, he offered to instruct them in the laws governing society and the relations of men. Every other Sunday the Doctor spoke before an ever-growing audience of townspeople of all classes. The lessons were entirely informal; there were frequent interruptions, questions, objections. Among the auditors were skeptics and troublemakers: M. Gagelin, the pharmacist, a fluent speaker and a hothead; Basset, the disgruntled cabaret proprietor, who saw his customers drift away to Dupré's Sunday talks. Since the lessons described in the book were offered in 1846-1847, Doctor Dupré was able to use the severe economic crisis of these years as a springboard for some of his discussions. When in spite of his wise counsels, some of the inhabitants of the town became involved in a riot for which they were tried and condemned, Dupré was able to draw the moral: "May this example serve as a lesson and teach us what the penalty is for violating divine and human laws."[85]

It is difficult to evaluate the influence of economics lectures, courses, and printed materials on the French working class. In one sense they can be called an unqualified failure, since the French working class, particularly its most active members, has refused up to the present day to accept the doctrines of liberal

[84]Rondelet, *Les mémoires d'Antoine*, 339-340.
[85]Rapet, *Manuel de morale*, 365.

economics. The problem, however, of the immediate success of the effort remains. Did workers attend or read courses and materials on economics? How did those who did attend or read react? The evidence is slight: infrequent comments by those involved in adult education and by workers themselves.

Nevertheless, once we penetrate the professional optimism of official reports and the wishful optimism of the organizers of popular economics instruction, the general impression is of disappointment, both in the number of workers attending the courses and the impact of the lessons upon them. Newspapers sympathetic towards economics instruction for workers told of the crowds, including workers, who attended the courses offered by the *Association Polytechnique* and *Association Philotechnique*. An official report stated that large numbers of interested workers followed the speakers at Vincennes.[86] But Perdonnet complained that more employees and clerks attended the various courses of the *Association Polytechnique* than artisans or factory workers.[87] Before a worker audience in 1868, the economist Horn felt it necessary to deny that he had lectured at Vincennes.[88] The future Communard Lefrançais referred mockingly to the economists at Vincennes and to the "banality" and "platitudes" of the doctrine they taught.[89] As we have seen, many economists harbored doubts concerning the value of speaking at the public meetings of the last two years of the Empire. A newspaper account of the reception given to the economist Joseph Garnier shows that the grounds for these doubts were quite real. Garnier was greeted with shouts of: "He is an economist." "He is a Jesuit." "A bore (*endormeur*)." It took courage, said the article, to admit that one

[86]*Conférences populaires*, 33-35.

[87]Duveau, *La vie ouvrière*, 455.

[88]Vitu, *Les réunions publiques*, 42-44.

[89]Gustave Lefrançais, *Souvenirs d'un révolutionnaire* (Brussels, 1902), 296-297.

was an economist before a public meeting.[90] The Catholic social reformer, François Beslay, probably best summed up the attitude of French workers to instruction in economics. Beslay admired "those persons who demonstrate economic truths in writing, at workers meetings," but he doubted that the lectures and books had much influence: "All instruction from above is suspected by French workers; therefore it is ineffective."[91]

[90]*Le peuple*, February 18, 1869.
[91]J.-B. Duroselle, *Les débuts du Catholicisme sociale en France (1822-1870)* (Paris, 1951), 636.

CONCLUSION

An Evaluation of Government Propaganda

How effective was government propaganda among workers during the Second Empire? Certainly, from the vantage point of an
age like our own that is far more skilled in manipulating people
than was the nineteenth century, there were some very striking
shortcomings and weaknesses in government propaganda during
the Second Empire. Some of these failures were due to inexpe-
rience with the techniques of mass indoctrination; others were
the result of differences among public officials on the role and
the objectives of propaganda. In general, propaganda among
workers during the Second Empire was a pale reflection of Bonapartist propaganda in 1848. This was, in part, inevitable; after
Louis Napoleon's arrival in power his propaganda had to be
more restrained than it was during the years of opposition. Nevertheless, memories of 1848 persisted, and when, in the 1860's,
an Imperial official criticized the extent and the skill of government propaganda, he urged a return to the "primitive vitality"
of the Bonapartist party.[1]

An example of the failure of the government to heed the lessons of 1848 was its press policy. In the year of Revolution one of
the most effective media of Bonapartist propaganda had been
newspapers founded specifically for working class readers. I have
not, however, seen a single pro-government newspaper published

---

[1] A.N. BB[30] 387, *procureur général* at Rouen to the Minister of Justice, April 18,
1868.

for workers during the Second Empire. Although *L'Opinion nationale* and the short-lived *L'Espérance* appealed to workers, both newspapers were equally interested in the liberal bourgeoisie. In 1853, a periodical *Le Journal des Ateliers*, was founded "to enlighten, to moralize, and to instruct the working class," and although the only issue to be found at the *Bibliothèque nationale* (June 1) included a few items favorable towards the government, the journal apparently had a very brief existence.[2] In 1868, Chabaud referred to a newspaper, *L'Union ouvrière*, which could be obtained at his home, and we can assume from his background that it was pro-government; however, this newspaper, also, did not survive very long.[3]

Another weakness of Imperial propaganda was lack of coordination so that it sometimes worked at cross purposes. The Press Bureau of the Ministry of the Interior did not, for example, despite the efforts of the government, have complete control of propaganda in the newspapers. "Every official newspaper," wrote Taxile Delord, "had its backer (*inspirateur*); these statesmen, hidden behind the newspapers, fought each other like the gods of Homer hidden behind the clouds."[4] Haussmann, Rouher and, as we have seen, the Prince Napoleon had newspapers which spoke for them. The Minister of the Interior Persigny twice issued warnings (*avertissements*) to newspapers for articles submitted by one of his fellow ministers.[5] On another occasion, he criticized ministers who permitted the press to attack the government but not themselves.[6]

Another reason for the contradictions of government propaganda was the fear of some ministers and officials that the new

[2]B.N. Lc² 21955.

[3]A.N. 45 AP⁶ (dossier 4), "Papiers de Rouher."

[4]Taxile Delord, *Histoire illustrée du Second Empire* (1880-1883), III, 288.

[5]Emile Ollivier, *L'Empire libéral* (Paris, 1895-1915), IX, 175-176.

[6]*Mémoires du duc de Persigny* (Paris, 1896), 400.

propaganda of the 1860's would incite class hatred and alienate upper class supporters of the regime. Thus, in an analysis of the 1863 elections to the *Corps législatif*, the *procureur général* at Aix criticized the campaign tactics of the defeated official candidate for his demagogy.[7] During the campaign, he wrote, "committees composed of workers or other men of little importance organized to support him had posted proclamations whose violence and impatience injured the cause that they claimed to serve." If such tactics had gained a few votes for the official candidate, they had lost him many more "among the men with influence and authority." The Minister of the Interior informed his liberal colleague, Victor Duruy, that he could not insert in the *Moniteur* a speech that the latter had made before workers attending the *Association Philotechnique* because it expressed "ideas contrary to the policy of the government."[8] The Prince Napoleon had to enlist the aid of Rouher and the Emperor himself to overcome the reluctance of the Prefect of Police Boitelle to permit workers to assemble and elect delegates to the London Exposition of 1862.[9] "I would rather have the law against associations repealed than see this trip [of workers to the Exposition]," objected the Prefect of Police. And even after he was finally forced to authorize meetings to elect delegates, he assured the worker Tolain that if he were master such things would not be permitted.[10] The difficulties of *L'Opinion nationale* with the administration also reveal the fear that the new propaganda would increase worker discontent rather than gain their support

7A.N. BB30 427, "Elections," *procureur général* at Aix to the Minister of Justice, June 8, 1863.

8Ollivier, *L'Empire libéral*, VII, 294. Ollivier adds the piquant detail that Duruy after listening very patiently to this colleague's objections produced a copy of his speech with the Empress' comment, "*Discours très politique.*"

9*Bibliothèque de l'Institut*, "Archives Le Play," letter of Prince Napoleon to Le Play (no date).

10E. E. Fribourg, *L'Association internationale des travailleurs* (Paris, 1871), 149.

for the regime. A file on *L'Opinion nationale* includes numerous letters from officials protesting against articles, news items, and letters printed by the newspaper.[11] The opposition of fearful officials also probably explains the frustrations of Lévy and Hugelmann. In a letter to Napoleon III, Lévy complained that, despite the favorable opinion of the Emperor, he had not received authorization to move his newspaper to Paris.[12] An official report urged the government to condemn Hugelmann's manifestos, speeches, and organization, activities that tended "to agitate the mass of workers and to arouse their hatred against the wealthy."[13] Hugelmann later charged that his effort to found a Bonapartist newspaper in the Department of the Gironde had been sabotaged by the prefect.[14]

Many officials, for whom memories of 1848 remained fresh, distrusted all workers, even those loyal to the Empire. In October 1861, the Minister of the Interior sent the Palais Royal brochure, *L'Organisation des travailleurs par les corporations nouvelles,* to the Minister of Justice for action, calling his attention to "the eminently socialist tendency of this publication."[15] The Minister of Justice replied that although the brochure contained "socialist ideas," its language was moderate and it did not violate any laws.[15a] Nevertheless, he suggested to his colleague that it might be advisable to forbid the sale of the brochure and others like it that were now at the publishers. He also advised keeping an eye on the workers who had signed the brochure and on the organi-

[11] A.N. F18 396. "*L'Opinion nationale.*" The newspaper's difficulties were due as much to its anti-clericalism and its ardent support of the cause of Italian nationalism as to its policy on workers' questions.

[12] A.N. F18 281, June 30, 1861.

[13] A.N. 45 AP6, "Note sur l'activité de la Société nationale pour l'extinction du paupérisme."

[14] B.N. Lb56 2007, Gabriel Hugelmann, *Vérité* (Paris, 1868), 20-21.

[15] A.N. BB18 1640 (A3 5713), Ministry of Justice, October 10, 1861.

[15a] A.N. BB 18 1640 (A3 5713), Ministry of Justice, October 16, 1861.

zation that they had formed. A report of the *Cour Impériale* at
Paris stated that A. Bazin, the contributor to the *"Chroniques
ouvrières"* and admirer of Napoleon III, had been fined 100
francs and costs on the charge that his brochure, *Deux questions
ouvrières* "excited hate and contempt of citizens for each other."[16]

The most serious weakness of government propaganda during
the Second Empire was its irregularity. It reached heights of in-
tensity in periods of crises, but when more normal conditions returned, government propaganda became relatively sparse and
colorless. At the time of the *Coup d'état*, during electoral periods,
and when worker opposition to the regime became very overt,
government propagandists were especially industrious. But in
the longer periods between there was not that constant hammer-
ing at the working class that twentieth century totalitarian regimes have learned is so necessary.

More impressive, however, than the weaknesses of Imperial
propaganda was the fact that contemporaries were well aware of
them. In fact, no better evidence exists that the age of propaganda
had arrived than the nature of the suggestions and programs for
more extensive and effective propaganda made by publicists and
officials during the Second Empire.

Many of these suggestions came from journalists and were not
always disinterested.[17] One journalist criticized the government
for not doing more to win the support of workers, especially since
this support could be won by whatever group made the greatest
effort to do so, something which the opposition understood very

16A.N. BB18 1647 (A3 6476), March 7, 1862; A.N. BB30 455, "Procès de presse,"
April 5, 1862.

17The editor of a provincial newspaper, after insisting upon the need for more
effective propaganda to combat "prejudices, errors in education, evil passions, ignorance," urged more government subsidies for loyal newspapers. B.N. Lb56 1230,
Amadée Matagrin, *De la nécessité d'une presse gouvernementale et des moyens de
l'organiser librement pour la défense de l'ordre social des institutions et de la politique impériale* (Périgueux, 1862).

well.[18] Specifically, he suggested that government newspapers devote more space to articles on institutions for workers.

Government officials involved in propaganda, particularly employees of the Press Bureau, were constantly seeking to improve communications with and to increase the influence of government newspapers. Thus, a memorandum of December 7, 1859, recommended that the administration provide a line ("*mot d'ordre*") on every issue that arose.[19] The Prefect of the Department of the Nord advised the government to take advantage of "the passion for reading of our young workers" by publishing low-priced and interesting material "for their moralization."[20] The *procureur général* at Lyons approved of the idea behind the *Moniteur du Soir*; a low-priced, well-edited newspaper, could be useful among the people.[21] However, the new government newspaper, he objected, failed to meet these tests; the form of type, the articles, the editors were poorly chosen.

The most remarkable and far-reaching program for the improvement of government propaganda was the work of the *procureur général* at Rouen who, in a series of reports to the Minister of Justice, outlined a plan for an all pervasive propaganda employing the entire state apparatus. In the first of these reports, in April 1866, the *procureur général* proposed a plan to combat the successes of the opposition.[22] The plan called for the cooperation of officials at all the levels of government. On the local level,

---

[18]A.N. 45 APIII (no date but probably in the late 1860's): "En ce moment, nos ouvriers seront à qui voudra et saura les prendre. Certains partisans politiques le comprennent fort bien, et, par leurs journaux s'y appliquent. Mais les amis du gouvernement semblent croire que la publication des actes populaires du gouvernement suffise; c'est une erreur."

[19]A.N. F18 310, "Division de la presse."

[20]A.N. F1c III, Nord 8, prefect to the Minister of the Interior, April 6, 1858.

[21]A.N. BB30 379, *procureur général* at Lyons to the Minister of Justice, July 3, 1864.

[22]A.N. BB30 387, April 13, 1866.

the mayors should continually propagate "dynastic ideas" by words and example. The sub-prefect must always be accessible to the people and preside over all kinds of meetings, such as municipal councils, organizations of firemen, choral societies, and mutual aid societies. He also urged the government to found low-priced, popular newspapers and suggested the kind of material that they should print: historical novels based upon the two Napoleonic Empires, news items, and a little politics, clearly and interestingly presented ("simple formulas and facts"). The Emperor's works should be distributed in large numbers through school and communal book stores. "In a word," summed up the *procureur général,* "all the forces which the government has at its command united and put into operation to maintain dynastic loyalty in the masses."

The following year the *procureur général* again complained of the inadequacies of government propaganda.[23] Because of its regularity the influence of the press was particularly important:

Every day and year on end the newspaper followed the subscriber, brought him its opinions ready made and without contradiction, repeated them in all ways and at every turn; the newspaper penetrated and succeeded in dominating the subscriber without his becoming aware of it. This imperceptible propaganda, whether by the written or spoken word, is the only really effective kind.

The government, he insisted, had the means to carry on such a campaign of "imperceptible propaganda," and it was a great fault not to have understood it. For fifteen years, he objected, the government had done nothing except on the eve of elections. Between elections no one sought to create "day by day and man by man a Napoleonic party united by interests and ideas, capable of opposing the progress of the opposition and reacting spontaneously to it." He also criticized government officials who enclosed

[23]A.N. BB[30] 387, April 7, 1867.

themselves in their homes rather than entering into close relations with the working masses and seeking to create among them a Bonapartist nucleus.

In another report, the *procureur général* urged Bonapartists "to descend into the electoral arena, to defend themselves by the press, by the spoken word, by public meetings, by all the means which arouse men, confirm them in their faith and render that faith contagious."[24] He reminded the government of the vast resources in personnel available to it for propaganda: primary school teachers, tax collectors, firemen, and other civil servants. And he again called upon government officials to work in associations of all kinds: agricultural committees, recreational associations, mutual aid societies. The *procureur général* also repeated his demand for a cheap popular press and recommended that the government subsidize newspapers for the different occupational groups.

When one looks at Bonapartist propaganda in its nineteenth century context, it is impressive both for the consciousness and determination with which the government set out to gain the loyalty of workers, and for its skillful use of the available media. It was, after all, a pioneering effort in the new field of mass indoctrination. Government officials and publicists made no secret of their belief that in the age of universal manhood suffrage the survival of the regime depended upon popular support.

Although there was not yet a "science" of propaganda, the publicists of the Second Empire had already arrived at some of the basic principles of mass indoctrination. They perceived that affirmations were more effective than discussion, that a simple statement or phrase was more convincing than a reasoned argument. They recognized the cumulative effect of repetition, and striking phrases from the works or speeches of the Emperor ap-

[24]A.N. BB[30] 387, April 8, 1868.

peared everywhere. Government propagandists also sought to satisfy popular curiosity concerning the personality and activities of the ruler, and understood the appeal of "human interest stories." They learned, particularly during the 1860's, to vary their message with the audience. This message had something for the politically naive worker who was satisfied by assurances that the government was charitable and kindly disposed towards him, as well as for the more thoughtful worker who read the serious journals, discussed the economic and social problems of his class, and who leaned towards republicanism. It was a relatively mobile propaganda, capable of changing with the political and economic policy of the government, and with new issues as they developed.

Bibliography

Research in an area like propaganda imposes a sampling technique rather than a careful survey of all the relevant sources. It was impossible, for example, to examine more than a small fraction of the newspapers and journals, both government and opposition, which, at one time or another, during the Second Empire published Imperial propaganda.

Materials are grouped under the following headings:

I. Bibliographies and Bibliographical Articles.

II. Works and Correspondence of Napoleon III.

III. Archival Material.

IV. Newspapers

V. Contemporary Pamphlets, Placards, and Handbills.

VI. Works by Contemporaries (memoirs, biographies, correspondence, articles, books).

VII. Secondary Works.

I. Bibliographies and Bibliographical Articles

Bourgin, Georges, "Bibliography of the French Press," *Bulletin of the International Committee of Historical Sciences*. Paris, 1934, 26-70; 109.

Dolléans, E., and Crozier, M., *Mouvements ouvrier et socialiste. Chronologie et bibliographie. Angleterre, France, Allemagne, Etats-Unis 1750-1918*. Paris, 1950.

Dunham, Arthur L., "The Economic History of France 1815-1870," *The Journal of Modern History*, XXI (1949), 121-139.

Hatin, Eugène, *Bibliographie historique et critique de la presse périodique française*. Paris, 1866.

Leuilliot, Paul, "Histoire industrielle et ouvrière de la France," *Revue de synthèse*, 63-64, "Nouvelle série" 22-23 (1948), 155-175.

———, "Recent French Writings in the Social and Economic History of Modern France," *The Economic History Review*, Second Series I (1948), 61-72.

Schnerb, Robert, "Napoleon III and the Second French Empire," *The Journal of Modern History*, VIII (1936), 338-355.

II. Works and Correspondence of Napoleon III

Much of Louis Napoleon's correspondence was lost in the disturbances of 1870-1871. According to Emerit *(Lettres de Napoléon III à Madame Cornu*, I, 139), the Emperor also purchased and destroyed some of the letters written before his arrival in power, particularly to the republican Joly and the journalist Degeorge. Correspondence in the hands of Napoleon's descendants is still largely unavailable to scholars.

Duchon, Paul, "Les élections de 1848 d'après les correspondances inédites du prince Napoléon et de M. de Persigny," *Revue de Paris*, 1936 (VII) 30-60; 381-410.

Emerit, Marcel, *Lettres de Napoléon III à Madame Cornu*. Paris, 1937, 2 v.

Fleury, Comte, "Napoléon III, Correspondance inédite avec Madame Cornu," *La Revue hebdomadaire*, 1906-1907.

Hauterive, Ernest d', *Napoléon III et le prince Napoléon, correspondance inédite*. Paris, 1925.

Oeuvres de Napoléon III, 5 v. Paris, 1856-1869. This official collection includes works, newspaper articles, and correspondence by Louis Napoleon before 1848, and public statements and correspondence after his arrival in power.

Peauger, Marc, "Lettres du fort de Ham," *La nouvelle revue* (1894).

The Secret of the Coup d'Etat. An Unpublished Correspondence of Prince Louis Napoleon, M.M. de Morny, de Flahaut, and others, 1848 to 1852. Edited by the Earl of Kerry. London, 1924.

III. ARCHIVAL MATERIAL

ARCHIVES NATIONALES

BB³⁰ 367-BB³⁰ 396. Reports of the *procureurs généraux* to the Minister of Justice.

These reports on public opinion, and the economic and political situation of the country, prepared by the *procureur general* at each court of appeals, were submitted regularly throughout the Empire, first, each month, then twice a year, and after 1858, three times a year. The reports vary in quality. Some are quite perfunctory, and the *procureurs* repeat themselves in report after report. Others, however, took the reports more seriously, and their conscientious accounts are among the most useful sources for the history of the Second Empire. The government attached considerable importance to the reports, summaries of which were prepared for the Emperor.

I have examined reports from courts of appeal in the following areas, all of which contained sizable agglomerations of workers:

BB³⁰ 370. Aix (includes Departments of Bouches du-Rhône, Var, Basses Alpes).

BB³⁰ 376. Colmar (includes Departments of Haut-Rhin and Bas-Rhin).

BB³⁰ 377. Douai (includes Departments of Nord and Pas-de-Calais).

BB³⁰ 378. Grenoble (includes Departments of l'Isère, Drôme, Hautes-Alpes).

BB³⁰ 379. Lyon (includes Departments of Rhône and Loire).

BB³⁰ 383-384. Paris (includes Departments of l'Aube, Eure et Loire, Marne, Seine et Marne, Seine et Oise, l'Yonne, Seine).

BB³⁰ 387. Rouen (includes Departments of Seine-Inférieure and l'Eure).

BB³⁰ 388. Toulouse (includes Departments of Tarn, Tarn et Garonne, Ariège).

BB³⁰ 367. "Circulaires, notes et pièces diverses relatives aux rapports politiques des *procureurs généraux*."

F¹ᶜ III. Correspondence of the prefects with the Minister of the Interior concerning public opinion, elections and specific questions.

Similar to the *procureurs'* reports to the Minister of Justice, these reports seem to have been more hastily prepared and are less useful than the former. I have examined reports from the following Departments:

Bouches-du-Rhône, Haut-Rhin, Isère, Nord, Pas-de-Calais, Rhône, Seine-Inférieure.

AB XIX 159-178. "Papiers des Tuileries."

A vast miscellany of reports, correspondence, personal files, demands for aid, etc. A commission established by the Government of National Defense (see section on printed archival materials) published a selection from the papers. Material by Napoleon III, published by the Commission, has, however, disappeared from the Archives.

45 AP. "Papiers de Rouher."

The papers of the Minister Rouher, who in the 1860's was called the Vice-Emperor, include both personal and official documents. They were removed to Germany after the war of 1870, and returned to France by the Treaty of Versailles. Of the twenty-four cartons, I found the following most useful:

> I. Notes of meetings of the Council of Ministers, 1865-1868.
>
> III. Included a file on the newspaper, *L'Etendard.*
>
> IV. Included a report on a newspaper founded by the Bonapartist worker Chabaud.
>
> V. Elections of 1863; police reports of public meetings in 1869.
>
> VI. Coalitions law; studies after passage of law.

F^{18}. The Press.

> F^{18} 10^c. File on *Moniteur des Communes.*
>
> F^{18} 277 and 281. Personal files in the Bureau of the Press; included dossiers on Hugelmann and Lévy.
>
> F^{18} 295. "Tirage des journaux politiques de Paris," 1852-1867.
>
> F^{18} 306. Press subventions, mostly for the years 1862-1863.
>
> F^{18} 307. "Presses départementales subvention," mostly for the years 1869-1870.

F^{18} 310. "Division de la Presse. Personnel et gratification. Travail des bureaux," 1847-1887.

F^{18} 319. File on *Avenir national.*

F^{18} 329. File on *Le Constitutionnel.*

F^{18} 350. Files on several newspapers.

F^{18} 396. File on *L'Opinion nationale,* including authorization reports of Prefect of Police, protests against articles by officials and magistrates, *avertissements* (warnings).

F^{18} 417. File on *Le Siècle.*

F^{18} 549. File on the newspaper *L'Espérance.*

BB^{18} 1471 (A 6703). "Manifestations, placards, etc. à l'occasion de l'élection du Président de la République."

BB^{18} 1567. "Elections législatives de 1857."

BB^{18} 1640 (A 35713). File on Palais Royal brochure, *L'organisations des travailleurs par les corporations nouvelles.*

BB^{18} 1644 (A 36166). Letter from Charles and A. Havas protesting against the organization of a rival press service.

BB^{18} 1647 (A 36476). File on brochure by Bonapartist worker, Bazin, *Deux questions ouvrières.*

BB^{30} 335. Correspondence of Minister of Justice on *Le Moniteur des Communes,* 1851-1852.

BB^{30} 366. "Affaires politiques diverses." Includes police reports for Emperor and Minister of the Interior on public opinion and activities of the opposition.

BB^{30} 393-423. "Série politique." Includes many reports on political opposition to regime, and on elections and plebiscites.

BB^{30} 426-430. Includes materials on elections.

BB³⁰ 455. "Pièces diverses concernant le plébiscite (1870)";
"Questions de presse. Pièces diverses (1850-1870)." "Procès de presse. Insertion au *Moniteur* (1858-1870)."

BB³⁰ 759. "Imprimerie nationale, histoire, règlement, organisation et gestion: dossier général (1787-1878)."

BIBLIOTHEQUE DE L'INSTITUT

Archives Le Play. The papers of the Catholic social reformer,
Frédéric Le Play, have only recently been deposited with the *Institut,* and an inventory was not yet available. Most interesting of
the six cartons in the *Archives* was one with letters from the
Prince Napoleon, some of them on the workers' delegations to
the London Exposition of 1862.

PRINTED ARCHIVAL MATERIAL

Bernard, Paul, "Le mouvement ouvrier en France pendant les
années 1852-1864 d'après les rapports politiques des *procureurs généraux.* Documents inédits." *International Review for Social History* IV (1939), 231-279. Excerpts from the
regular reports of the *procureurs généraux.*

Papiers et correspondance de la famille impériale. Paris, 1870-
1872, 2v. Published by the commission established by the
Government of National Defense and based upon the "Papiers des Tuileries." Many other selections from the "Papiers
des Tuileries" were printed commercially in 1870 and 1871.
Usually they repeat the documents in the official collection
from which they were probably taken. Some of the titles were
quite sensational, and the works went through numerous
editions, for example, B.N. Lb⁵⁶. 481. *Les documents secrets
du cabinet de Badinguet et du gouvernement du Bas-Empire*
(1851-1870), 8th ed. Brussels 1871. Badinguet was a con-
temptuous nickname for Napoleon III.

IV. Newspapers

I have consulted the following newspapers, paying particular attention to issues dealing with significant events and problems, elections, workers' delegations to London, discussion of coalitions law, etc.

Le Capital. A Bonapartist newspaper founded in 1839; disappeared in 1840.

Le Constitutionnel. "Journal politique, littéraire universel."

Démocratie napoléonienne. First issue January 27, 1852; on February 21, title changed to *La France napoléonienne*; disappeared after March 21, 1852.

L'Ecole du peuple. "Journal hebdomadaire. Histoire, littérature, sciences, agriculture, droit public, hygiène, arts industriels." Edited by a committee of workers, but apparently had no connection with the government.

La France. A weekly; appeared September 3, 1857-December 1861.

L'Espérance. "Journal international quotidien," Armand Lévy's journal.

L'Etincelle. Editor Florian Pharaon.

Le Moniteur universel.

Le Moniteur universel du soir (appeared 1864).

L'Opinion nationale.

La Patrie.

Le Pays.

La Petit journal.

Le peuple.

La Revue de l'Empire. Authorized to discuss political and social questions on December 14, 1862.

A l'Empereur Napoléon III. Manifeste des ouvriers. Paris, n.d. An appeal to the Emperor for reforms.

Anselme, M., *Les idées de l'Empereur Napoléon III.* Paris, 1863. A poem in praise of the Emperor by an inspector of primary instruction.

Arrivée de S.M. l'Emperor à Lyon. Secours aux victimes de l'inondation. Lyon, 1856. A four-page account of an Imperial visit.

Association fraternelle. Comité napoléonien. Paris, n.d., placard.

Auprès de la villa Eugénie. L'Ange de l'avenir. Bayonne, 1858. In praise of the Empress.

Aux électeurs. La Guillotière, n.d., placard.

Aux ouvriers de la maison Guérin et Jouault. A letter to the employees of the firm urging vote for government candidates.

Baudrillart, H., *Luxe et travail.* Paris, 1866. This and the following brochure are lectures in the "Conférences populaires faites à l'asile impériale de Vincennes sous le patronnage de S.M. l'Impératrice."

———, *La propriété.* Paris, 1867.

Bazin, A., *L'Opposition, le Gouvernement et les classes ouvrières.* Paris, 1865. By a worker friendly to the Empire.

Bibliothèque Nationale. Le[77]. 1 to Le[77]. 443. This is a bound collection of electoral placards, programs, and brochures for the years 1852-1859. Similar material for elections after 1859 may be found in the following cartons:

$$
\begin{array}{ll}
30\text{—Le}^{64}. & 1237\text{—Le}^{77}. 606 \text{ A} \\
31\text{—Le}^{77}. & 608\text{—Le}^{77}. 883 \\
32\text{—Le}^{77}. & 884\text{—Le}^{77}. 1096 \\
33\text{—Le}^{77}. & 1097\text{—Le}^{77}. 2863
\end{array}
$$

L.-*Napoléon Bonaparte. Fondation d'une caisse de retraite en faveur des manufactures nationales, telles que Sèvres, les Gobelins, et Beauvais.* Paris, n.d. (probably 1852). A propaganda placard.

Brillard, Norbert, *Le groupe de l'Empereur à l'Exposition universelle.* Paris, n.d. (probably 1867).

Brochures ouvrières.

A l'Empereur, les cahiers populaires I. Paris, 1861.

A l'Empereur, les cahiers populaires II. Paris, 1861.

Coutant (ouvrier typographe), *Du salaire des ouvriers compositeurs. Tarif des prix de main d'oeuvre.* Paris, 1861.

Les délégations ouvrières à l'Exposition universelle de Londres en 1862. Paris, 1862.

Des intérêts typographiques devant la conférence mixte. Des maitres imprimeurs et des ouvriers compositeurs. Paris, 1861.

L'Organisation des travailleurs par les corporations nouvelles. Paris, 1861.

Le peuple, l'Empereur et les anciens partis. Paris, 1861.

Voeux et besoins des ouvriers corroyeurs. Paris, 1862.

Candidature de Louis Napoléon Bonaparte. (Paris, 1848). One-page electoral statement.

Chevalier, Michel, *Question des travailleurs.* Paris, 1843.

Clémence et bienfaits de S.M. Napoléon III, Empereur des Français. Paris, n.d. (probably 1853).

Comité des ouvriers de Paris et de la banlieue. Proclamation de l'Empire. Paris, 1852. A propaganda placard containing a letter of congratulations to the Emperor and his reply.

Comité électoral napoléonien. Lyons, n.d. Placard.

Conférences populaires sous le patronage de S.M. l'Impératrice. Paris, 1867.

Cours d'économie industrielle. Paris, 1866-1868. These are series 1, 5 and 6 of the courses offered by *l'Association Polytechnique.*

Coutant, A., *Les candidatures ouvrières.* Paris, 1869. Pamphlet.

————. *A M.M. les électeurs du départment de la Somme.* Péronne, 1848. Electoral placard.

————. *Organisation du travail. Discussion entre le Journal Le Globe et un ouvrier typographe.* Paris, 1844. Pamphlet.

————. *Propriété et travail association.* Paris, 1868. Pamphlet.

Détails sur le voyage de S.A. le prince Louis-Napoléon Bonaparte. Lyons, n.d. (probably 1852). Propaganda placard.

Discours de S.M. l'Empereur prononcé au Conseil d'Etat en faveur de la classe ouvrière pour la suppression des livrets d'ouvriers. Paris, 1869.

Discours de M. le Président de la République sur les améliorations à apporter au bien-être des classes ouvrières. Paris, n.d. (Probably 1850.)

Distribution des prix aux élèves réunis des deux associations polytechniques. Paris, 1862.

Distribution solennelle des prix-Napoléon aux ouvriers les plus méritants de l'agriculture et de l'industrie de la Loire. Saint-Etienne, 1857. An eight-page propaganda brochure.

Durand, Jacques, *Mémoire adressé à la réunion générale des coupeurs et brochures en chaussure de la ville de Paris.* Paris, n.d. (probably after 1864). Durand, a radical and anti-clerical worker who fought in the Commune, seems to have been pro-Empire.

Duval, Jules, *Les sociétés coopératives de production*. Paris, 1867. A course offered at the convalescent home for workers at Vincennes.

Election du président de la République. Paris, 1848. A placard.

Essai de conciliation, des démocrates républicains avec les démocrates napoléoniens. Paris, 1865. Pamphlet.

La France nouvelle. Clémence et bienfaits de S.M. Napoléon III. Paris, n.d. (probably 1853). A large placard containing excerpts from *Le Moniteur*.

Histoire et bienfaits de Sa Majesté Napoléon III Empereur des français. Avignon, 1859. Twelve pages.

Hugelmann, G., *Le Panthéon du travail. M. Rouher*. Paris, 1866. Pamphlet.

————. *Le Salut c'est la dynastie*. Paris, 1870. Pamphlet.

————. *Vérité*. Paris, 1868. Pamphlet.

Invalides civils de France, fondés par l'initiative nationale. Paris, 1867. Pamphlet concerning Hugelmann's organization.

Laity, Armand, *Relation historique des évènements du 30 octobre 1836. Le Prince Napoléon à Strasbourg*. Paris, 1836.

Lefèvre, André, *Les finances particulières de Napoléon III. D'après les documents recueillis aux Tuileries pendant le siège de Paris (Septembre 1870-Février 1871)*. Paris, 1873.

Lévy, Armand and Valleton, Henri (Présidents de club), *Démocratie sociale*. Paris, 1849. Brochure in favor of the Social Republic.

———— ————, (Présidents de club), *Les émeutiers! Les deux lundis*. Paris, n.d. (probably 1849). Two pages.

Lévy, Armand, *La loi contre les coalitions et la liberté des travailleurs*. Paris, 1864. Against coalitions law.

————, *Mémoire pour les ouvriers typographes*. Paris, 1862. Defense of printers tried for violations of the coalitions law.

Martin, Jean. *Les travailleurs et le plébiscite*. Bordeaux, 1870. This was in a carton: "Pièces diverses concernant le plébiscite (1870)." A plea for a "yes" vote in the 1870 plebiscite.

Matagrin, Amédée, *De la nécessité d'une presse gouvernementale et des moyens de l'organiser librement pour la défense de l'ordre social, des institutions et de la politique impériales.* Périgeux, 1862.

Les murailles révolutionnaires de 1848. 17th ed. Paris, 1868. Posters of the year of Revolution.

Perdonnet, Auguste, *De l'utilité de l'instruction pour le peuple.* Paris, 1867.

————, *Notice sur les associations polytechnique et philotechnique.* Paris, 1867.

Pose de la première pierre de l'asile impérial de Vincennes pour les ouvriers convalescents. Paris, 1855. A placard.

Reboul-Daneyrol, *Aperçu historique sur l'asile et les conférences.* Paris, 1867.

Régnault, *Recueil de proclamations, manifestes et discours du prince L. Napoléon Bonaparte.* Imprimerie des ouvriers associés. Bordeaux, 1852. Pamphlet.

Relation du passage de Louis-Napoléon dans la Meurthe à l'occasion de l'inauguration du chemin de fer de Paris à Strasbourg. Juillet, 1852. Nancy, 1852.

Relation du voyage de Son Altesse Impériale Monseigneur le prince Louis Napoléon dans le midi de la France. Paris, n.d. Placard.

Réponse de Louis-Napoléon Bonaparte. Paris, 1848. Pamphlet also published at the workers' suburb of Lyons, La Guillotière.

Ribeyre, Félix, *Voyage en Lorraine*. Paris, 1867.

Richard, Albert et Blanc, Gaspard, *L'Empire et la France nouvelle. Appel du peuple et de la jeunesse à la conscience française*. Brussels, 1872. Richard, one of the founders of the International at Lyons and a refugee after the Commune, urges a restoration of the Empire and lauds Napoleon III. He later abandoned Bonapartism.

Robert, Charles, *Les améliorations sociales du Second Empire*. 2 v. Paris, 1868. Courses offered at the convalescent home at Vincennes. A good enumeration of the accomplishments of the Second Empire in favor of the working class.

————, *Considérations générales sur le groupe X*. Paris, 1868. Concerning the section on paternalistic activities at the Paris Exposition of 1867.

————, *Enquête ouverte par la réunion des bureaux du 10ème groupe de l'Exposition Universelle de 1867 sur les institutions crées par les chefs d'industrie en faveur de leurs·ouvriers*. Paris, 1866. Reprinted from *Le Moniteur*.

S.M. Napoléon III à Lyon. Lyons, 1865.

Séjour à Lyon du Prince-Président. Cérémonies et fêtes. Lyons, 1852. Four pages.

Société nationale pour l'extinction du paupérisme. Compte-rendu de la séance extraordinaire du 9 Septembre 1866 et de l'installation des bureaux d'arrondissement. Paris, 1866. This and the following brochure, both intended for public distribution, were in the "Papiers de Rouher."

Société nationale pour l'extinction du paupérisme. Assemblée générale de Février, 1867. Paris, 1867.

Soirées populaires. Lettre adressée par Sa Majesté l'Empereur Napoléon III à son Ministre d'Etat en faveur de la classe ouvrière. Paris, 1866. Eight pages.

Tréfu, *Un ouvrier à ses frères de Paris*. Paris, 1858. Scolds Parisian workers for their indifference towards Orsini assassination attempt.

Visite du prince Louis Napoléon faite aux métiers de tissage à Elbeuf. Bordeaux, 1852. Four pages.

Voyage de Leurs Majestés l'Empereur et l'Impératrice dans les départements du nord. Paris, 1867. Twenty pages, illustrated.

Voyage de Louis Napoléon en France. Paris, 1849. A placard.

Voyage de Loüis Napoléon en Sologne. Bourges, 1852. A pamphlet.

Wolowski, L. *Notions générales d'économie politique*. Paris, 1868.

VI. Works by Contemporaries

Albiot, J., *Annales du Second Empire. Les campagnes électorales (1851-1869)*. Paris, 1869. An interesting account of Imperial elections; propaganda, pressure, repression.

Ambès, Baron d', *Intimate memoirs of Napoleon III*. Tr. 2 v. London, n.d. By the Senator Heeckeren, an intimate of Napoleon III. Although not always reliable and apologetic, important because of Heeckeren's interest in economic and social questions. Insists upon Napoleon III's preoccupation with the social problem. It was Heeckeren who killed the poet Pushkin in a duel.

Audiganne, A., *Mémoires d'un ouvrier de Paris, 1871-1872*. Paris, 1873. Prepared from notes by a foreman, Pierre Bruno. The views of Bruno are very much like Audiganne's; he is moderate and opposed to vague formulas for social reform.

——, *Les populations ouvrières et les industries de la France*. 2nd ed. 2 v. Paris, 1860. A survey of the condition of labor and industry. An important source of information by a quite conservative observer.

Aumale, Henri d'Orléans, duc d', *Ecrits politiques (1861-1868)*. Brussels, 1868. Includes the *Lettre sur l'histoire de France adressée au prince Napoléon*.

Barrot, Odilon, *Mémoires posthumes*. 4 v. Paris, 1875. Useful for relations with Louis Napoleon before 1848 and during the Second Republic. Includes revealing comment by Louis Napoleon on *Extinction du paupérisme*.

Bavoux, Evariste, *La France sous Napoléon III. L'Empire et le régime parlementaire*. 2 v. Paris, 1870. A collection of author's writings, largely from various journals.

Blanc, J.-J., "Les hommes et les souris." *Almanach de la coopération* (1870), 96-102.

Blanc, Louis, *Histoire de dix ans (1830-1840)*. 5 v. Paris, 1846. An indispensable and still interesting work.

————, *1848: Historical Revelations: Inscribed to Lord Normanby*. London, 1858. Written in English. Interesting to us for Blanc's account of his relations with Louis Napoleon.

Blanqui, Jérôme Adolphe, *Des classes ouvrières en France pendant l'année 1848*. 2 v. in one. Paris, 1849. Results of a study for *L'Académie des Sciences Morales et Politiques*. An indispensable survey of the condition of the working class.

Broglie, A.-L. Duc de, "Rapport sur le concours Félix de Beaujour relatif au manuel de morale et d'économie politique," *Séances et travaux de l'Académie des Sciences morales et politiques*. v. 4 (1857).

Castille, Hippolyte, *M. Baroche*. Paris, 1859. An Imperialist publicist with an eye to "human interest" stories.

————, *M. Achille Fould*. Paris, 1859.

————, *E. de Girardin*. Paris, 1858.

————, *Les journaux et les journalistes depuis 1848 jusqu' aujourd'hui*. Paris, 1858.

————, *Les Frères Péreire.* Paris, 1861.

————, *M. de Morny.* Paris, 1859.

————, *Napoléon III, Empereur des français.* Paris, 1856.

————, *Le prince Napoléon.* Paris, 1859.

————, *Le-vicomte de la Guéronnière.* Paris, 1860.

Chevalier, Michel, *Cours d'économie politique fait au Collège de France.* 2nd ed. Paris, 1855.

————, *L'exposition universelle de 1862.* Paris, 1862.

————, *Exposition universelle de 1867. Rapports du jury international. Introduction.* Paris, 1868.

Corbon, A., *Le secret du peuple de Paris.* Paris, 1863. An extremely interesting description of the ideas of the Parisian working class, particularly the new attitude towards reform which emerged in the 1860's.

Correspondence and Conversations of Alexis de Tocqueville with Nassau William Senior from 1834 to 1859, ed. by M. C. M. Simpson. 2 v. London, 1872. Tocqueville's observations on Louis Napoleon and the Second Empire are interesting, but it should be kept in mind that he was a foe of the regime.

Dabot, Henri, *Souvenirs et impressions d'un bourgeois du quartier latin de mai 1854 à mai 1869.* Péronne, 1899.

Dameth, H., *Introduction à l'étude de l'économie politique.* 2nd ed. Paris, 1878.

————, *Le mouvement socialiste et l'économie politique.* Paris, 1869.

Darimon, Alfred, *Histoire d'un parti. Les Cinq sous l'Empire (1857-1860).* Paris, 1885. Although Darimon exaggerates his own role, this and the following volumes are among the most useful memoirs so far as economic and social problems are concerned. Darimon, with one foot in the opposition and the other in the Palais Royal, was very concerned with social problems; he claimed to be a socialist.

————, *Histoire d'un parti. Les irréconciliables sous l'Empire (1867-1869)*. 2nd ed. Paris, 1888.

————, *Histoire d'un parti. Le Tiers Parti sous l'Empire (1863-1866)*. Paris, 1887.

————, *L'Opposition libérale sous l'Empire (1861-1863)*. Paris, 1886.

————, *A travers une révolution (1847-1855)*. Paris, 1884.

Delaroa, Joseph, *Le duc de Persigny et les doctrines de l'Empire*. Paris, 1865. Circulars, speeches, and works by Persigny with a biographical notice by Delaroa.

Delord, Taxile, *Histoire illustrée du Second Empire*. 6 v. Paris, 1880-1883. One of the first histories of the Empire; the author was a moderate republican journalist. The first edition appeared in 1869.

Du Camp, Maxime, *Souvenirs d'un demi siècle*. v. I. *Au temps de Louis-Philippe et de Napoléon III, 1830-1870*. Paris, 1949.

Duruy, Victor, *Notes et souvenirs (1811-1894)*. 2 v. Paris, 1901. Valuable as the testimony of one of the leading figures of the Liberal Empire. Lauds Napoleon III's efforts in behalf of the working class.

Economie politique. Discours et rapports du prince Napoléon. Paris, n.d. A collection of speeches and statements.

Falloux, Comte de, *Mémoires d'un royaliste*. 2 v. Paris, 1898. A conservative Catholic reformer.

Ferrère, Aristide, *Révélations sur la propagande Napoléonienne faite en 1848 et 1849 pour servir à l'histoire secrète des élections du prince Napoléon-Louis Bonaparte*. Turin, 1863. The author called this Volume I, but apparently wrote no other volumes. Although open to suspicion, this is one of the few sources for Bonapartist propaganda in 1848. Ferrère perhaps exaggerated his own role in the Bonapartist campaigns of 1848.

Ferry, Jules, *La lutte électorale en 1863*. Paris, 1863. Important for Imperialist and Republican electoral campaigns.

Fribourg, E. E., *L'Association internationale des travailleurs*. Paris, 1871. By one of the founders of the French section of the First International. Interesting to us for relations between Empire and First International.

Garnier-Pagès, Louis-Antoine, *Histoire de la Revolution de 1848*. v. X-XI. Paris, 1872.

Granier de Cassagnac, A., *Souvenirs du Second Empire*. 3 v. Paris, 1881-1884. Publicist, deputy, friend of Napoleon III and a "true believer" in Bonapartism.

Guéroult, Adolphe, *La liberté et les affaires. La cherté des loyers et les travaux de Paris*. Paris, 1861.

Haussmann, Georges-Eugène, *Mémoires du baron Haussmann*. 3 v. Paris, 1890-1893. One of the most useful memoirs. Although Haussmann's name is most closely associated with the work on Paris, as Prefect of the Seine he was concerned with all the problems of the Department.

Hubner, Comte de, *Neuf ans de souvenirs d'un ambassadeur d'Autriche à Paris sous le Second Empire 1851-1859*. Paris, 1904.

Hugelmann, Gabriel, *La IVème Race*. 2 v. Paris, 1863. In praise of the Bonapartist dynasty which is destined to bring about the age of equality.

Joly, Maurice, *Dialogue aux enfers entre Machiavel et Montesquieu ou la politique de Machiavel au XIXème siècle*. Brussels, 1864. A bitter attack upon Napoleon III by a political exile. Includes perceptive satire on Bonapartist propaganda.

Laveleye, Emile de, "De l'instruction du peuple au dix-neuvième siècle," *Revue des deux mondes,* January 1, 1866.

Lebey, André, *Dix lettres inédites de Persigny (1834, 1841, 1842, 1843).* Paris, 1909. Interesting for Persigny's ideas on socialism and reformers.

Lefrançais, Gustave, *Souvenirs d'un révolutionnaire.* Brussels, 1902.

Leroy-Beaulieu, Anatole, "La politique du Second Empire," *Revue des deux mondes,* 98, 2nd period (April 1, 1872), 536-572.

Leroy-Beaulieu, Paul, *De l'état moral et intellectuel des populations ouvrières et de son influence sur le taux des salaires.* Paris, 1868.

———, *La question ouvrière au XIXème siècle.* 3rd ed. Paris, 1871.

Lescarret, J. B., *Conférences sur l'économie politique faites en 1867-1868 à Bordeaux et à Bayonne.* Paris, 1869.

Levasseur, Emile, "Résumé historique de l'enseignement de l'économie politique et de la statistique," *Journal des économistes* (November, 1882).

———, *Résumé historique de l'enseignement de l'économie politique et de la statistique en France de 1882 à 1892.* Paris, 1893.

Marx, Karl, *The Eighteen Brumaire of Louis Bonaparte.* Moscow, 1948.

Melun, Armand de, *Mémoires du vicomte Armand de Melun.* 2 v. Paris, 1891. "Revue et mise en ordre par le comte de Camus." A conservative Catholic reformer who at the beginning of Napoleon's rule advised him on social problems, particularly mutual aid societies. Has interesting observations on Napoleon III and social problems.

Mémoires du duc de Persigny. Paris, 1896. Biographical notice by J. Dalaroa. Indispensable for the growth of Bonapartist ideology during the Second Empire. There is a grain of truth in the remark attributed to Napoleon III that Persigny was the only Bonapartist. This work includes speeches, letters, memoranda.

Mémoires de la reine Hortense. v. III. Paris, 1927. Published by the Prince Napoleon.

Merruau, Charles, *Souvenirs de l'Hôtel de Ville de Paris (1848-1852)*. Paris, 1875. Merruau was Secretary General of the Prefecture of the Seine, a member of the Municipal Council of Paris, a Councilor of State, and a journalist.

Mirecourt, Eugène de, *Timothee Trimm*. Paris, 1867. A popular biography of the columnist.

Molinari, M. G., *Le mouvement socialiste et les réunions politiques avant la révolution du 4 Septembre 1870*. Paris, 1872.

———, *Napoléon III publiciste*. Brussels, 1861.

Morny, A. de, "Quelques réflexions sur la politique actuelle," *Revue des deux mondes*, 21 (1848), 151-162.

Nadaud, Martin, *Mémoires de Léonard ancien garçon maçon*. Bouraneuf, 1895. Nadaud, a mason, was a member of the legislature during the Second Republic. He was exiled after December 2.

Ollivier, Emile, *L'Empire libéral*. 17 v. Paris, 1895-1915.

———, *Journal, 1846-1867*. 2 v. Paris, 1961.

Passy, Frédéric, *Les machines et leur influence sur le développement de l'humanité*. Paris, 1881.

Pessard, Hector, *Mes petits papiers 1860-1870*. v. I. Paris, 1887. An opposition journalist friendly to the Empire. Includes incidents revealing relations between the opposition and the Government.

Poulot, Denis, *Question sociale. Le Sublime.* 3rd ed. Paris, 1887. A highly interesting description of the Parisian working class by one close to them.

Pierre et Paul, "Armand Lévy," *Hommes d'aujourd'hui* (1882). A three-page biography.

Proudhon, P.-J., *De la capacité politique des classes ouvrières.* New ed. by C. Bouglé and H. Moysset. Paris, 1924. Inspired by the workers' candidacies of 1863-1864 which Proudhon regarded as evidence of the maturity of the working class.

——, *La Révolution sociale démontrée par le coup d'état du 2 décembre.* New ed. by C. Bouglé and H. Moysset. Paris, 1937. Proudhon advances the theory that because of his origin and the objective situation Louis Napoleon must be revolutionary.

Rondelet, Antonin, *Les Mémoires d'Antoine ou notions populaires de morale et d'économie politique.* Paris, 1860.

——, *Petit manuel de l'économie politique.* Paris, Lyons, 1867.

Rousseau, P., *Opinion du peuple sur les questions politiques et économiques du jour présentée à Sa Majesté Napoléon III, Empereur des Français.* Paris, 1866.

Saveney, Edgar, "Les délégations ouvrières à l'Exposition universelle de 1867," *Revue des deux mondes,* 77, Second Period (October 1868), 586-621.

Senior, Nassau William, *Conversations with Distinguished Persons during the Second Empire from 1860 to 1863.* 2 v. London, 1880. Most of the "distinguished persons" were Orleanist or other foes of the Second Empire who believed and repeated every anti-government incident they heard.

——, *Conversations with M. Thiers, M. Guizot, and other Distinguished Persons during the Second Empire.* 2 v. London, 1878.

Stein, Lorentz von, *Geschichte der socialen Bewegung in Frank-reich von 1789 bis auf unsere Zeit*. 3 v. Leipzig, 1850. A classic. Shows the influence of non-economic forces upon the development of French social thought.

Stern, Daniel (pseud. for Countess d'Agoult), *Histoire de la Révolution de 1848*. 2nd ed. 2 v. Paris, 1862. An excellent account based upon personal observations. Mildly liberal.

Thiers, Adolphe, *De la propriété*. Paris, 1848.

Tocqueville, Alexis de, *The Recollections of Alexis de Tocqueville*. A. T. de Mattos tr.; J. P. Mayer ed. London, 1948.

Villeneuve-Bargemont, Alban de, *Economie politique chrétienne ou recherches sur la nature et les causes du paupérisme en France et en Europe et sur les moyens de le soulager et de le prévenir*. 3 v. Paris, 1834.

Villermé, M., *Tableau de l'état physique et moral des ouvriers employés dans les manufactures de coton, de laine et de soie*. 2 v. Paris, 1840. The most famous survey of the condition of the working class.

Villiers, George W. F. (pseud. for Lord Clarendon), *Ten Years of Imperialism. Impressions of a "Flaneur."* Edinburgh, 1862. Some very perceptive observations on the economic and social policy of the Second Empire.

Vingtain, Léon, *De la liberté de la presse*. Paris, 1860. Includes a very useful appendix: "Avertissements, suspensions, suppressions encourus par la presse quotidienne ou périodique depuis 1848 jusqu'à nos jours."

Vitu, Auguste, *Les réunions publiques à Paris 1868-1869*. Paris, 1869.

VII. Secondary Works and Articles

Altick, Richard, *The English Common Reader. A Social History of the Mass Reading Public.* Chicago, 1957.

Armengaud, André, *Les populations de l'Est-Aquitain au début de l'époque contemporaine.* Recherches sur une région moins développée (vers 1845-vers 1871). Paris, 1961.

Artz, Frederick B., "Bonapartism and Dictatorship," *The South Atlantic Quarterly,* XXXIX (1940), 37-49.

Avenel, Henri, *Histoire de la presse française depuis 1789 jusqu'-à nos jours.* Paris, 1900. Despite its inadequacies, the only work on the subject. Histories of the press and of the individual journals are lacking.

Barbier, J.-B., *Mensonges sur le Second Empire.* Paris, 1959. A fervent Bonapartist work.

Berger, Georges, *Les Expositions universelles internationales (leur passé, leur rôle actuel, leur avenir).* Law thesis. Paris, 1901.

Berl, Heinrich, *Napoleon III, Demokratie und Diktatur.* Munich, 1947. Napoleon III was a copy of Napoleon I; the first Napoleon was a great creator, Napoleon III an imitator. A better than average biography.

Berthet-Leleux, François, *Le vrai prince Napoléon (Jerôme).* Paris, 1932.

Bertier de Sauvigny, G. de, *La Restauration.* Paris, 1955. The most recent scholarly account of the period.

Blanchard, Marcel, *Le Second Empire.* Paris, 1950. *Collection Armand Colin.* An excellent brief synthesis, particularly of economic life.

Bloch, Maurice, *Trois éducateurs alsaciens.* Paris, 1911. One of the "educators" is August Nefftzer, founder of *Le Temps.*

Boon, H. N., "Les idées économiques et sociales de Napoléon III," *Bulletin de la société d'histoire moderne*, 8th series, no. 3 (April, 1935), 77-82.

————, *Rêve et réalité dans l'oeuvre économique et sociale de Napoléon III*. The Hague, 1936. A very interesting interpretation of Napoleon III's social policy; insists upon his concern with people. Like others who have worked upon the social policy of the Second Empire (including this writer), Boon has had difficulty in determining the personal role of the Emperor in much of the legislation and activities of his government.

Bourgin, Georges, "La législation ouvrière du Second Empire," *Revue des études napoléoniennes*, IV, 220-236.

————, *1848, Naissance et mort d'une république*. Paris, 1948.

————, *Napoleon und seine Zeit*. Stuttgart, 1925.

————, "Neutralité gouvernementale et conflits ouvriers à Lyon au début du Second Empire," *Revue d'histoire économique et sociale*, 1921, 92-102.

Bramstedt, E. K., *Dictatorship and Political Police. The Technique of Control by Fear*. London, 1945. A sociological study of how modern dictators employ terrorism as an instrument of rule. Starts with Napoleon I and III.

Bremer, Karl Heinz, "Der sozialistische Kaiser," *Der Tat*, XXX (June, 1938), 160-171. Finds similarities between ideas of Napoleon III and National Socialism. However, criticizes the Emperor for emphasizing only material welfare and for failing to create a new ethos.

Byrnes, Robert F., *Antisemitism in Modern France. The Prologue to the Dreyfus Affair*. New Brunswick, New Jersey, 1950.

Calman, Alvin R., *Ledru-Rollin and the Second French Republic*. New York, 1922.

The Cambridge Modern History. v. XI. *The Growth of Nationalities*. New York, 1909.

Case, Lynn C., *French Opinion on War and Diplomacy during the Second Empire*. Philadelphia, 1954.

La censure sous Napoléon III. Rapports inédits et en extenso (1852 à 1866). Paris, 1892. Interesting account of censorship of theatre.

Chapman, J. M. & Brian, *The Life and Times of Baron Haussmann. Paris in the Second Empire*. London, 1957.

Charlety, Sébastien, *La Monarchie de Juillet (1830-1848)*. Paris, 1921. v. 5 in Lavisse, E., *Histoire de France contemporaine*.

Chauvet, P., "Le coup d'état vu par un ouvrier," *1848-Revue des révolutions contemporaines*, 189 (December, 1951), 148-152. Memoirs of a typographical worker written in 1896. Seeks to explain why there was not more worker opposition to the *coup d'état* of Louis Napoleon.

Cheetham, F. H., *Louis Napoleon and the Genesis of the Second Empire*. London, 1909. An early account; no longer very useful.

Chrétien, Paul, *Le duc de Persigny (1808-1872)*. Toulouse, 1943. An able law thesis, but Persigny is still awaiting a biographer.

Clapham, J. H., *The Economic Development of France and Germany, 1815-1914*. 3rd ed. Cambridge, (Engl.), 1928. A solid standard work.

Clough, Shepard B., *France a History of National Economics (1789-1939)*. New York, 1939.

Cogniot, Georges, *Proudhon et la démagogie bonapartiste*. Paris, 1958. Subtitle: "Un 'socialiste' en coquetterie avec le pouvoir personnel."

Collins, Irene, *The Government and the Newspaper Press in France 1814-1881*. London, 1959.

Corley, T. A. B., *Democratic Despot, a Life of Napoleon III*. London, 1961.

Cuvillier, A., *Un journal d'ouvriers, "l'Atelier" 1840-1850*. Paris, 1914. An interesting monograph of the first successful workers' journal in France.

Dansette, Adrien, *Louis Napoléon à la conquête du pouvoir*. Paris, 1961.

Dechamps, Jules, *Sur la légende de Napoléon*. Paris, 1931. On the growth of the legend.

Dolléans, Edouard, *Histoire du mouvement ouvrier*. v. I. 1830-1871. 3rd ed. Paris, 1947.

————, "Vie et pensée ouvrières entre 1848 et 1871," *Revue historique*, 198 (1947), 62-78. A review article on Duveau's, *La vie ouvrière*.

Dommanget, Maurice, *Blanqui et l'opposition révolutionnaire à la fin du Second Empire*. Paris, 1960.

Dreyfus, Ferdinand, *L'Assistance sous la Seconde République (1848-1851)*. Paris, 1907. Deals with social reform and social theory as well as assistance.

Driencourt, Jacques, *La Propagande nouvelle force politique*. Paris, 1950.

Droz, Jacques; Genet, Lucien; Vidalenc, Jean, *L'époque contemporaine. Restaurations et révolutions (1815-1871)*. In *Collection Clio*. Paris, 1953.

Dunham, Arthur L., *The Anglo-French Treaty of Commerce of 1861 and the Progress of the Industrial Revolution in France*. Ann Arbor, 1930.

———, "Industrial Life and Labor in France 1815-1848," *The Journal of Economic History*, III (1943), 117-151. An excellent "mise au point."

———, "Unrest in France in 1848," *The Journal of Economic History*, VIII (1948, supplement), 74-84.

Duroselle, J.-B., *Les débuts du Catholicisme social en France (1822-1870)*. Paris, 1951. A very useful work.

Duval, Georges, *Napoléon III, enfance, jeunesse*. Paris, 1899.

Duveau, Georges, "Comment étudier la vie ouvrière: les méthodes d'investigation," *Revue d'histoire économique et sociale*, 26 (1940-1947), No. 1, 11-21.

———, "L'ouvrier de Quarante-huit," *La Revue socialiste* (January-February, 1948), 73-79.

———, *La pensée ouvrière sur l'éducation pendant la Seconde République et le Second Empire*. Paris, 1947.

———, *La vie ouvrière en France sous le Second Empire*. Paris, 1946. An excellent study of the French worker at the shop and factory, at home, his recreations, his psychology. However, Duveau was only incidentally interested in the activities of the government in this work.

Les élections de 1869. Bibliothèque de la révolution de 1848, v. XXI. Paris, 1960.

Emerit, Marcel, "L'égerie de Napoléon III, Madame Cornu," *Revue de Paris*, 1937 (v. 3), 550-575; 794-825.

———, "Les sources des idées sociales et coloniales de Napoléon III," *Revue d'Alger*, III, no. 9 (1945), 427-437. Suggests how Louis-Napoleon may have been influenced by Saint-Simonism before his arrival in power.

Fisher, H. A. L., *Bonapartism*. Oxford, 1908. An interpretation.

Fougère, Henry, *Les délégations ouvrières aux expositions universelles sous le Second Empire*. Montluçon, 1905. A very useful law thesis. His conclusions on the motives for government encouragement of the delegations differ from those of Fournier.

Foulon, Maurice, *Eugène Varlin relieur et membre de la Commune*. Clermont-Ferrand, 1934.

Fournier, Pierre-Léon, *Le Second Empire et la législation ouvrière*. Paris, 1911. A law thesis. Able account of Imperial social legislation and activities. States that liberal measures of the 1860's were the result of pressure from the opposition.

Fournière, Eugène, *Le règne de Louis-Philippe (1830-1848)*. Paris, 1906. v. VIII in *Histoire socialiste*, ed. by Jaurès J.

Gaumont, Jean, *Histoire générale de la coopération en France*. v. I. Paris, 1924.

————, *Un républicain révolutionnaire romantique. Armand Lévy (1827-1891)*. Paris, 1932.

Girard, Louis, *La politique des travaux publics du Second Empire*. Paris, 1952. Indispensable for the economic history of the Second Empire. The author traces the rise and fall of what he has called "the political economy of December 2."

Gonnard, Philippe, *Les origines de la légende napoléonienne. L'oeuvre historique de Napoléon à Sainte-Hélène*. Paris, 1906. Good upon the elaboration and the content of the Napoleonic legend. Little on its growth and dissemination.

Gooch, G. P., *The Second Empire*. London, 1960.

Guérard, Albert, *Napoleon III*. In *Makers of Modern Europe*, ed. by Donald C. McKay and Dumas Malone, Cambridge, Mass., 1943. An interpretation. Napoleon III was above all interested in improving the condition of the working class and in the liberation of oppressed nationalities.

————, *Reflections on the Napoleonic Legend*. New York, 1924. The growth of the legend.

Guériot, Paul, *La captivité de Napoléon III en Allemagne (Septembre 1870-Mars 1871)*. 3rd ed. Paris, 1926.

Guest, Ivor, *Napoleon III in England*. London, 1952. Mostly on relations with nobility. However, some remarks on his more serious activities.

Hachet-Souplet, Pierre, *Louis-Napoléon, prisonnier au fort de Ham*. Paris, 1893.

Holtman, Robert B., *Napoleonic Propaganda*. Baton Rouge, 1950. Interesting account of Napoleon I's propaganda message and machinery.

Hunt, H. J., *Le Socialisme et le Romanticisme en France. Etude de la presse socialiste de 1830 à 1848*. Oxford, 1935.

Jerrold, Blanchard, *The Life of Napoleon III*. 4 v. London, 1874. This early biography is still sometimes useful. Jerrold used family correspondence and the testimony of members of the Imperial government and entourage.

Kelso, Maxwell R., "The French Labor Movement during the Last Years of the Second Empire." In McKay, Donald C., *Essays in the History of Modern Europe*. New York, 1936.

Kent, Sherman, *Electoral Procedure under Louis Philippe*. Yale, 1937.

Kuczynski, Jurgen, *France 1700 to the Present Day*. v. 4 of *A Short History of Labour Conditions under Industrial Capitalism*. v. 4. London, 1946.

Labrousse, C.-E., *Le mouvement ouvrier et les idées sociales en France de 1815 à la fin du XIXème siècle*. Les cours de Sorbonne. Paris, n.d. (the course was offered in 1948-1949). Keen insights and interpretations.

Lacour-Gayet, G., "Les idées libérales et sociales de l'Impératrice." *La Revue du XIXème siècle. Napoléon.* XXVI (1926), 177-180.

La Fuye, Maurice de, and Babeau, Emile A., *Louis Napoléon Bonaparte avant l'Empire (1808-1851).* Amsterdam, 1951.

La Gorce, Pierre de, *Histoire du Second Empire.* 7 v. Paris, 1899-1905. A major history, but the royalist author is not very much interested in social problems.

Lamy, Etienne, "Le Second Empire et les ouvriers," *La Revue de Paris*, II (May 1, 1894), 1-35; III (May 15, 1894), 100-135.

Laronze, Georges, *Le Baron Haussmann.* Paris, 1932. An important biography.

Lebey, André, *Louis Napoléon Bonaparte et la Révolution de 1848.* 2 v. Paris, 1907-1908. This and the following work are important for Louis Napoleon before the Empire.

———, *Les trois coups d'état de Louis-Napoléon Bonaparte. Strasbourg et Boulogne.* Paris, 1906.

Ledré, Charles, *Histoire de la presse.* Paris, 1958.
———, *La presse à l'assaut de la Monarchie 1815-1848.* Paris, 1960.

Leonard, Charlene, *Lyon Transformed. Public Works of the Second Empire.* Berkeley, Calif., 1961.

Leroy, Maxime, *Histoire des idées sociales en France.* v. II. *De Babeuf à Tocqueville.* 2nd ed. Paris, 1950. One of the best surveys.

Leuilliot, Paul, *L'Alsace au début du XIXe siècle. Essais d'histoire politique, économique et religieuse (1815-1830).* 3 v. Paris, 1959-1960.

Lhomme, Jean, *La Grande bourgeoisie au pouvoir (1830-1880).* Paris, 1960.

Levasseur, E., *Histoire des classes ouvrières et de l'industrie en France de 1789 à 1870*. v. II. 2nd ed. Paris, 1904. Despite its age this work by a liberal economist remains essential.

Loliée, Frédéric, *La fête impériale*. Paris, 1912.

———, *Rêve d'Empereur, le destin et l'âme de Napoléon III*. Paris, 1913.

Loubère, Léo, *Louis Blanc. His Life and his Contribution to the Rise of French Jacobin-Socialism*. Evanston, Illinois, 1961.

Louis, Paul, *Histoire de la classe ouvrière en France de la Révolution à nos jours*. Paris, 1927.

Lucas-Dubreton, J., *Le Culte de Napoléon*. Paris, 1960.

McKay, Donald C., *The National Workshops. A Study in the French Revolution of 1848*. Cambridge, Mass., 1933.

Maritch, Sreten, *Histoire du mouvement social sous le Second Empire à Lyon*. Paris, 1930. A fine study based upon national and local archival material.

Mathiez, A., "Le prince Louis-Napoléon à Strasbourg," *La Revue de Paris*, XXII (November 15, 1899), 294-322.

Maurain, Jean, *Un bourgeois français au XIXème siècle. Baroche ministre de Napoléon III*. Paris, 1936. An outstanding biography of an Orleanist who for class interests rallied to the Empire. Maurain considers Baroche a representative of the liberal bourgeoisie.

———, *La politique éclésiastique du Second Empire de 1852 à 1869*. Paris, 1930.

Merlat-Guitard, Odette. *Louis-Napoléon Bonaparte de l'éxile à l'Elysée*. Paris, 1939. An able account.

Morienval, Jean, *Les créateurs de la grande presse en France*. Paris, 1934. A history of the origins of the popular press told by means of three biographies; Emile de Girardin, H. de Villemessant, and Moïse Millaud.

Morazé, Charles, *La France bourgeoise, XVIII-XX siècles.* Paris, 1946.

Palm, Franklin C., *England and Napoleon III. A Study of the Rise of a Utopian Dictator.* Durham, N.C., 1948.

Perivier, A., *Napoléon journaliste.* Paris, 1918.

Perreux, G., *La propagande républicaine au début de la Monarchie de Juillet.* Paris, 1931.

Pilenco, Alexandre, *Les moeurs du suffrage universel en France (1848-1928).* Paris, 1930.

Pimienta, Robert, "La propagande bonapartiste en 1848," *La Révolution de 1848,* VI (1909), 404-415; VII (1910-1911), 42-60; 90-104; 145-160; 257-271; 306-325; 375-388. A very useful study of propaganda in Paris.

Pinkney, David H., *Napoleon III and the Rebuilding of Paris.* Princeton, N.J., 1958.

Ponteil, Félix, *L'opposition politique à Strasbourg sous la monarchie de Juillet (1830-1848).* Paris, 1932. First rate. Useful for Ponteil's account of Louis Napoleon's Strasbourg attempt.

Prolès, Charles, *Charles Delescluze, 1830-1848-1871.* Paris, 1898.

Quentin-Bauchard, Pierre, *La crise sociale de 1848. Les origines et la Révolution de Février.* Paris, 1920. A very capable analysis. About half the work deals with economic change and the social movement before 1848. Author seems to be a moderate conservative.

Reclus, Maurice, *Emile de Girardin le créateur de la presse moderne.* Paris, 1934.

Rémond, René, *La droite en France de 1815 à nos jours.* (Paris, 1954).

Renard, Edouard, *La vie et l'œuvre de Louis Blanc.* Toulouse, 1922.

Renard, Georges, *La République de 1848 (1848-1852)*. Paris, 1907; v. IX in *Histoire socialiste*, ed. by Jaurès, J.

Rigaudias-Weiss, Hilde, *Les enquêtes ouvrières en France entre 1830 et 1848*. Paris, 1936.

Rocquain, Félix, *Notes et fragments d'histoire*. Paris, 1906. Chapter on "La police politique" good on the activities of secret police. After the fall of Napoleon III the government charged Rocquain with the study of the archives of the political police.

Rubel, Maximilien, *Karl Marx devant le Bonapartisme*. Paris, 1960.

Salmon, Lucy M., *The Newspaper and the Historian*. New York, 1923.

Shapiro, J. Salwyn, *Liberalism and the Challenge of Fascism*. New York, 1949. Includes Napoleon III among the "Heralds of Fascism."

Schmidt, Charles, *Les journées de Juin 1848*. Paris, 1926.

Schnerb, Robert, "La côte d'Or et l'élection présidentielle du 10 décembre 1848," *La Révolution de 1848*, XX (1923-1924), 376-411; XXI (1924-1925), 74-93.

————, *Rouher et le Second Empire*. Paris, 1949. A very able biography. Stresses the economic and social views of Rouher.

See, Henri, *Histoire économique de la France*. 2 v. 2nd ed. Paris, 1951.

Seignobos, Charles, *La Révolution de 1848. Le Second Empire (1848-1859)*. Paris, 1921; v. VI in *Histoire de France contemporaine*, ed. by Lavisse, E.

————, *Le déclin de l'Empire et l'établissement de la 3e République (1859-1875)*. Paris, 1921; v. VII in *Histoire de France contemporaine*, ed. by Lavisse, E.

Siegfried, André, *Tableau politique de la France de l'ouest sous la Troisième République.* Paris, 1913. Shows the persistence of Bonapartist political doctrine and manifestations of it within other movements such as Boulangism.

Simpson, F. A., *Louis Napoleon and the Recovery of France.* 3rd ed. London, 1951. This and the following work are probably the best in English. Mildly pro-Napoleon.

————, *The Rise of Louis Napoleon.* 2nd ed. London, 1929.

Tchernoff, I., "Les candidatures ouvrières sous le Second Empire," *La Revue socialiste,* XLIII (January-June 1906), 161-167. A summary account.

————, *Le parti républicain au coup d'état et sous le Second Empire.* Paris, 1906. The best account of the repressive activities of the Empire and the republican and worker opposition. However, Tchernoff was unable to consult archival material for the late 1850's and the 1860's.

————, *Le parti républicain sous la Monarchie de Juillet.* Paris, 1901.

Thirria, H., *Napoléon III avant l'Empire.* 2 v. Paris, 1895. Still useful despite its age.

Thomas, Albert, *Le Second Empire (1852-1870).* Paris, 1907; v. X in *Histoire socialiste,* ed. by Jaurès, J. In many ways still the best account of relations between the Second Empire and the working class.

Thompson, J. M., *Louis Napoleon and the Second Empire.* New York, 1955.

Tudesq, A., "La légende napoléonienne en France en 1848," *Revue historique,* v. CCXVIII (1957), 64-85.

Ulin, Robert P., *Prince Louis Napoleon and the Workers' Vote in 1848. A Study in Modern Revolution*. An unpublished honors thesis. Harvard, 1943. Bonapartist propaganda during the Second Republic.

Weill, Georges, *Histoire du Parti républicain en France (1814-1870)*. 2nd ed. Paris, 1928.

————, *Le journal, origines, évolution et rôle de la presse périodique*. Paris, 1934. A rapid survey. The bibliographies on the French press provide additional evidence of the need for more work.

————, "Les journaux ouvriers à Paris (1830-1870)," *Revue d'histoire moderne et contemporaine*, (1907), 89-103.

Windelband, Wolfgang, "Die historische Figur Napoleons III," *Deutsche Rundschau* (August, 1936), 97-103. Insists upon differences between the Second Empire and National Socialist Germany, but points out that Second Empire made a cautious start upon paths leading to the new Nazi society.

Wright, Charles R., *Mass Communication*. New York, 1959.

Wright, Gordon, "Public Opinion and Conscription in France, 1866-1870," *Journal of Modern History*, XIV (1942), 20-45.

Zevaès, Alexandre, "Les candidatures ouvrières et révolutionnaires sous le Second Empire," *La Révolution de 1848*, XXIX (1932), 132-154.

Index

Académie des sciences morales et politiques, 173, 177, 191

d'Ambès, baron, pseud. *See* Heeckeren

Amis du peuple, republican club, 14

Anti-Semitism, 33-34, *n*116

Article 1781, Civil Code, 121, 165, 167

Association Philotechnique, propaganda and adult education, 87-88; awards to workers, 160; economics courses for workers, 182-187; 195, 199

Association Polytechnique, propaganda and adult education, 87-88; awards to workers, 160; economics courses for workers, 182-187; lectures in pamphlet form, 189, 195

Association pour la défense du travail national, 177

L'Atelier, 26, 27

Ateliers nationaux, 31

d'Aumale, duc, 132, 133

Barbès, Armand, 108-109

Baroche, Jules, 94, 111-112

Bastiat, Frédéric, 177

Batbie, A. P., 188

Baudrillart, Henri, 187-188

Bazin, A., 130, 152-153, 201

Beslay, François, 196

Bibliothèque de connaissances utiles, workers' textbook, 189

Bibliothèque utile, workers' textbook, 189

Blanc, J. J., 127

Blanc, Louis, social views, 20, 26, 28, 36-37, 124; social workshops, 177

Blanqui, Louis-Auguste, 162

Bonaparte, Jerôme. *See* Prince Napoleon

Bonaparte, Louis Napoleon. *See* Napoleon III

Bonaparte, Napoleon. *See* Napoleon I

Brochures ouvrières, 128, 130, 131, 132, 143

Bureau de l'esprit public, propaganda agency, 41

Buret, Eugène, 26

Canrobert, Marshal, 85

Cassaignac, Granier de, 62, 67, 81, 96, 114

Castile, Hippolyte, 81

Cavaignac, Gen. Louis Eugène, 37, 107, 168

Chabaud, 125, 128, 129, 133, 136, 152, 153, 189

Charles X, 10, 13

Charnier P., 13

Chateaubriand, vicomte de, 5

Chevalier, Michel, 123; attacks socialist theories, 177, 179

Cité Napoléon, workers housing, 100, 101

Clémence et bienfaits de S. M. Napoléon III, (pamphlet) , 83

Coalitions law, 151, 152

Cobden-Chevalier Treaty of 1860, 136, 158, 174

Committee of the rue de Poitiers, 177

Communism, 11, 178

Campagnes glorieuses du régne de Napoleon III, (by Muraour) , 50

Compagnonnage, 10

Le Constitutionnel, 47, 48, 49, 50, 60, 67, 95, 104, 121, 151, 153, 164--169 passim

Cooperatives, organization of, 121, 122, 123-124, 148

Coquard, 136

Cornu, Mme., 26, 29

Cours d'économie industrielle, (pamphlets), 189

Coutant, 129, 136, 142, 152, 153, 162

Dameth, Henri, 171, 175, 181-182, 190

Darboy, Archbishop of Paris, 186, 187

Darimon, Alfred, 112, 124, 125, 138, 147-148, 155

David, Jerôme, 111-112

De la propriété, (by Thiers) , 177

De Lesseps, Ferdinand, 63

Delord, Taxile, 60, 156, 198

Deux questions ouvrières, (pamphlet by Bazin), 201

Durand, Jacques, 130
Duruy, Victor, 171, 178, 199
Dusautoy, 61-62
Duvernois, Clément, 51-52; founded *Le Peuple français*, 51; government subsidy, 51; 167, 169

L'Ecole mutuelle, cours complet d'éducation populaire, (workers' textbook), 189
Elections, use of placards, 31-32; procedure, 114-119; government propaganda, 115-117; role of press in, 116; candidates, 116-119; appeals to working class, 115-119; 122, worker candidates, 162, 163
L'Empereur Napoléon III et les principautés roumaines, (pamphlet), 139
L'Empereur Napoléon III et l'Italie, (pamphlet), 92
Enfantin, Barthélemy-Prosper, 144, 154
L'Epoque, 51; generous subsidy, 61-62; Emperor sets policy, 91; 92
L'Etincelle, 51, subsidized, 62; addresses workers, 76
Eugénie, Empress, 54, 71, 74, 84, 92, 100, 105, 110, 112, 187
L'Extinction du paupérisme, 28-30, 32, 35, 78, 132, 146

Faure, Jules, 42
Ferrère, 32
Ferry, Jules, 155
First International. *See* International Workingman's Association
Fould, Achille, 94
Fourier, Charles, 144
Fourneaux du prince impérial, (soup kitchens), 100
Fribourg, E. E., 149

Garnier, Joseph, 185; on public debating of social problems, 188-189; 195
Gaumont, Charles, 52, 152, 166
Girardin, Emile de, 41, 45

Gloires de l'Empire, Les, (Muraour), 50
Grenier, A., nom de plume of Napoleon III, 92
Guéroult, Adolphe, 154-162

Havas, A. and Charles, 56
Havas Press Agency, government subsidized, 55-56
Havin, 59-60, 125
Heeckeren (Baron d'Ambès), 4 and n6, 8
Heine, Heinrich, on bourgeoisie, 11; on Napoleon II, 20
Henry, J., 153
Hortense, Queen, on propaganda, 3-4
Hugelmann, Gabriel, 143-144; *Société nationale pour l'extinction du paupérisme*, 145-147; 149, 200

L'Idée napoléonienne, 24
Idées napoléoniennes, Les, Bonapartist party platform, 23-24, 78
International Workingman's Association, The First International, 44; Tolain on workers' need to read, 44; 127-128, 148 and n96-150, 154, prison terms for membership in, 161
Invalides civils, old-age retirement plan, 146
Italian independence, 58; supported by Prince Napoleon, 121, 125; Catholics oppose, 122

Jews, under the Second Empire, 33-34 and n116
Joly, Maurice, 37, 42, 56, 98
July Monarchy, x, 6, 7; denunciation of, 8, 16-17; the press under, 41; newspaper *Débats*, 41
July Revolution, 10-11, 14

Lafayette, marquis de, 5
La Gorce, Pierre de, 60, 95
Lamartine, Alphonse de, 27
Leçons d'économies politiques . . ., (2 vols.) Passy, 180

Ledru-Rollin, Alexandre Auguste, 26, 28
Lefrançais, Gustave, 195
Legitimists, 12; propaganda, 13-14; newspapers *La Quotidienne,* 13, and *L'Union,* 31
Leroy-Beaulieu, Paul, 172, 173, 174
Les machines et leur influence . . . , lectures for workers, (Passy), 180
Lescarret, J.-B., 191, 193
Lévy, Armand, 126, 137-143, 141, 144, 156, 159, 200
Limayrac, Paulin, 67
Livret law, 77, 95-96, 121, 152, 165, 167
Louis Philippe, working class under, 10, 12; repression under, 13; 134

Magne, 94
Malinowski, Jacques, 139
"Manifesto of the Sixty," (1864), 154, 162-163, 164
Manuel d'artillerie, 6
Manuel de morale et d'économie politique à l'usage des classes ouvrières (Rapet), 173; into two editions, 191; won first prize, 191; 194
Marx, Karl, 92, 111
Melun, Armand de, 111
Les mémoires d'Antoine . . . (Rondelet), 173; propaganda story for working class on economics, 193-194
Millaud, Moïse, 52-53, 60
Mirecourt, Eugène de, 81-82
Mirès, 60
Molinari, Gustave de, 189
Moniteur (universel), Le, official propaganda organ, 3, 41; circulation, 1860, 44, 45-47; reorganized, 45; *Le Petit moniteur,* 46; 53-54, 67, 68, 70, 75, 78, 83, 91, 92, 95, 101-108 passim, 199
Morny, Charles, duc de, 38, 105; warns against Communism, 178
Muraour, Emile, 50

Napoleon I, on propaganda, 3; dictatorship of, 6; belief in equality, 17, 19; working class support, 18-20; 27
Napoleon III, views on popular support, 4-5; *Manuel d'artillerie,* 6; propaganda-1830's, 6; *Rêveries politiques,* 6; working class support, 18-20; United States, 22; England, 22; *Les idées napoléoniennes,* 23; attempted *coups,* 7-8, 25, 32; at Ham, 25-30; *L'Extinction du paupérisme,* 28-30; Jews under, 33-34 and *n*116; concern for workers, 35; the press, 48, 49, 51; socialism, 88; tariff treaty, 88; propaganda-2nd Empire, 91-93; propaganda novel planned, 93; "cult of the hero," 107, 110-112; amnesty for political prisoners, 108-109; contributes funds to producers' cooperatives, 123-124; proposes economics classes for workers, 178, 199
New York Times, The, 91-92
Newspapers, subsidized, propaganda media. "Literary," *Le Petit journal,* 44, 52, 53, 54, 93; *Le Petit national,* 52; *La Petite presse,* 52, 53. "Political," *L'Atelier,* 26, 27; *Bibliothèque historique,* 16; *Le Capitole,* 16, 17; *Le Commerce,* 16; *Le Constitutionnel,* 47, 48, 49, 50, 60, 67, 95, 104, 121, 151, 153, 164, 166, 168, 169; *Le Concorde,* 104; *Courrier de l'Isère,* 67, 75; *Courrier de Marseille,* 103; *Dix Décembre,* 91, 92; *L'Echo de Vaucluse,* 21; *L'Epoque,* 51, 61-62, 91, 92; *L'Espérance,* 141-143; *L'Etendard,* 50; *L'Etincelle,* 51, 62, 76; *Gazette de Lyon,* 181; *La Gironde,* 63; *Hebdomadaire de Vichy,* 61; *Industriel Alsacien,* 58; *Journal des ateliers,* 198; *Journal des Basses Alpes,* 61; *Journal des débats,* 58; *Journal du Loiret,* 26; *Minerve,* 16; *Le Moniteur universel,* 3, 41, 44-78 passim, 101-108 passim, 199; *Moniteur de la*

Meurthe, 168; *Le Moniteur du soir*, 46, 91, 202; *Le Nain jaune*, 15-16, 144; *Le Napoléonien*, 34; *Le Napoléon républicain*, 32, 33; *Le National*, 42; *L'Opinion nationale*, 52, 56, 130, 154-162, 163-164, 166, 198-200; *L'Organisation du travail*, 34; *La Patrie*, 47, 48, 49, 67; *Le Pays*, 47, 48, 50, 60, 62, 91, 95, 119, 121, 128, 151, 152, 153, 166; *Petit Marseillais*, 63; *Le Peuple*, 17, 92, 166; *Le Peuple français*, 51-52, 62; *Phare de Marseille*, 63; *La Presse*, 155; *Le Progrès*, 148, 158, 181; *Progrès du Pas-de-Calais*, 26; *La Réforme*, 14, 15, 42; *La République*, 154; *Revue de L'empire*, 50, 151, 164; *La Ruche populaire*, 129; *Le Salut public*, 58, 104; *Le Siècle*, 49, 59-60, 67, 82; *L'Union bourguignonne*, 104; *L'Union ouvrière*, 198

Ollivier, Emile, 40, 57 and *n*63-58, 59, 69, 73, 111-112; on elections, 115; 123

L'Opposition, le gouvernement et les classes ouvrières, (pamphlet), 153

L'Opinion nationale, a worker and liberal bourgeoisie paper, 52, 56, 154; some independence, 157; Bonapartist propaganda in, 158-162; opposes class concept, 164, 166, 167, 169, 198, 199, 200

L'Organisation des travailleurs par les corporations nouvelles, 200

Le Panthéon du travail (Hugelmann) (pamphlet), 145

Palais Royal group, 126-137; publications, 131-137; London Exposition-1862, 135-136; 152, 159

Papiers et correspondance, published outline of Emperor's propaganda novel, 93

Paris, Count of, 124

Passy, Frédéric, 176, 180, 184, 185, 188

La Patrie, 47, 48, 49, 67

Le Pays, 47-50 passim, 60, 67, 95, 104, 121, 151, 153, 164-169 passim

Perdonnet, Auguste, director *Association Polytechnique*, 183-186, 195

Péreire, Isaac, 97, 155

Persigny, Victor Fialin, duc de, statement at 1840 trial, 17; 20, 31-32, 35, 36, 40, 50, 60, 65, 73, 81, 94, 100; on elections, 115; 143, 146-147, 198

Le peuple, l'empereur et les anciens partis, (pamphlet)), by Palais Royal group, 132

Pharaon, Florian, 51, 62

Placard, *Moniteur des communes*, 79

Planty, marquis du, 146

Prince Napoleon, symbol of liberal Bonapartism, 54, 58, 82, 124; opposed 1851 *coup d'état*, 125; assisted workers' movement, 125; London Exposition-1862, 125; Palais Royal group, 126-137; 139, 141, 198, 199

Press *(see also* Newspapers*)*, workers' papers, 32, 33; anti-Semitism, 33-34; government subsidies, 41-68; decline of government press, 48-49; the "political" press, 52-53; the "literary" press, 52; provincial, 54, 63; subservience of, 55; propaganda value of opposition papers, 57, 58, 59; profit motivation, 60; government regulations of, 63-68; publish workers' demands, 151; workers' letters to, 152; propaganda role of, 156-162; weaknesses as propaganda tools against working class, 197-201

Press Bureau, Ministry of the Interior, elaborate machinery of, 38; national reports on public opinion, 38-40; surveillance and direction of newspapers, 64-67 and *n*106; use of propaganda placards, 76-80; *Moniteur des communes* founded, 79; use of pamphlets, 80-84; writers as pamphleteers, 81; secret activities, 91; attempts to rally workers to Empire, 98-113;

"cult of the hero," 111, 112; divide and conquer, 122-125; London Exposition, 136; secret use of former revolutionary writers and intellectuals, 137; Armand Lévy, 137-143; attempts to stem class consciousness, 163-169; declining influence, 202; weaknesses of propaganda, 203-204

Proudhon, Pierre-Joseph, 37, 107, 125, 147

Quinet, Edgar, 26

Rapet, J. J., 173, 191, 192, 194
Renan, Ernest, 9-10
Republicans, 14; propaganda, 14-15; newspaper *La Réforme*, 14; pamphlets, 14; propaganda theatre, 14; evening courses for workers, 14; 18; newspapers, 26-27
Restoration Monarchy, x; use of propaganda, 12-13; the press under, 41
Rêveries politiques, 6 and n11, 78
Revue de l'Empire, 50, 151, 164
Richard, Albert, 130-131 and n34
Robert, Charles, 190
Rondelet, Antonin, 173, 190-191, 193
Rothschild, House of, anti-Semitism, 33
Rouher, Eugène, 67, 82, 91, 94, 123, 145, 149-150, 198, 199
Royal tours, as propaganda technique, 69-76; claques employed, 73; security measures for, 73-74; visits to factories and workshops, 74-75

Saint-Simon, comte de, 144, 154
Le Salut c'est la dynastie (pamphlet), 145
Sand, George, 26
Say, Jean-Baptiste, 26
Le Siècle, circulation, 49; popular with workers, 59; 60, 67, 82
Simon, Jules, 124

Smith, Adam, 26
Social Catholicism, and the working class, 12, 13
Socialism, 88, 162, 163, 177; public debate on, 188-189; attempts to stem spread of, 170-196
Société d'économie politique, 171; economics courses to define workers' conduct, 175, 185, 188
Société du Prince Impérial (credit union), 100
Société nationale pour l'extinction du paupérisme, 145-146, 149
Société Philomatique, 180
Sorbonne, La, 187
Stadler, Eugène de, 81
Strasbourg, 7-8, 32
Strike, right to, 88-89, 112, 121, 122-123, 129; call for legalization, 140-141; *L'Opinion nationale* supports, 161; 167, 174, 178
Strikes, 10, 11, 151, 161, 163, 166-167
Suffrage, universal manhood, x, propaganda resulting from, 30, 32, 113-114, 134, 204

Tariffs, under July Monarchy, 26; 1860 Treaty, 136, 158; propaganda for acceptance, 174, 178
Taxes, under July Monarchy, 25
Thiers, Adolphe, 144, 168, 177
Thomas, Albert, 127-128
Thomas, Emile, 31
Titres de la dynastie napoléonienne, (pamphlet), 83
de Tocqueville, Alexis, on social revolution, 12
Tolain, 127, 149, 199
Trade, under July Monarchy, 25
Trade unions, 121, ban on, 129; 152, 162
Trimm, Timothée, 53
Triomphes de l'empire, (Muraour), 50
Tristan, Flora, 26
Turcs en Europe, propaganda tract, 92
L'Union ouvrière (Flora Tristan), 26

Vésinet convalescent home for workers, inaugurated 158; 168
Villeneuve-Bargemont, Alban de, 11-12
Vincennes home for convalescent workers, 54; instruction and propaganda at, 88; 99, 168, 186-187, 190, 191, 195
Vitu, Auguste, 50-51, 168

Walder, Mélanie, 81
Wanschooten, 136
Wollfers, de, Bonapartist agent, 148
Working class, x, xi; growth of, 8-9; poverty of, 9-10; trade unions, 10; strikes, 11; press propaganda, 17; Bonapartist sentiment of, 18-20; newspapers for, 18-19, 44-45, 50, 51; under Napoleon I, 24; under July Monarchy, 25; under Napoleon III, 32-33; aid to needy, 53-54; royal tours, 69-76; organizations coopted by government, 84-87; mutual aid societies, 85-87 and n72; adult education for, 87-88, 171-196; employer electoral propaganda, 89-90; government concern for, 95-97; nurseries, 96; old age retirement fund, 96; private charity, 98, 110-112; cradle to grave institutions, 99-101; public works program, 101-102; electioneering among, 115-119; class consciousness, 120-121; votes republican, 122; wooed by more liberal legislation, 122-125; Palais royal movement, 126-137; delegation to London Exposition, 136; *Le Pays* prints letters of, 152-154; livrets, 152; *L'Opinion nationale* propaganda, 156-162; propaganda to counter demands of, 163-166; liberal opposition woos, 167-169; economic courses to stabilize social order, 171; to prevent strikes, 172; to improve morality, 172-173; to assist religion, 173; to accept increased mechanization, 174, 193; to accept low tariffs, 174; to blunt strike weapon, 174; to refute socialist doctrines, 175-196; economics pamphlets, books and courses for, 182-194; effectiveness of propaganda, 194-205.